POSTCARD HISTORY SERIES

Hanover Milestones

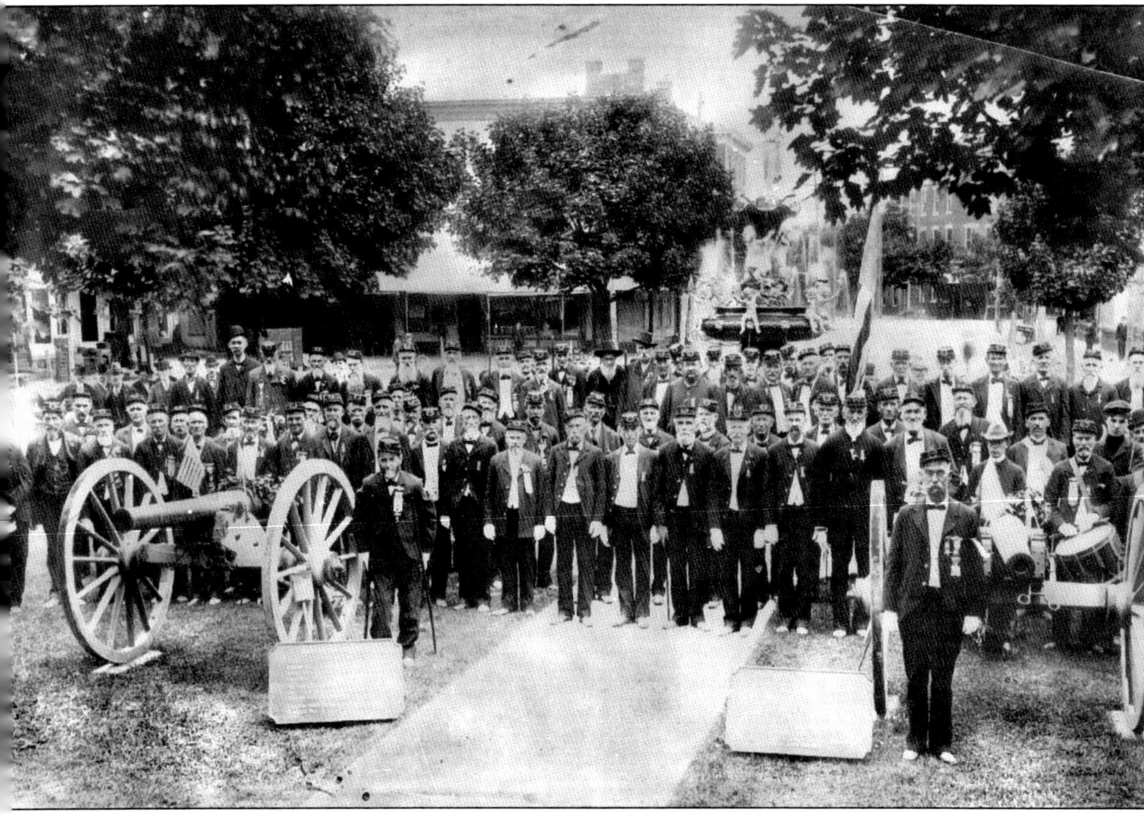

The Hanover area Civil War veterans held frequent reunions up until about 1915 and often participated in Hanover parades. This group of members of Major Jenkins Post No. 99, Grand Army of the Republic, many in uniform, gathered about the fountain on Center Square in Hanover in 1899, facing toward the Frederick Street entrance with Broadway in the background. Standing in front of the cannon on the right is Cdr. Frank A. Zeigler, and beside the cannon on the left is Joel Henry. Seen here are the following, from right to left: (first row) Rev. Emory Weeks, Maj. Joseph A. Renaut, drummer Mahlon H. Naill, Harry Hershey, Jerre Kohler, unidentified bearded veteran, Jacob Kline, N. B. Carver, Charles Young, Jacob Bender, Charles Z. Thomas, Dr. Nathan Stambaugh, Jacob Lau, Silas Beard, Dan F. Stair, William Lau, Dan Withers, and Henry Becker (with wooden leg); (second row) George Kline (fifer), L. B. Johns, unidentified, David Forney, James Gordon, George Koehler, Charles T. Kump, George Carl, William Dresher, William Small, James Miller, Jacob Shultz, William Bair, Frank Roberts, unidentified, Henry Trone, John Kline, and two unidentified at left end; (third row, not in order) David E. Winebrenner, Adolphus Baughman, Lewis Renaut, ? Feeser, Isaac Wagner, John Zinn, Albert Anthony, Samuel Trone, Daniel Snyder, Dr. O. T. Everhart, Michael Bucher, Henry K. Wentz, Peter Resh, Alfred Koller, ? Biddle; (fourth row) M. O. Smith, standing beneath the cupid of the fountain, and, to his right, Joe McKinney and Daniel Carter. Others in the rear include Christ Bange, Calvin Shultz, and Charles Emig.

POSTCARD HISTORY SERIES

Hanover Milestones

Hanover Area Historical Society

ARCADIA
PUBLISHING

ISBN 978-0-7385-3918-8

Published by Arcadia Publishing
Charleston, South Carolina

Printed in the United States of America

Library of Congress Catalog Card Number: 2005931162

For all general information contact Arcadia Publishing at:
Telephone 843-853-2070
Fax 843-853-0044
E-mail sales@arcadiapublishing.com
For customer service and orders:
Toll-Free 1-888-313-2665

Visit us on the Internet at www.arcadiapublishing.com

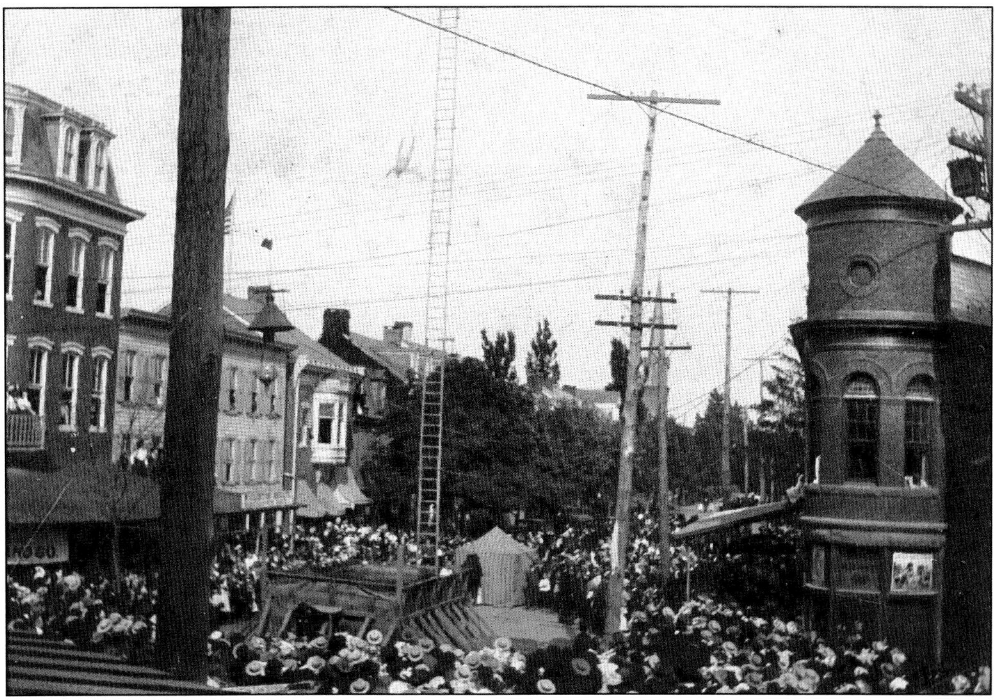

Within these pages are images of many major Hanover celebrations, including the 1915 centennial and 1932 Washington bicentennial. There were numerous annual occasions for entertainment as well, such as the Hanover Fair, which is included, and carnivals, like this image. June 1, 1903, was the start of Carnival Week. The Hatch-Adams Carnival Company arrived in town via the Pennsylvania Railroad. Six tents were erected on the square, as was a Ferris wheel. Main streets were also set up with attractions. Broadway featured Lunette, the flying lady, and on York Street at Broadway was the high dive act, as the photograph demonstrates. He made two descents from his lofty ladder to the tank below on June 3, 1903, and can be seen in midair in this image. Also, each evening there was a balloon ascension from Wirt Park.

Contents

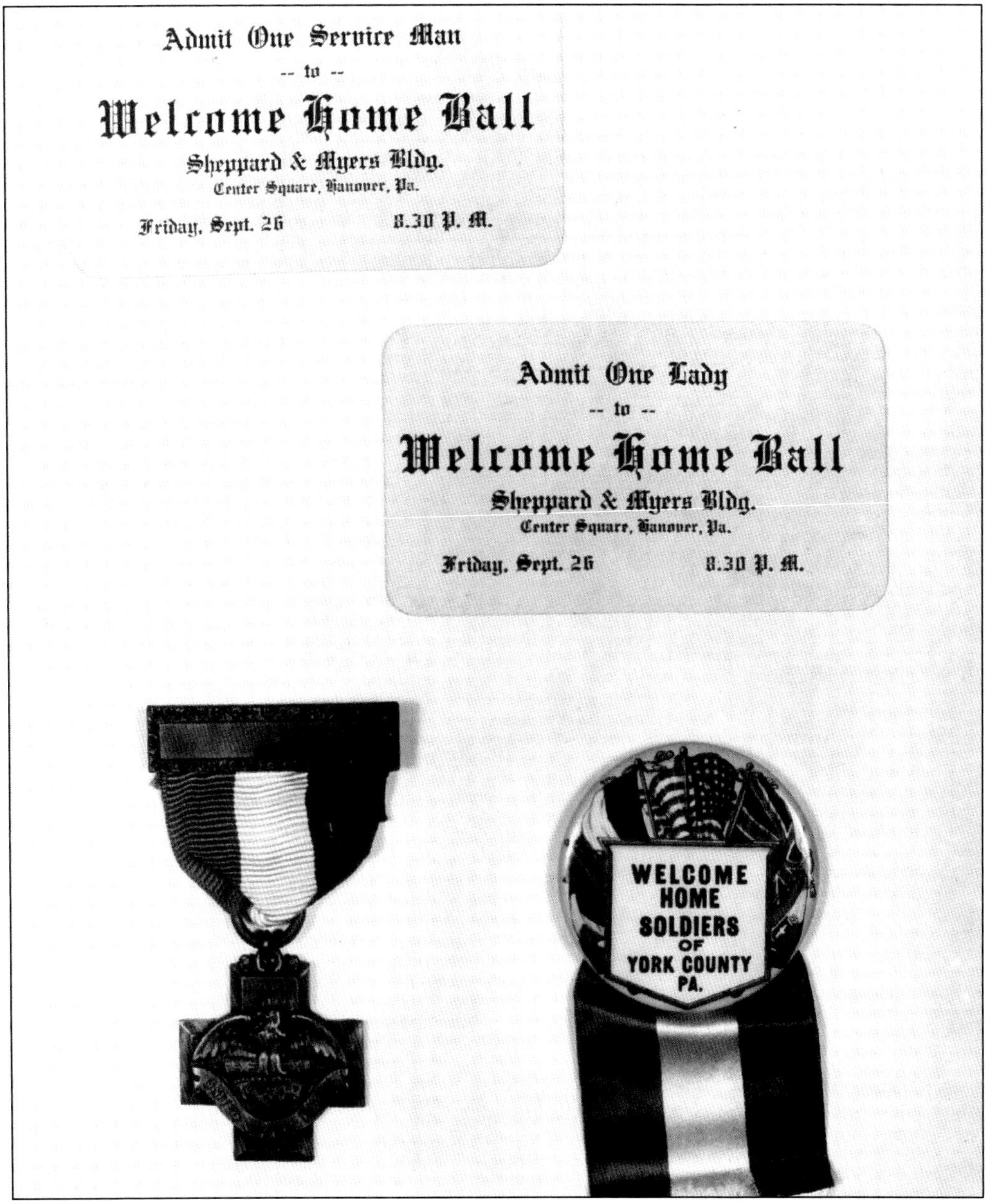

The United States entered World War I in April 1917, having declared war on Germany on Good Friday, April 2. The first U.S. divisions landed in France on June 25, 1917. Ultimately Germany surrendered on November 11, 1918. Hanover and York County contributed mightily to the war effort. Native servicemen were treated with enormous respect and gratitude. This memorabilia reflects such recognition. On November 11, 1919, a county-wide Welcome Home celebration was held. Hanover also honored its servicemen with a September 26 ball for which these admission tickets were issued. York County issued a Welcome Home ribbon that was manufactured by the Whitehead and Hoag Company of Newark, New Jersey. Hanover issued its own medal imprinted on the rear with "in grateful recognition of patriotic service rendered during the World War." The badges are shown here and were presented to Roy F. Brillhart of Porters Sideling, who was an infantry private. Chapter five provides more information on the recognition of their war efforts.

ACKNOWLEDGMENTS

The Hanover Area Historical Society is pleased to have this opportunity to publish its second volume of Hanover postcards. This publication is primarily focused on events rather than buildings and street scenes, as in the first book. The vast majority of this collection of postcards reveals Hanover society from about 1905 to 1932. A defining moment for the citizens of the proud hardworking community occurred in 1915. Extravagant plans were materializing for a centennial celebration to be held in September 1915, including six parades over the course of a week. However, nature would first have to be reckoned with since on August 21, 1915, a severe, crippling tornado struck. Large sections of town received massive damage, including downtown areas to the south of major street arteries leading from the community's Center Square. Both of these events are amply reflected in postcards, of which many are found in this publication.

Perhaps the most unique collection of Hanover postcards in existence is the documentation of the 1932 Washington bicentennial celebration. Chapter six records that part of the town's history with postcards that are known to exist in only two collections. Therefore, they are rare indeed, and this publication may well represent the only lifetime opportunity for the public to view their content. Numerous other parades and celebrations are likewise covered, including the town's patriotic support for its soldier's World War I efforts.

This book begins with a record of many of the early-20th-century popular musical groups performing in town and a number of the parks and fairs available to its citizens for social, spiritual, and recreational use.

The Hanover Area Historical Society owes an enormous debt of gratitude to local collectors Austin Ruth and William (Bill) Marquet, who have generously provided the vast majority of both volumes' images. Without them, this would not have been possible. Other contributors deserving recognition for their support through additional postcards and memorabilia are Andrew Crooks, CPA; John (Jack) Tanger III and Tanger's Hardware; Hanover Ice Company; and Romaine Haar. The society is indebted to the following individuals: Austin Ruth, Bill Marquet, Allen Haar, Mark S. Tome, and Barbara Weimer of Stambaugh Ness for untold hours spent selecting and arranging postcards, and researching, identifying, and preparing text. Your recognition of their efforts will be appreciated.

The Hanover Area Historical Society welcomes you to the fruits of their labors found between the pages of these two postcard publications.

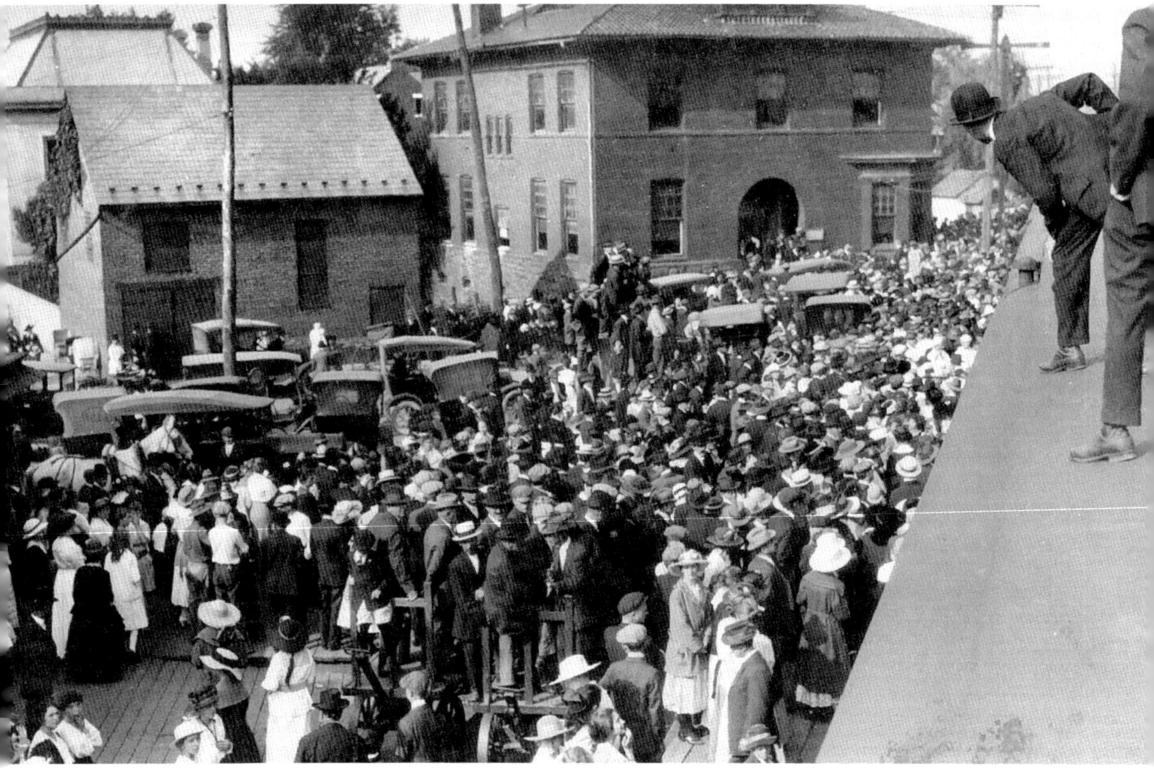

Hanover recognized the initial wave of men drafted for service in World War I on September 19, 1917, with this display of support. The newly inducted servicemen departed from the Union Depot train station on Railroad Street behind the Hanover Public Library, visible in the rear of this scene. Both buildings in the center have since been razed—the one on the right having been the Western Maryland Railroad telegraph office, which was torn down in 1981. The roof of the train station is on the left edge, and the men on the right are standing on train cars. One hundred and thirty drafted men assembled at the Red Cross headquarters at 127 Broadway. There each man was presented with comfort kits purchased by the residents of Hanover and the surrounding areas. Attached to the kits were a tin cup, a towel, and soap, which the draft officials were asked to provide each man. The soldiers then marched to the train station, escorted by the Sons of Veterans' drum corps and 16 veterans of the Civil War, who also marched in the parade rather than riding despite their advancing ages. At the train station, the Grand Army Civil War veterans formed a double column while the new army passed through. They boarded a train shortly after 9:00 a.m. and departed for Camp Meade. The previous day, the draftees were recognized with a parade through town headed by chief of police William W. Smeach, officer Jesse Crabbs, and chief marshal Philip N. Forney. The drafted men marched behind cars carrying the Grand Army of the Republic men. The Grand Army of the Republic members included Charles Ryder, C. T. Kump, Dr. O. T. Everhart, Jacob Clive, O. F. Neely, Adam McKinney, John I. McKinney, Henry K. Wentz, Henry L. Trone, George Trone, J. Wagner, George C. Harman, J. F. Gordon, D. E. Winebrenner Sr., Jason Shultz, William Bair, and Charles Young. The draftees were each given a wristwatch during the day's festivities. Another postcard photograph taken of the event at the station was published by the *Evening Sun* newspaper October 29, 1981, and records the new inductees marching to the train station east on Library Place from Carlisle Street. Additional images of the recognition given the World War I servicemen can be found in chapter five.

One

Local Entertainment and Recreation

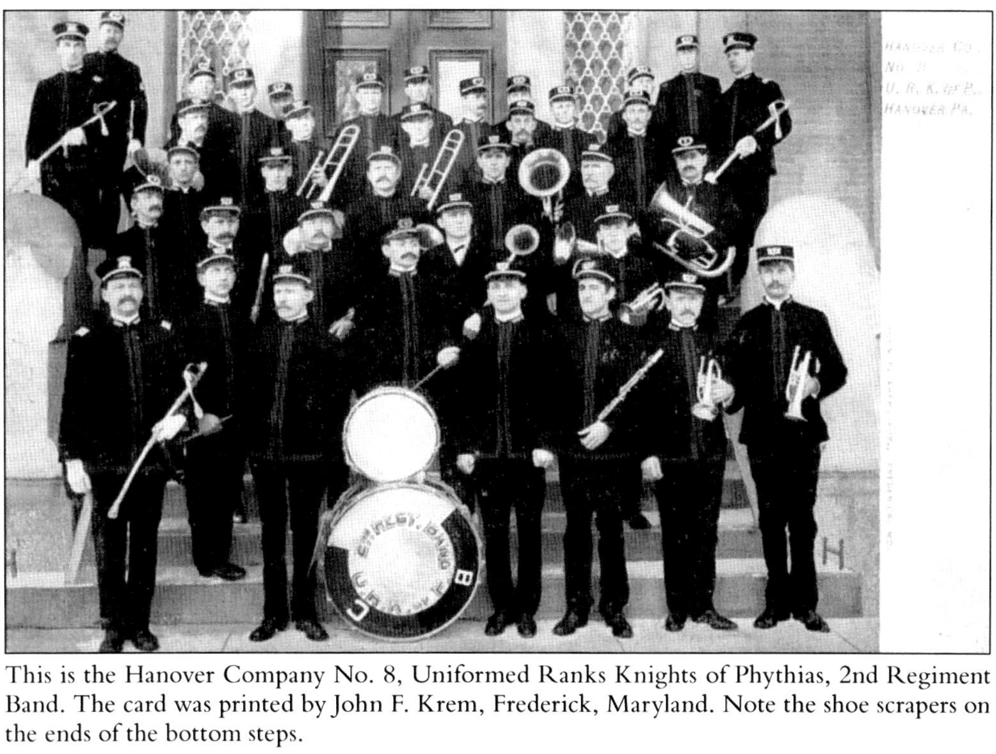

This is the Hanover Company No. 8, Uniformed Ranks Knights of Phythias, 2nd Regiment Band. The card was printed by John F. Krem, Frederick, Maryland. Note the shoe scrapers on the ends of the bottom steps.

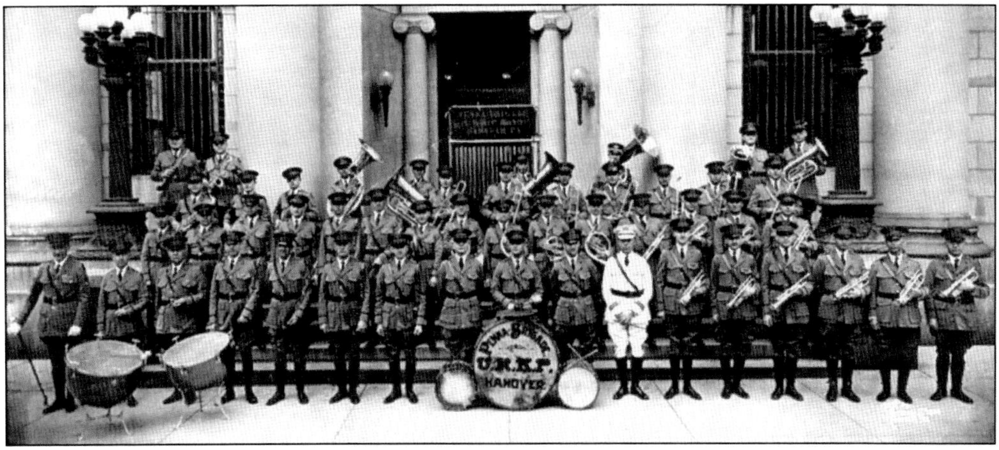

The *c.* 1940 Uniformed Ranks of Knights of Phythias, Pennsylvania Brigade band is in front of the former Hanover Saving Fund Society Bank on Carlisle Street, later the Bank of Hanover and now Sterling Financial Bank.

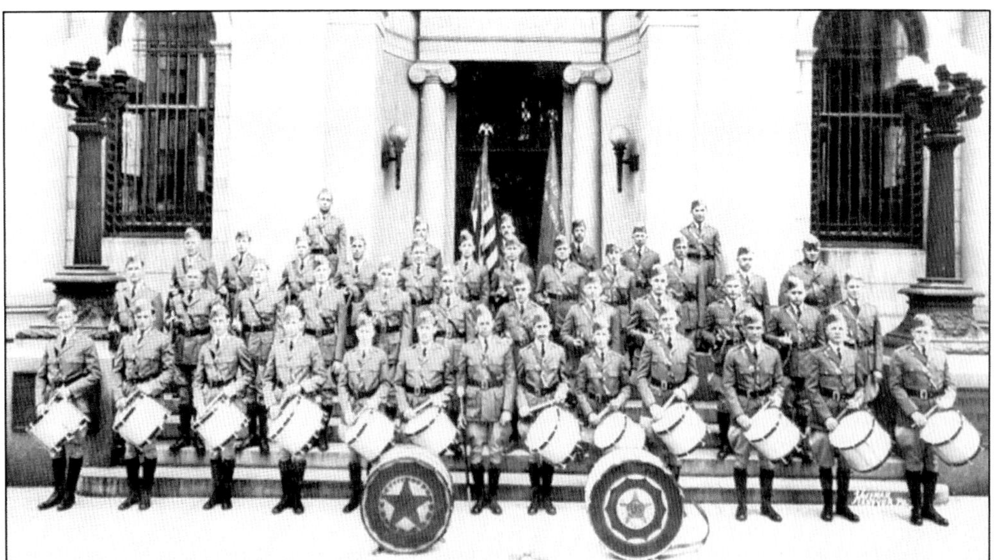

The Harold H. Bair Post 14, American Legion Drum and Bugle Corps is shown in front of the former Hanover Saving Fund Society Bank in the 1930s. The photograph is by Hoffman Studios, Hanover, Pennsylvania.

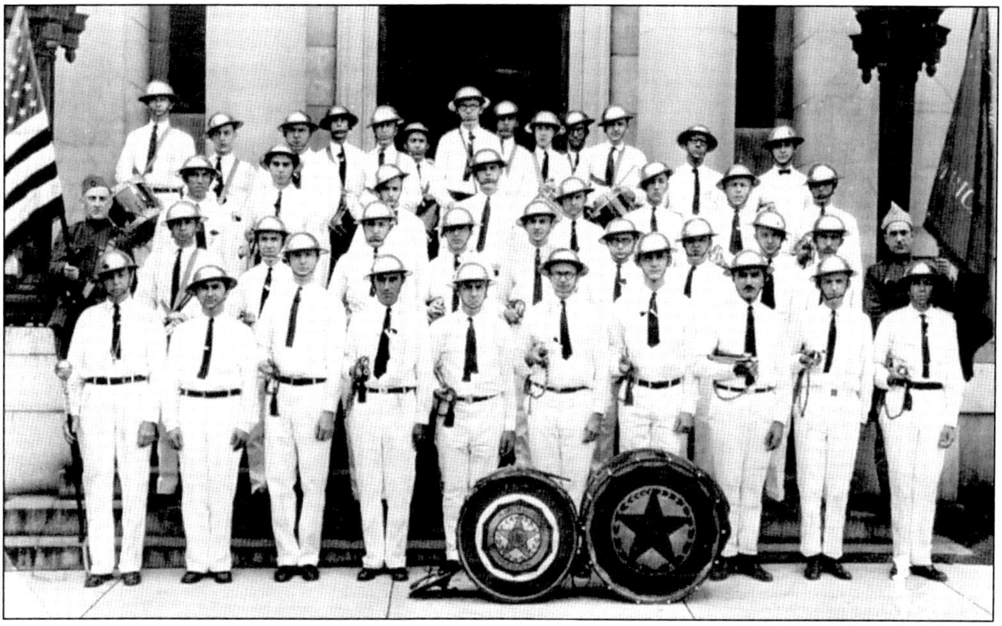

This image of the American Legion Post 14, Hanover, Pennsylvania, Drum and Bugle Corps was taken in the 1930s in front of the former Hanover Saving Fund Society Bank. The bank is now Sterling Financial Bank. The photograph is by Hoffman Studios, Hanover, Pennsylvania. Note the World War I surplus helmets as part of the uniform.

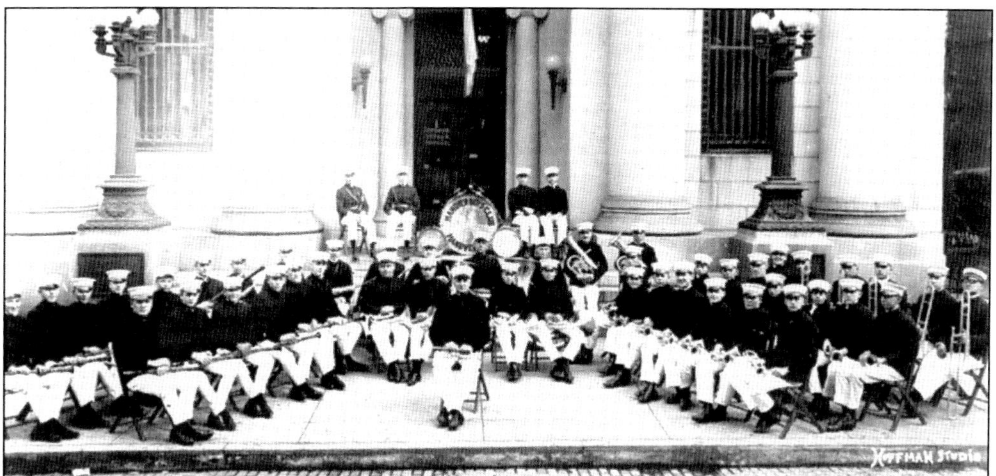

The Hanover, Pennsylvania, Boys Club Band was photographed in front of the former Hanover Savings Fund Society Bank in the 1930s. The photograph is by Hoffman Studios, 113 Broadway, Hanover, Pennsylvania.

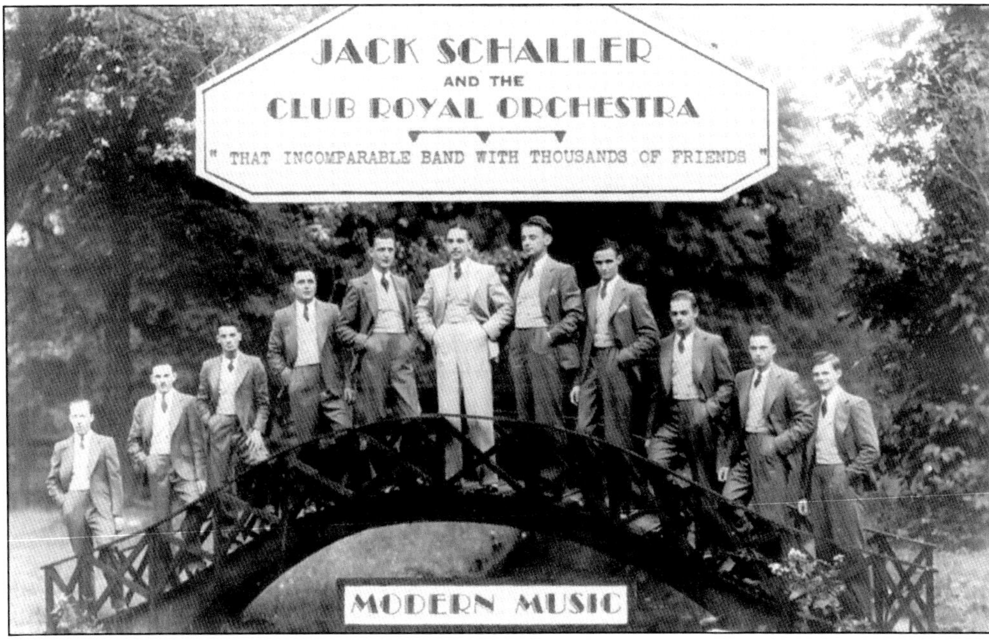

This is Jack Schaller and the Club Royal Orchestra with Dick Feeser, second from the left. Their motto was "that incomparable band with thousands of friends." The stamp box indicates that the card was printed between 1927 and 1942.

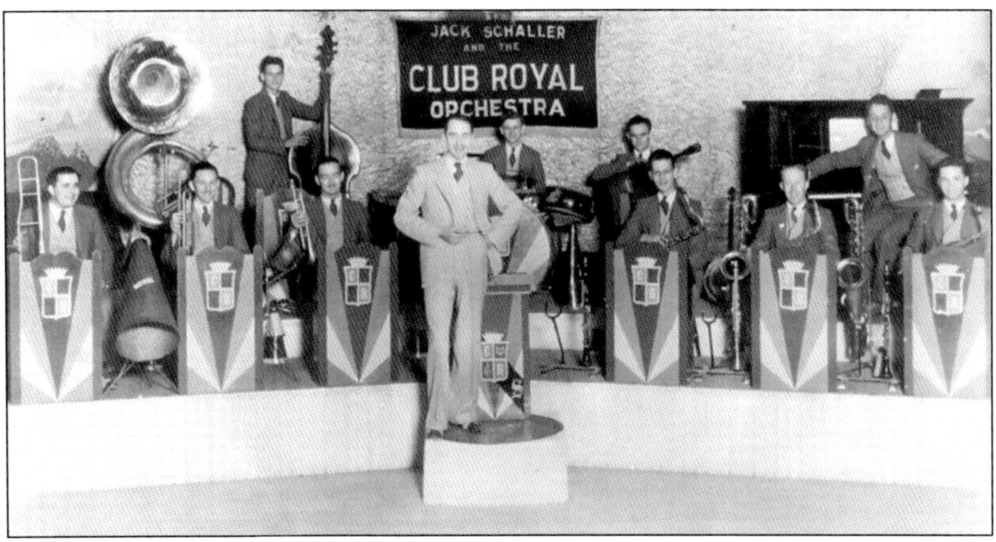

Another picture of Jack Schaller and the Club Royal Orchestra with Dick Feeser, second from the left, was used to secure bookings for the band. The stamp box indicates the card was printed between 1927 and 1942.

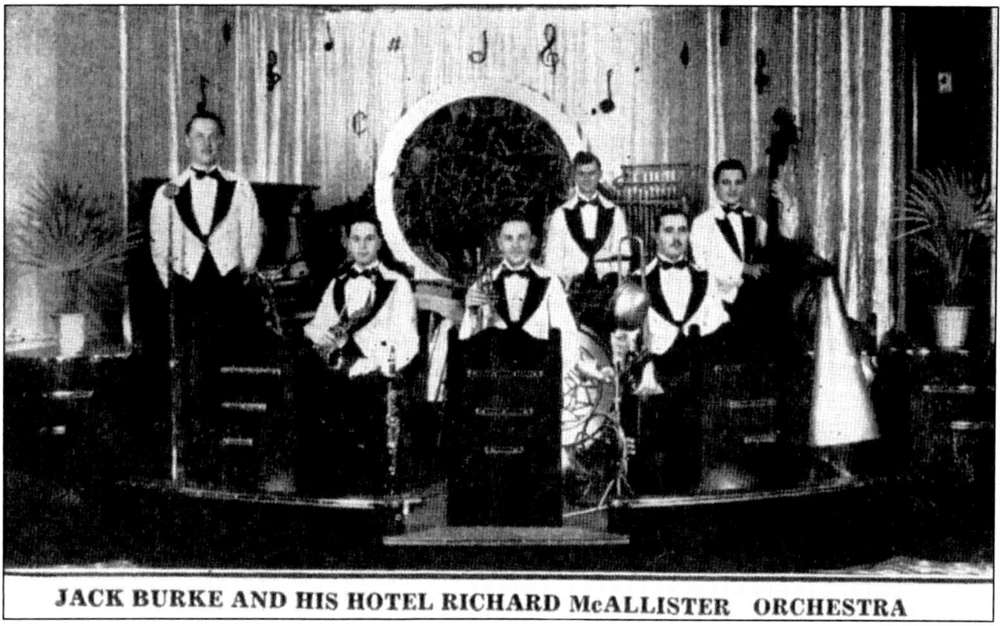

Jack Burke and his Hotel Richard McAllister Orchestra included Dick Feeser, in the middle with the trumpet. This was a booking card for the band. The card was never mailed but required 1¢ postage.

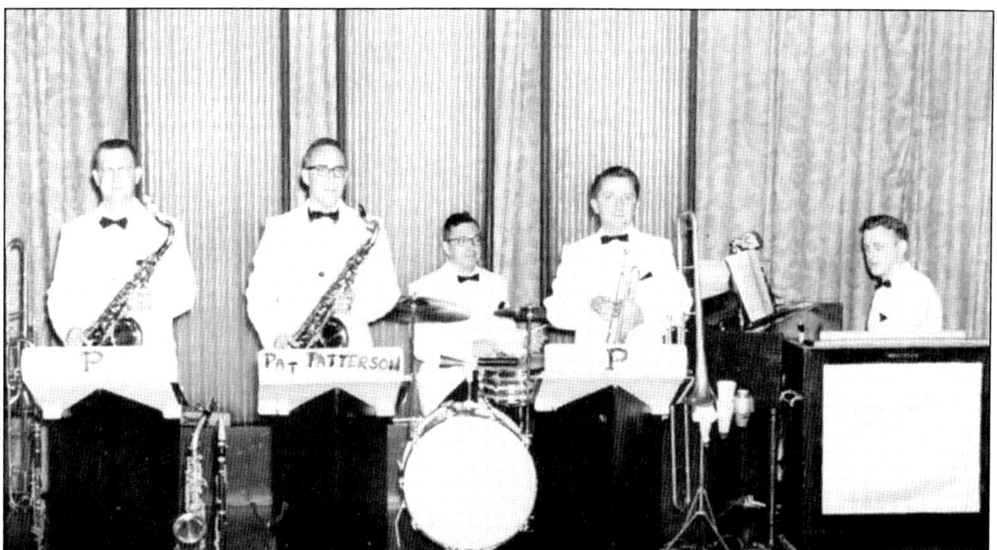

The Pat Patterson Orchestra was located at 24 Third Street in Hanover. The card was printed by National Press, Inc., Chicago, Illinois, and was used as a promotional card.

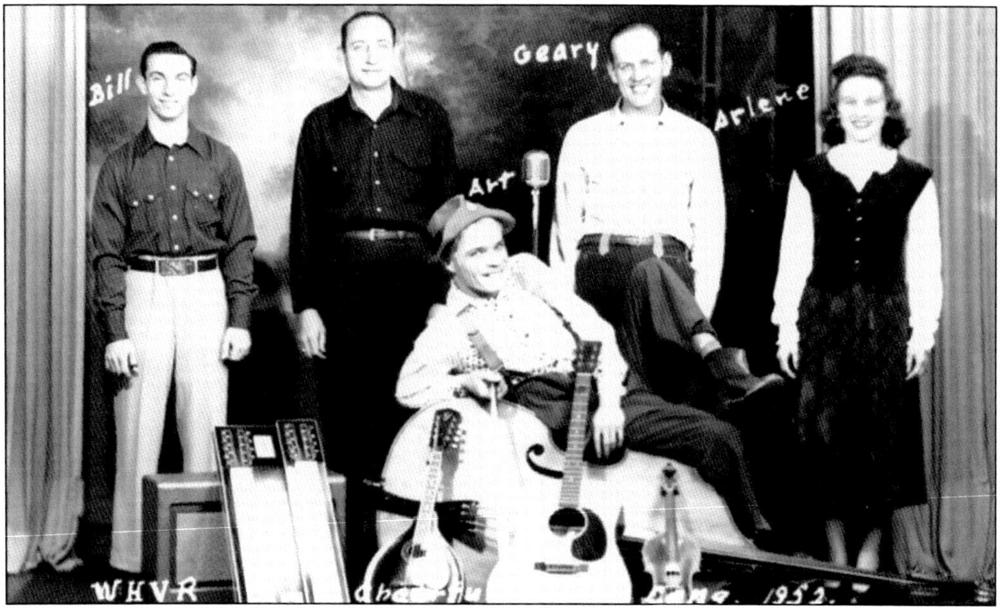

The Cheerful Valley Gang, a country musical group, entertained on the Hanover AM radio station, WHVR, in 1952.

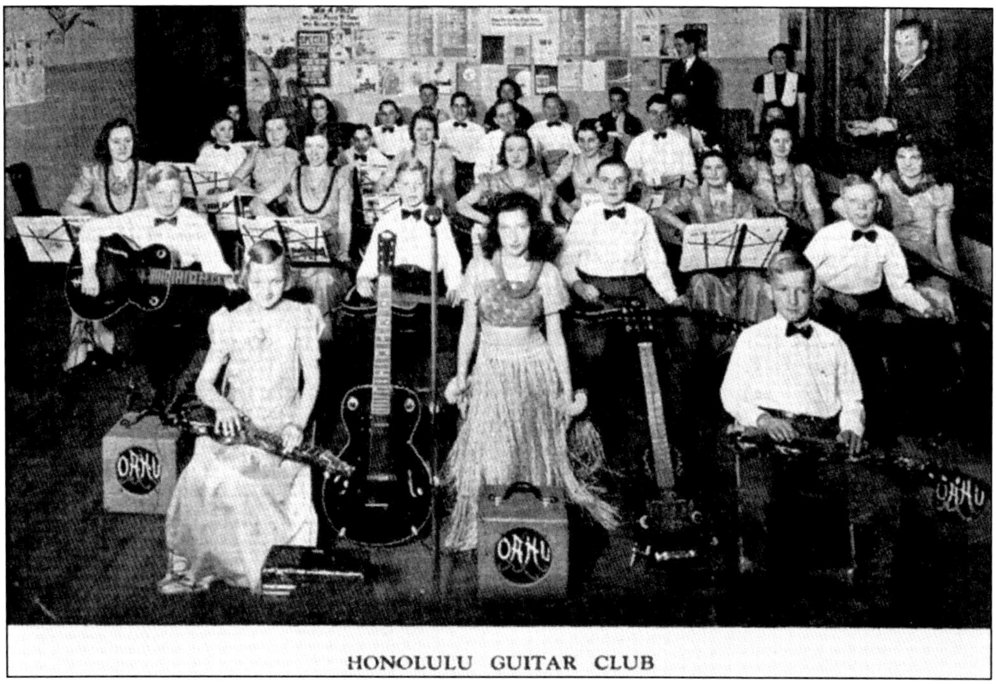

The Honolulu Guitar Club was part of the Honolulu Conservatory of Music, located at 22 Carlisle Street. The back of this card was devoted to advertising.

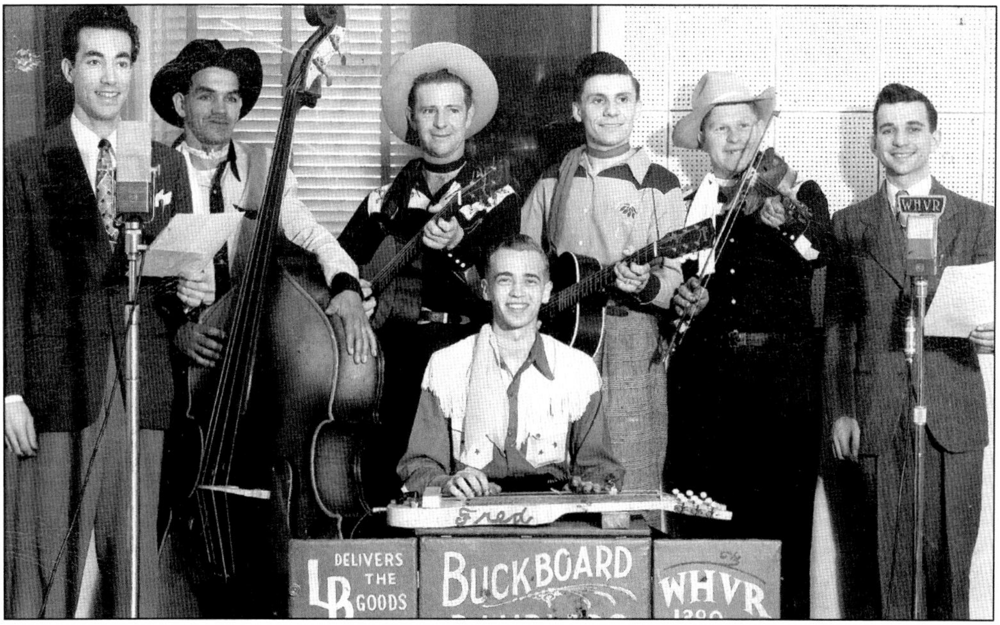

The Buckboard Ramblers was a country music group that entertained on the AM radio station WHVR in Hanover in the early days of the station during the late 1940s. The announcer on the left is longtime local personality Ned Rutledge, and the announcer on the right is "Chuck" Zink. The card was mailed March 1, 1948.

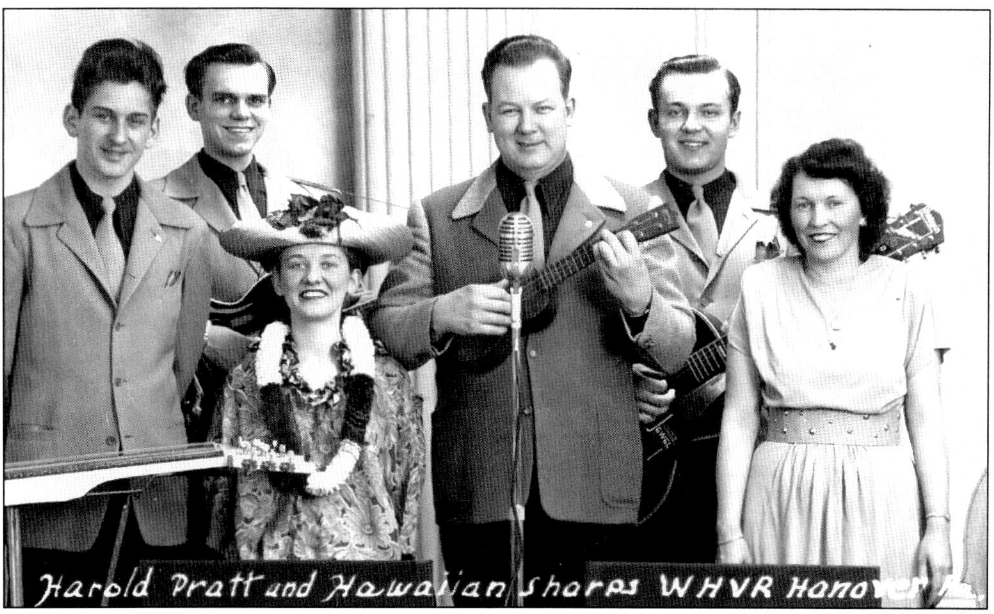

Harold Pratt and Hawaiian Sharps were an instrumental and vocal group that entertained on WHVR in the early days of the station.

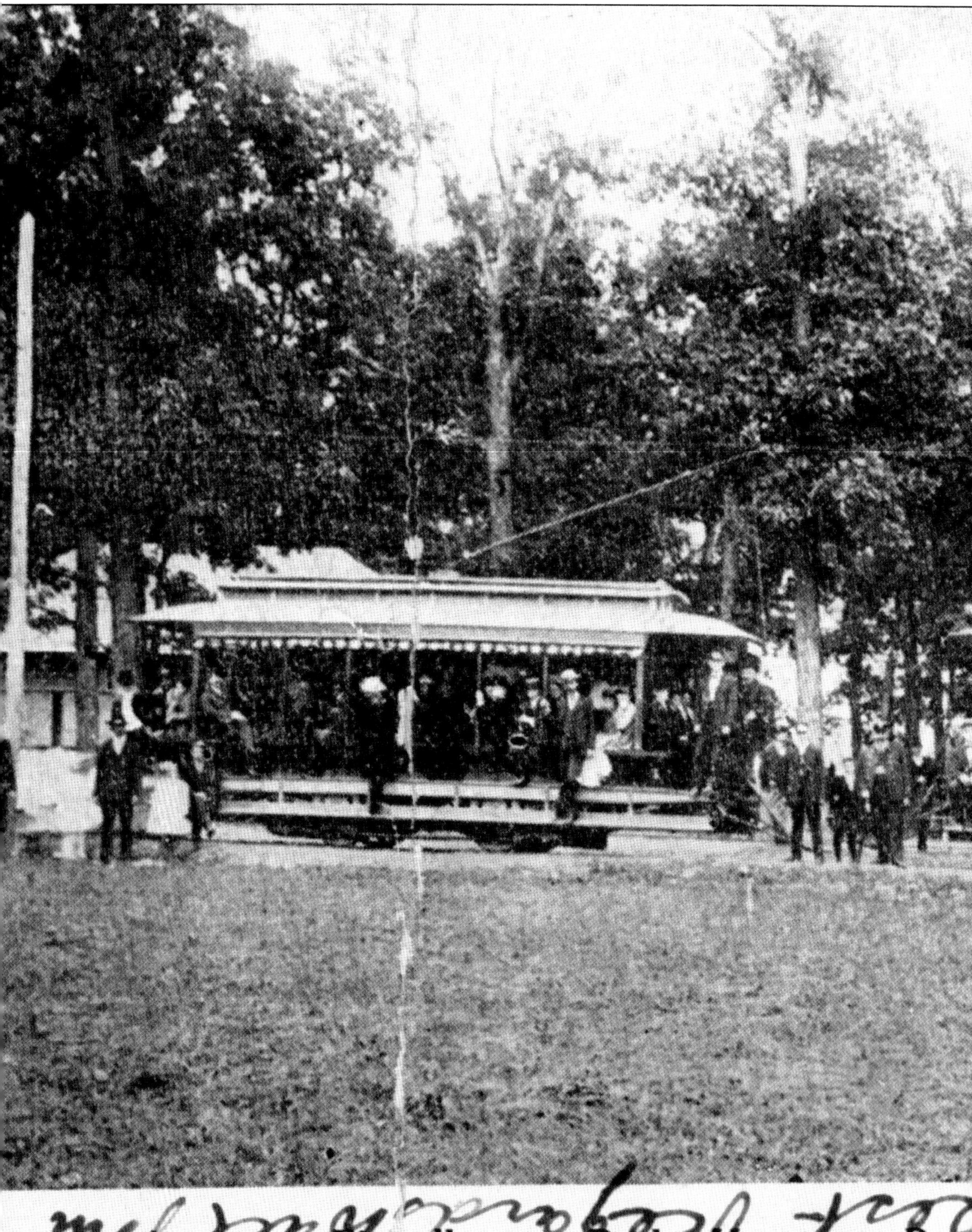

Eichelberger Park was at the end of the trolley line on Baltimore Street. The card was by Swords Brothers Photographers, Hanover, Pennsylvania. This is an interesting card showing

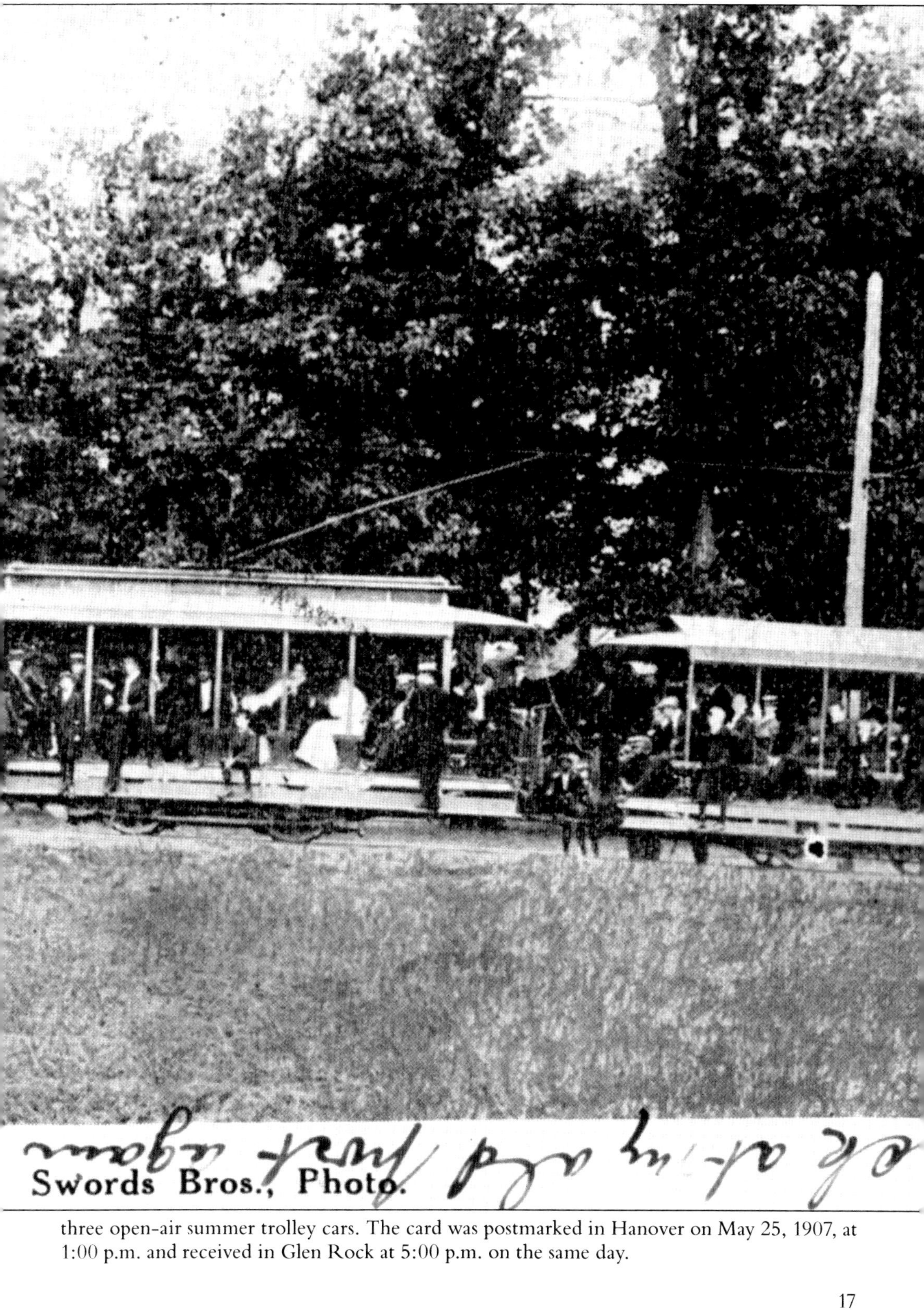

three open-air summer trolley cars. The card was postmarked in Hanover on May 25, 1907, at 1:00 p.m. and received in Glen Rock at 5:00 p.m. on the same day.

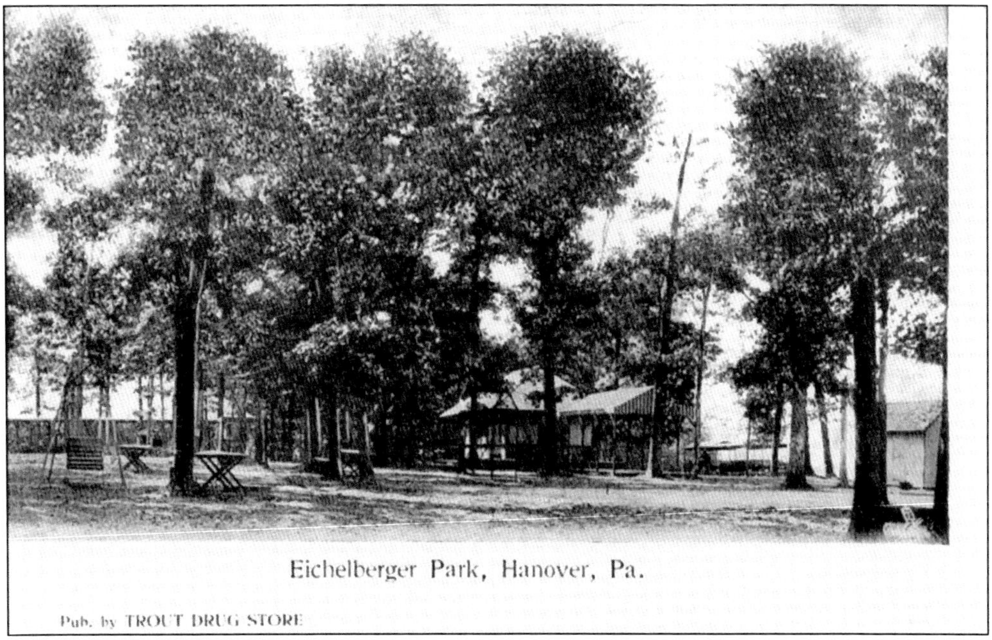

The Eichelberger Park was established by the Hanover and McSherrystown Street Railway Company and was located at the south end of the trolley line on Baltimore Street. The trolley line was extended to the park in 1904. The card was published by Trout Drug Store, Hanover, Pennsylvania. The card was postmarked in Hanover at 9:00 a.m., October 20, 1906, and stamped as received in Ephrata, Lancaster County, on the same day at 7:00 p.m. That is not a bad delivery time for 1906.

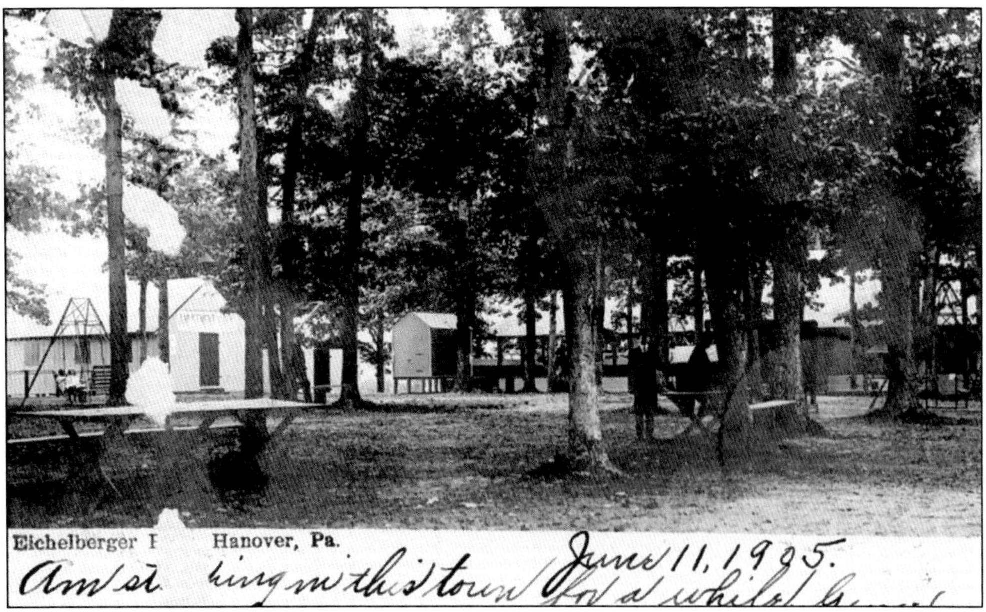

Eichelberger Park, which opened June 25, 1904, was taken by Swords Brothers Photographers, Hanover, Pennsylvania. The card was postmarked in Hanover at 9:00 a.m. on June 12, 1905, and stamped as received in Manchester, Massachusetts, at 8:00 a.m. the next day, June 13, 1905. How did they do it?

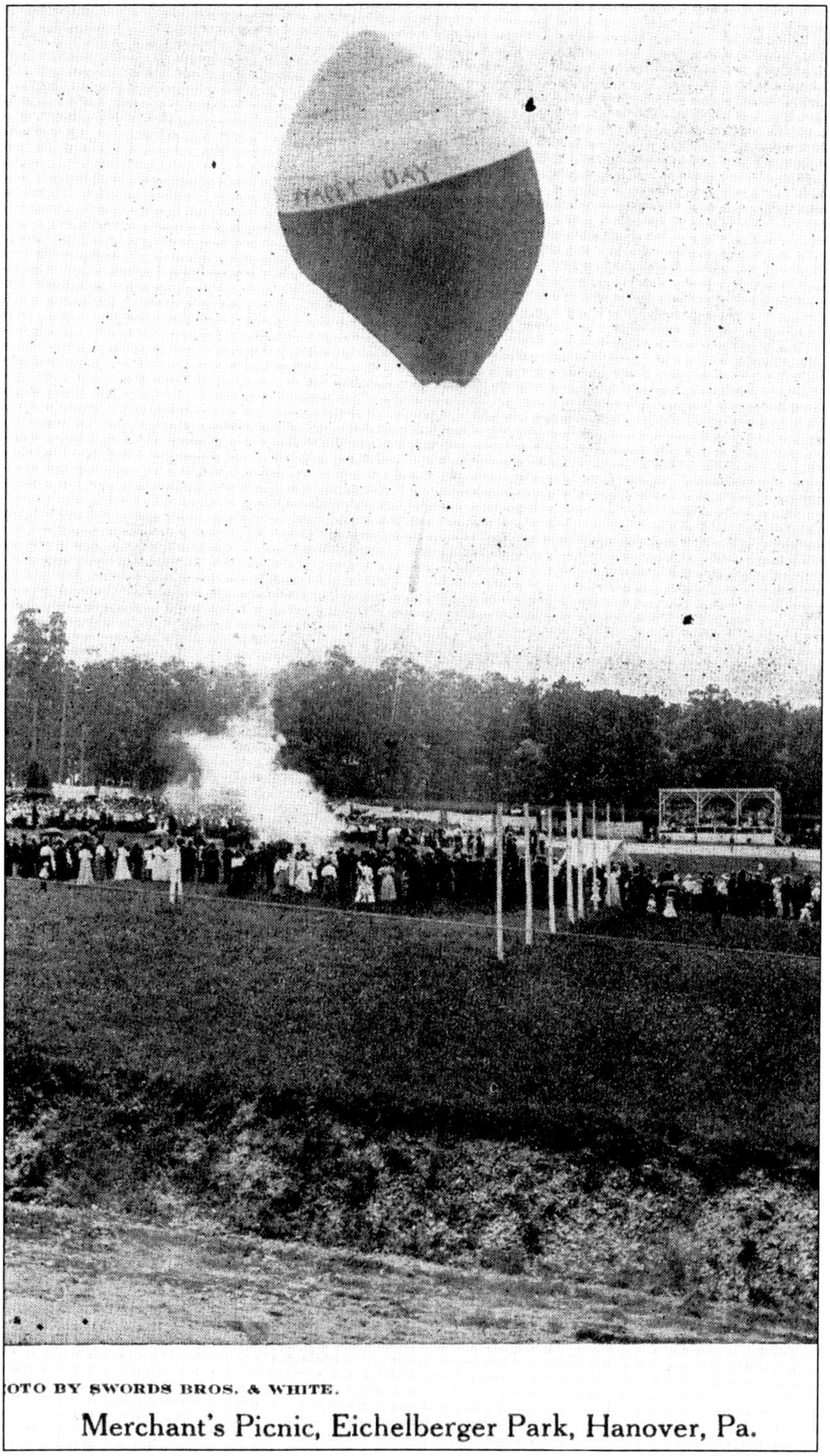

A merchant's picnic was held at Eichelberger Park at the south end of the trolley line on Baltimore Street. Balloon ascensions were popular events of the era. The photograph is by Swords Brothers and White, Hanover, Pennsylvania.

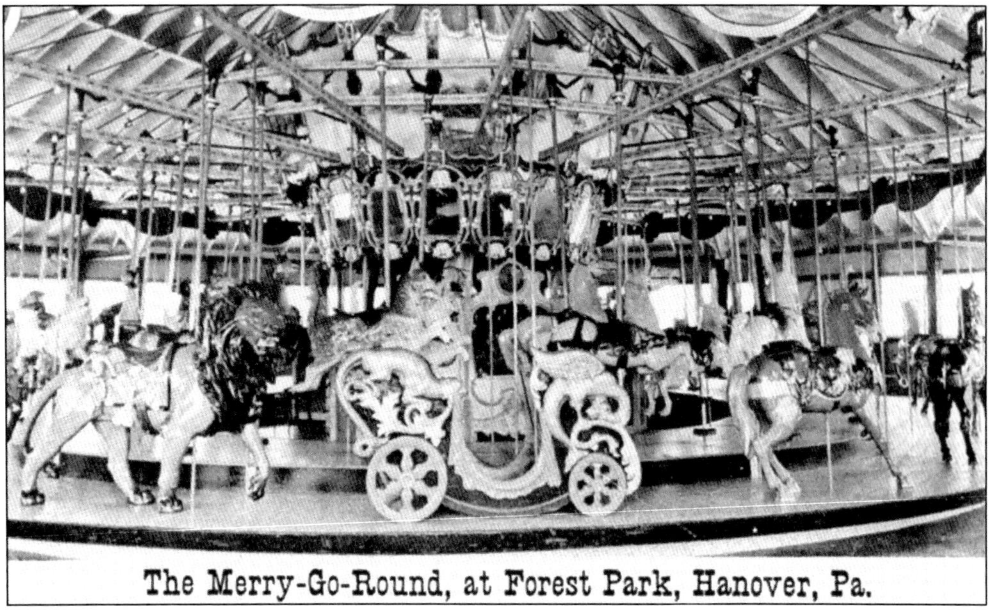

The merry-go-round at Forest Park was located at the former Eichelberger Park at the end of the trolley line on Baltimore Street. The card is by Raum Printing, Philadelphia, Pennsylvania, for August Karst, the park owner.

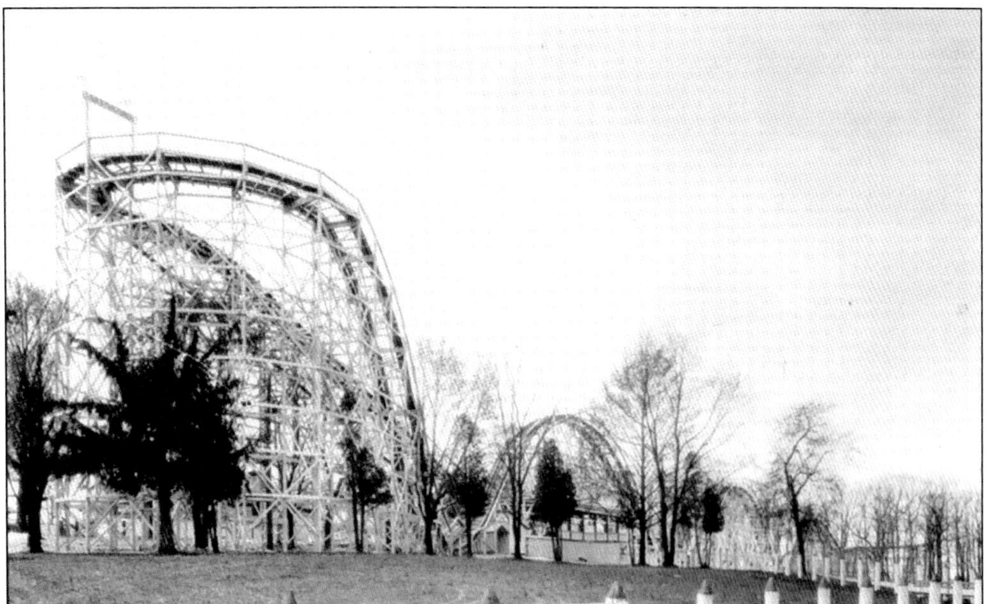

In 1926, A. Karst and Sons of Philadelphia purchased Eichelberger Park and operated it as Forest Park until 1967, when the real estate was sold to accommodate a shopping center. The popular roller coaster ride named the Greyhound opened in 1930.

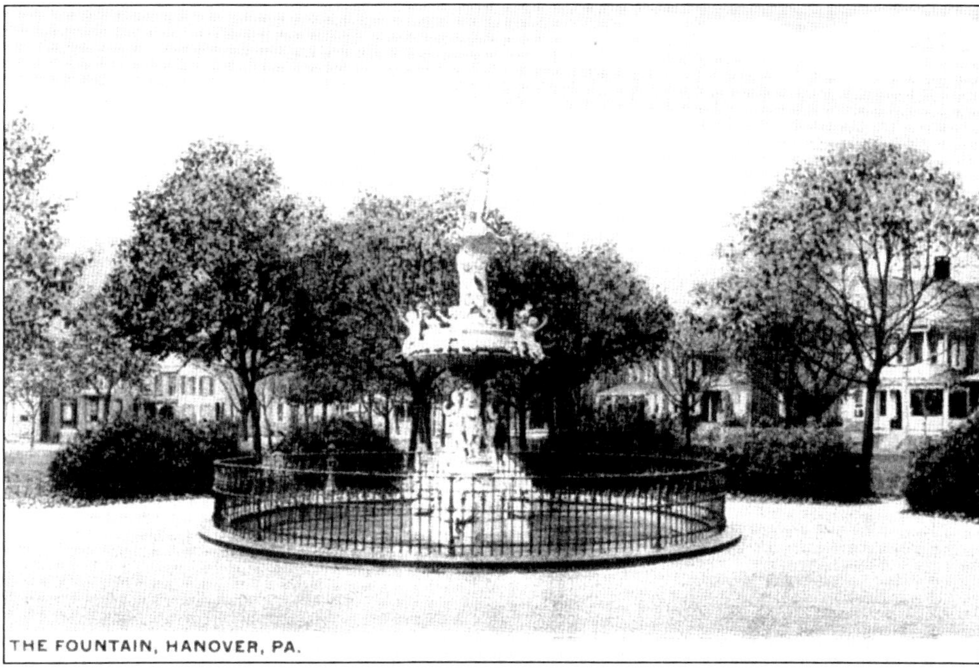

This fountain was formerly located on Center Square in Hanover. It was then moved to Wirt Park, bounded by High Street in the background and Park Avenue on the right. The fountain has since been sold to a Florida restaurant. Card No. 102405 was published by David Kauffman from Baltimore, Maryland.

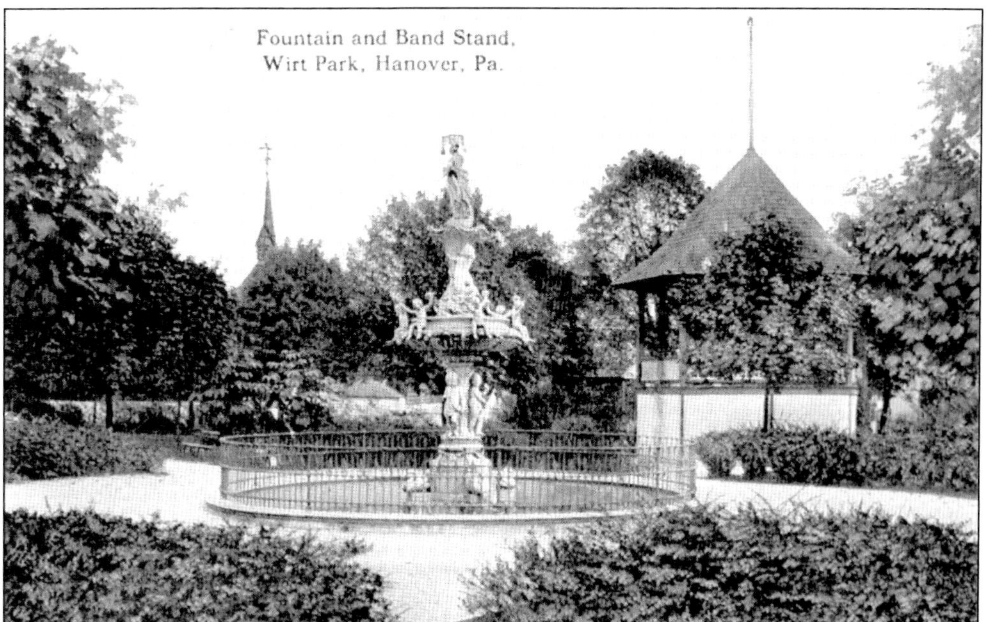

This is the fountain and bandstand at Wirt Park in Hanover. The card was published by the Fair and Square Bargain House, York, Pennsylvania. It was postmarked June 5, 1916.

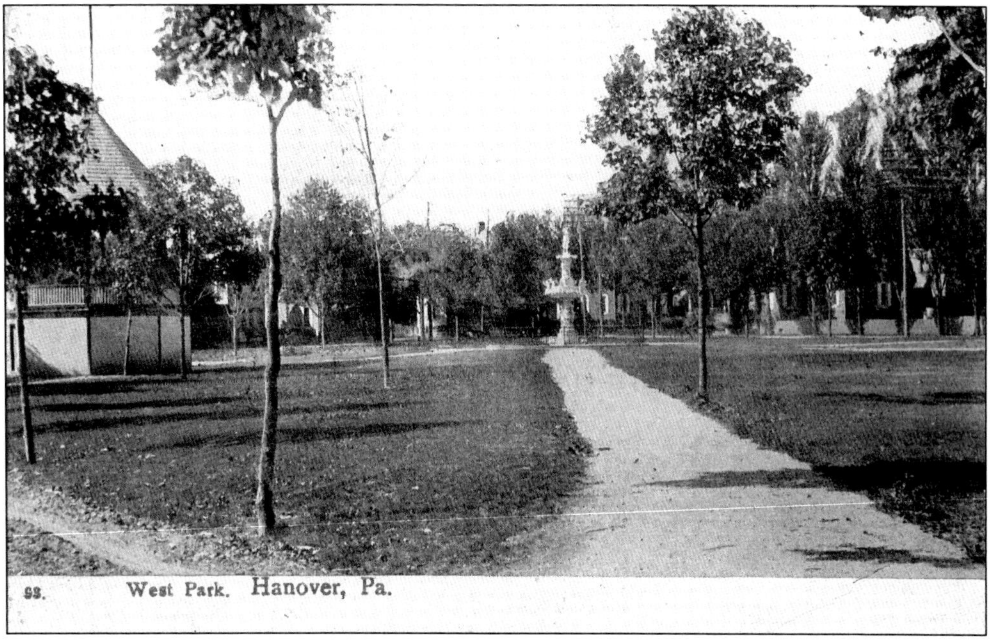

This card has a printing error. It says it is West Park, but it should be Wirt Park. Wirt Park is bounded by High Street, Park Avenue, North Franklin Street, and Gail Street. The card was published by Wheelock, Peoria, Illinois. The card was printed in Germany as Card No. 93.

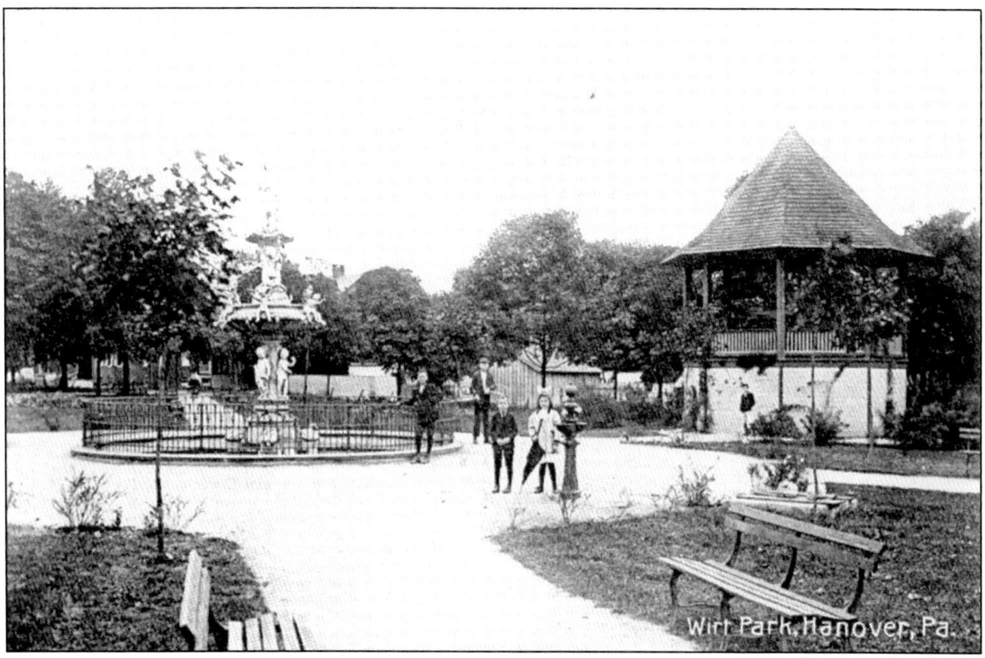

Wirt Park was a popular destination to relax by the fountain and to be entertained by bands at the bandstand on the right. This card was mailed in 1909.

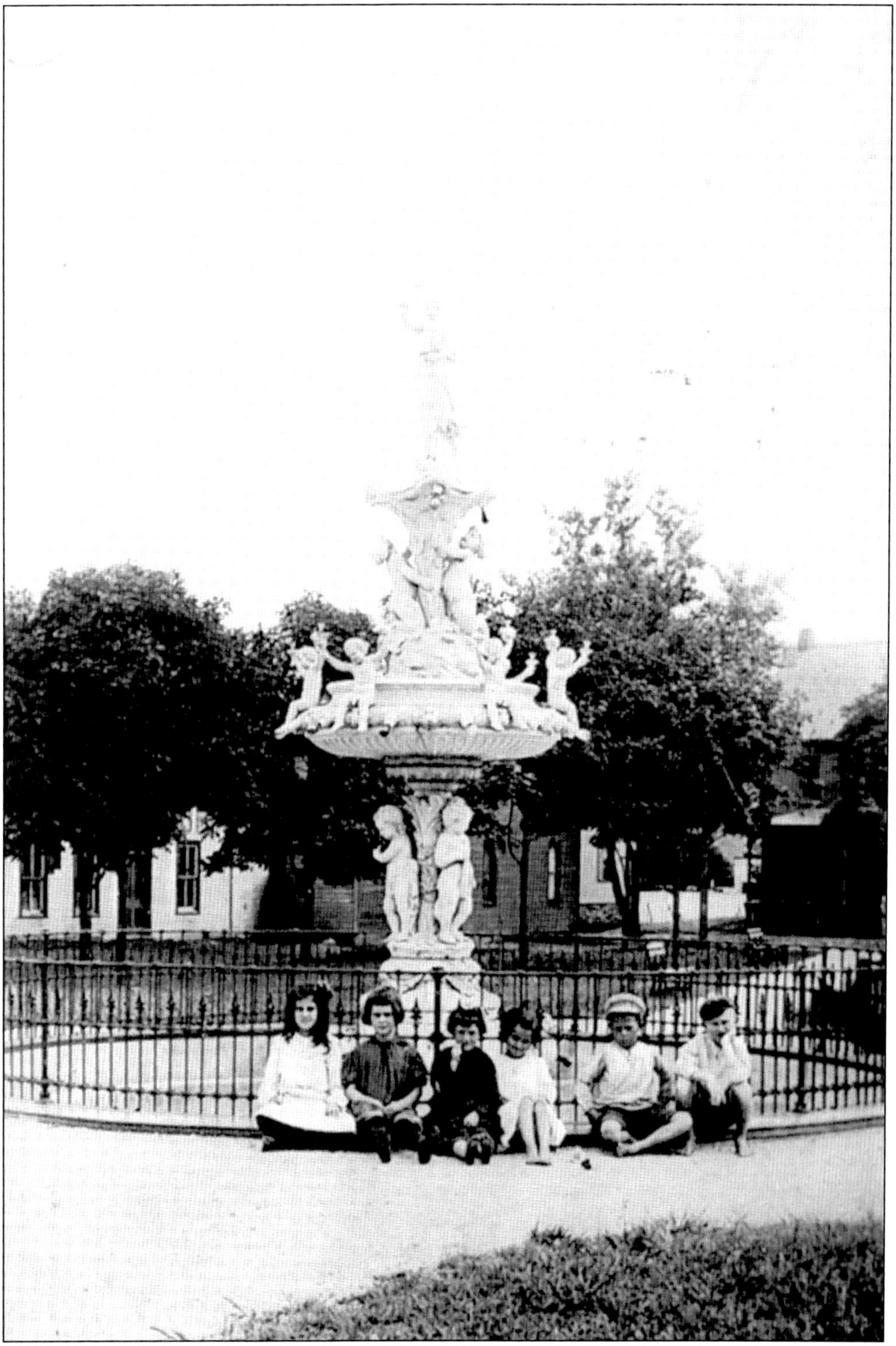

Card No. 57834 of the Wirt Park Fountain is by the Rotograph Company, New York, New York. It was printed in Germany, and it was mailed on September 10, 1910.

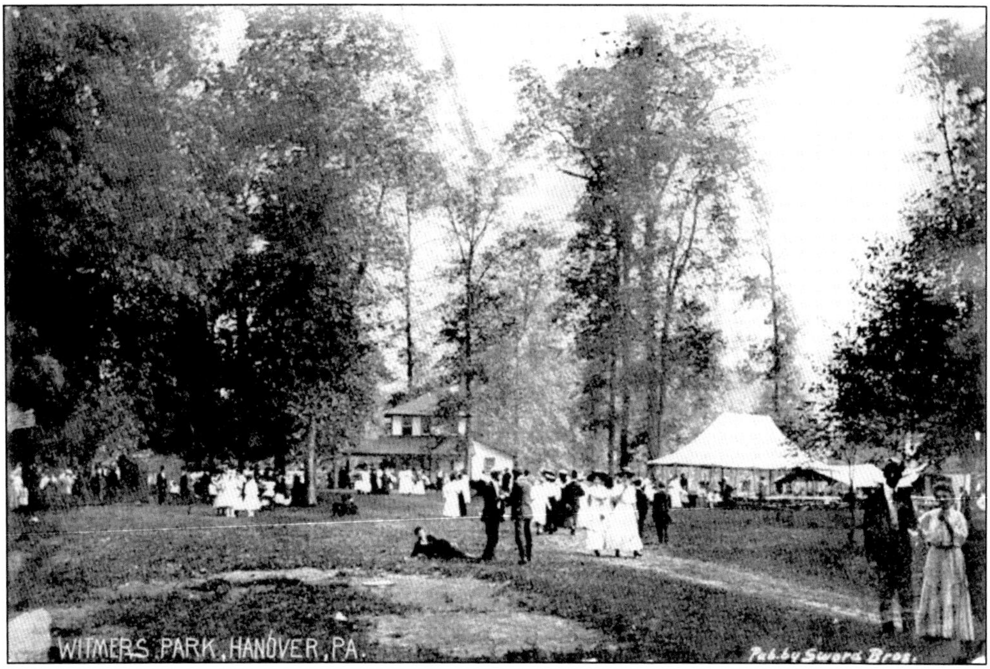

Witmer's Park was located two miles south of McSherrystown on the Conewago Creek in Hanover. The trolley company established this park around 1908. The color-tinted card is by Swords Brothers, Hanover, Pennsylvania. The card was postmarked July 4, 1912.

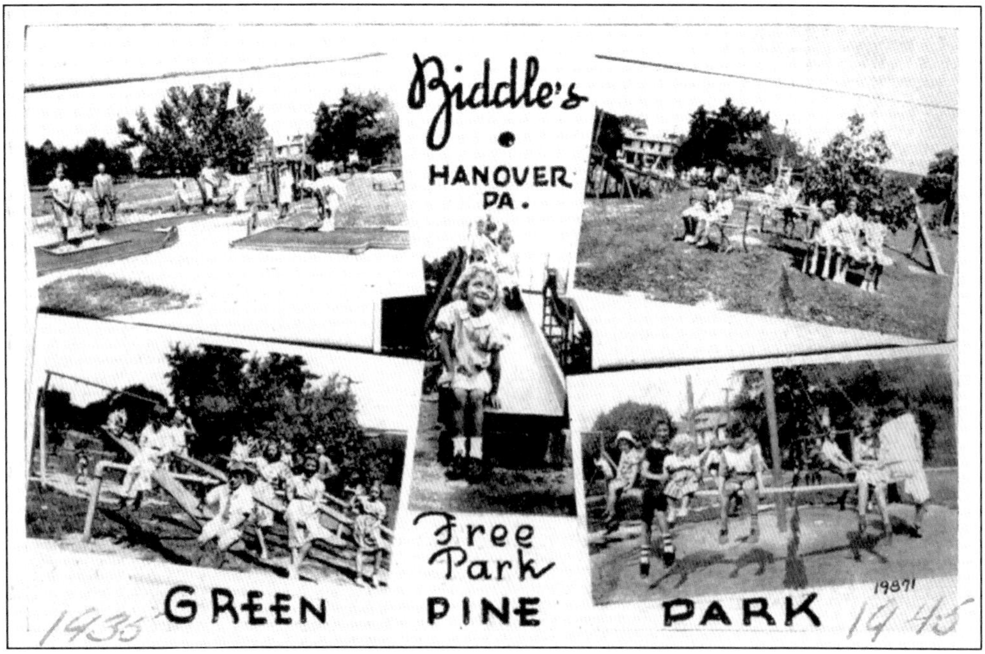

Biddle's Free Green Pine Park was located at Stock, Penn, and George Streets in Hanover. The use of this park was free to Sunday schools, family reunions, and children. The card was printed by Kaiser and Blair, Cincinnati, Ohio. The card was hand dated 1935–1945.

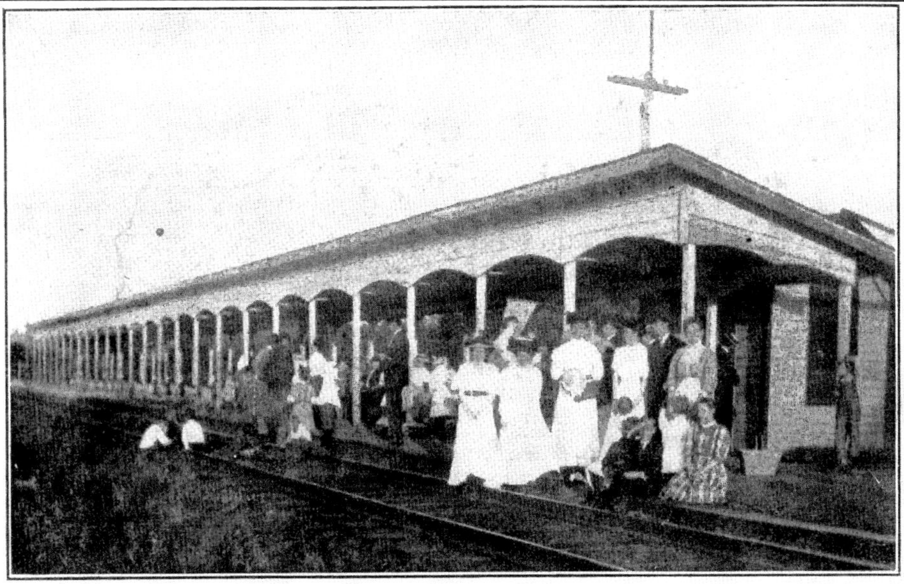

PENN GROVE CAMP STATION

Penn Grove Camp Station was located near Smith's Station along the main line of the Western Maryland Railroad from Baltimore to Hagerstown, Maryland. Penn Grove Camp was a religious summer camp meeting grounds that was very well attended, as indicated by the size of the station. The card was postmarked 1911.

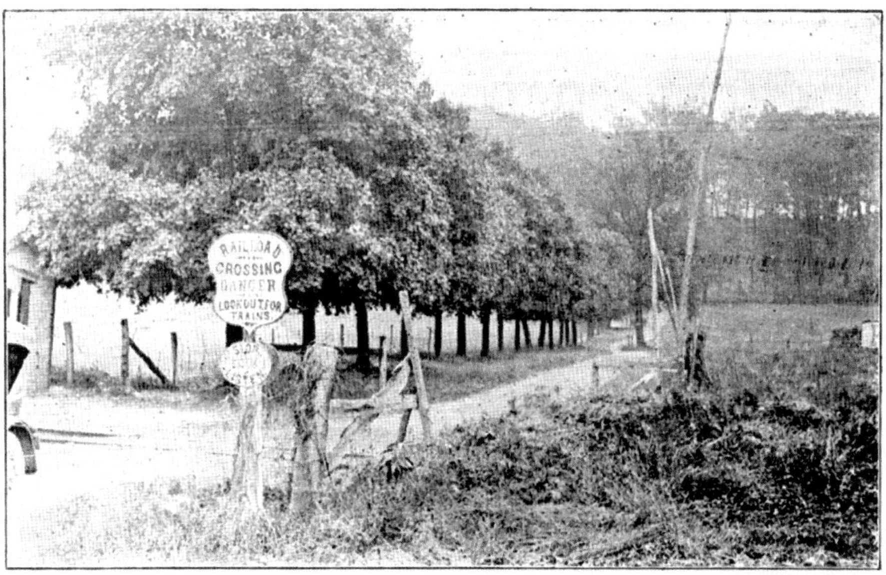

Path from Station to Grove (Penn Grove Camp) **Smith's Station, Pa.**

The path from the train station led to the Penn Grove Camp near Smith's Station, Pennsylvania. It is a religious summer camp located near Smith's Station, north of the Blooming Grove Road.

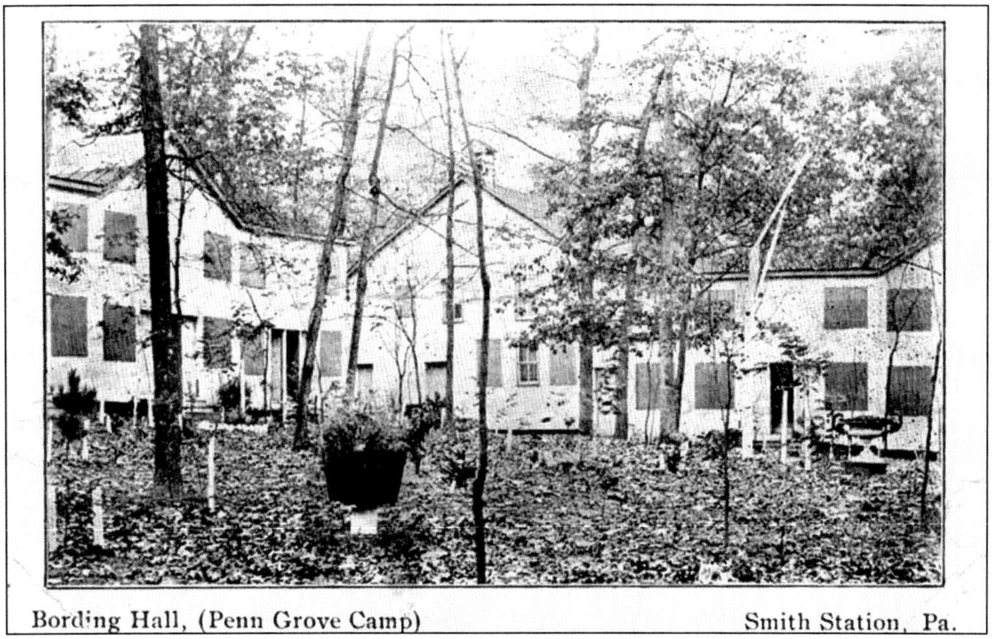

The boarding hall at Penn Grove Camp was near Smith's Station, Pennsylvania. The card was postmarked June 24, 1926. The camp is still in operation today.

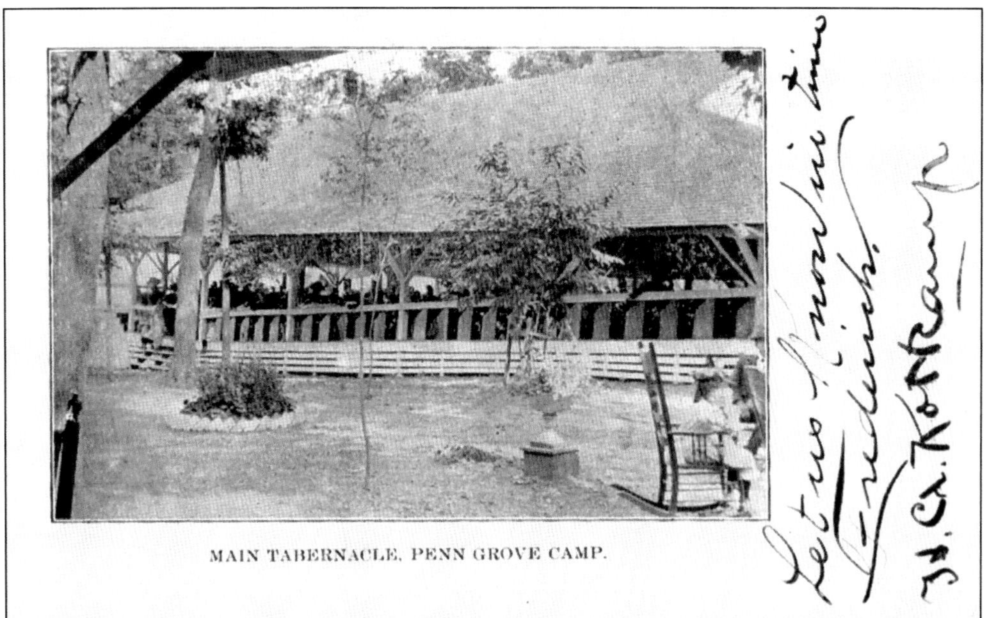

The Main Tabernacle at Penn Grove Camp was part of a summer church camp near Smith's Station. The card was printed for the camp store. The card was mailed July 3, 1905.

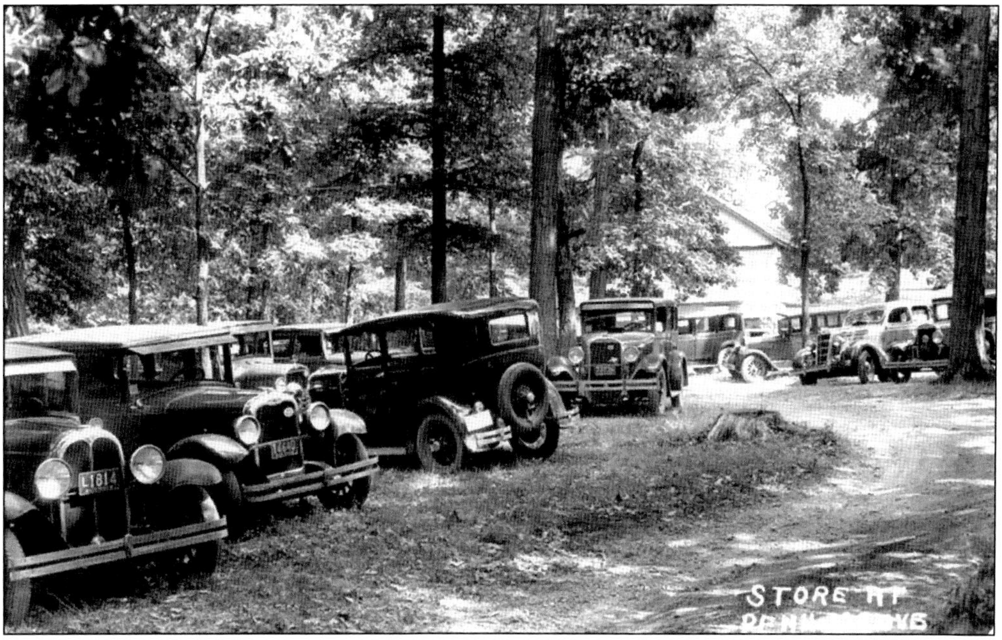

This is the store at Penn Grove Camp, a summer church camp near Smith's Station, Pennsylvania. The card was postmarked August 7, 1939.

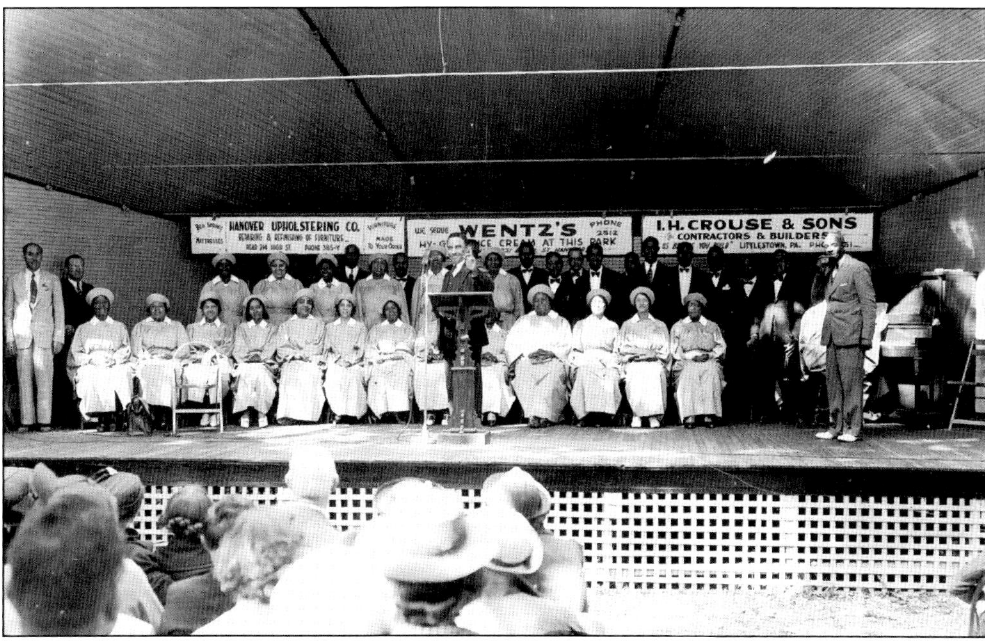

The local band stage could be at Penn Grove church camp. Advertisers include Hanover Upholstering Company at the rear of 214 High Street, Wentz Ice Cream, and I. H. Crouse and Sons, contractors and builders of Littlestown, on the inside rear of the pavilion wall.

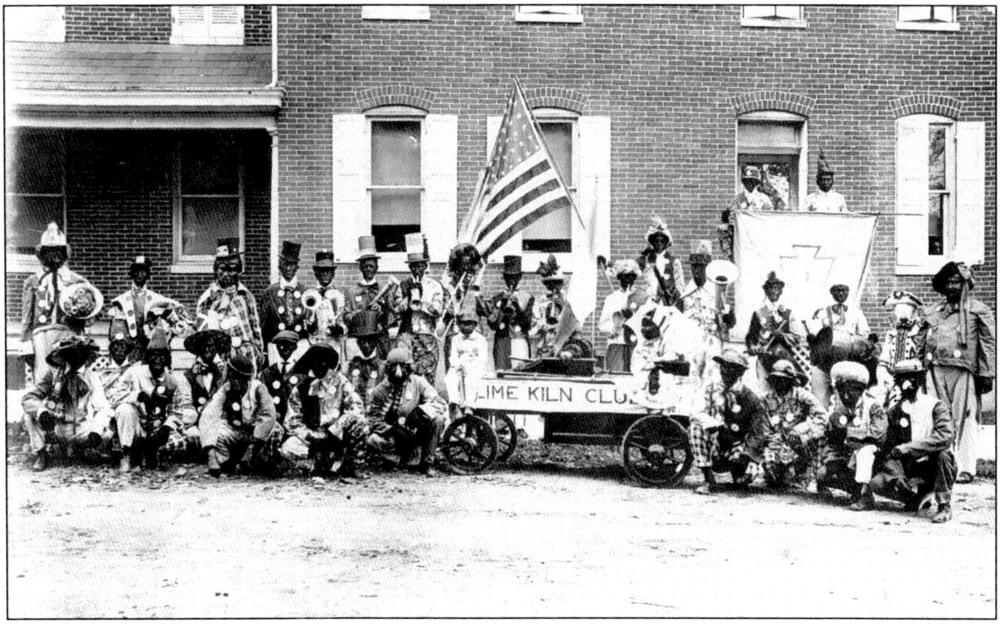

The Lime Kiln Club was organized in November 1894 by the members of the Hanover Fire Company to prepare for the Thanksgiving Day parade and to add interest to the fire company organization, according to the newspaper. With costumes and black-painted faces, they often marched in parades. A parade scene can be found on page 86.

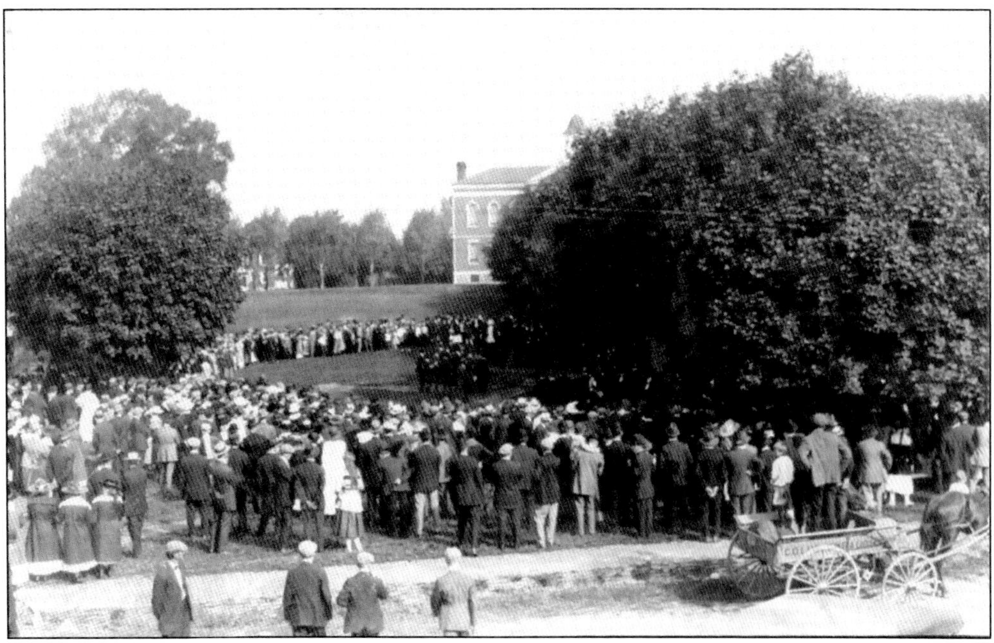

This early event (date unknown) occurred at the Eichelberger High School campus, with a portion of the building in the upper center evident. This view is from North Street with McCosh Street on the right corner. The homes to the upper left are on Eichelberger Street.

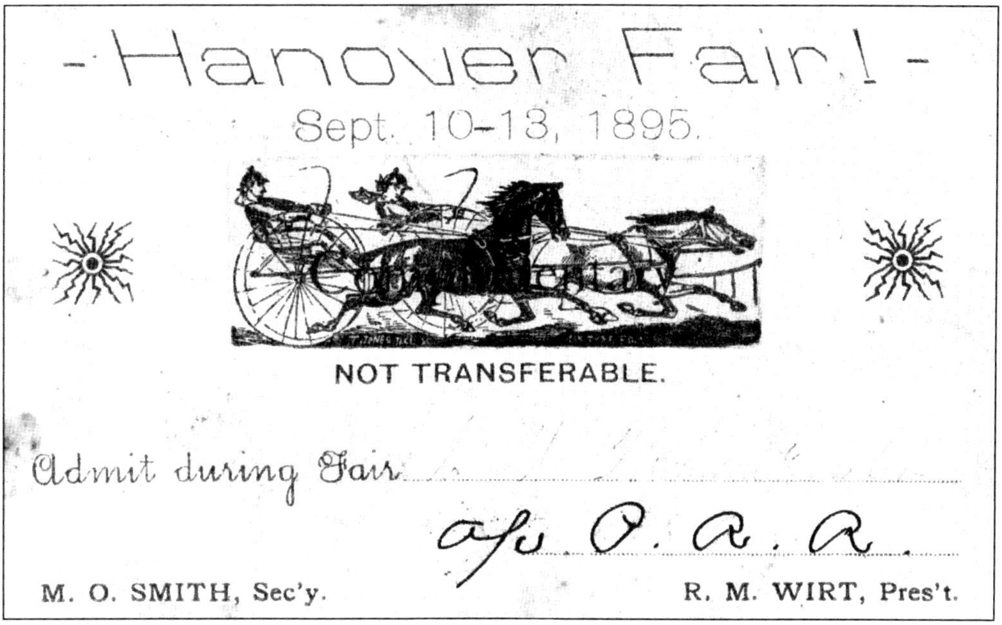

The Hanover Agricultural Society was organized in 1884, and 27 acres were purchased between York and Baltimore Streets for $125 per acre. This is an admission ticket to the September 1895 fair.

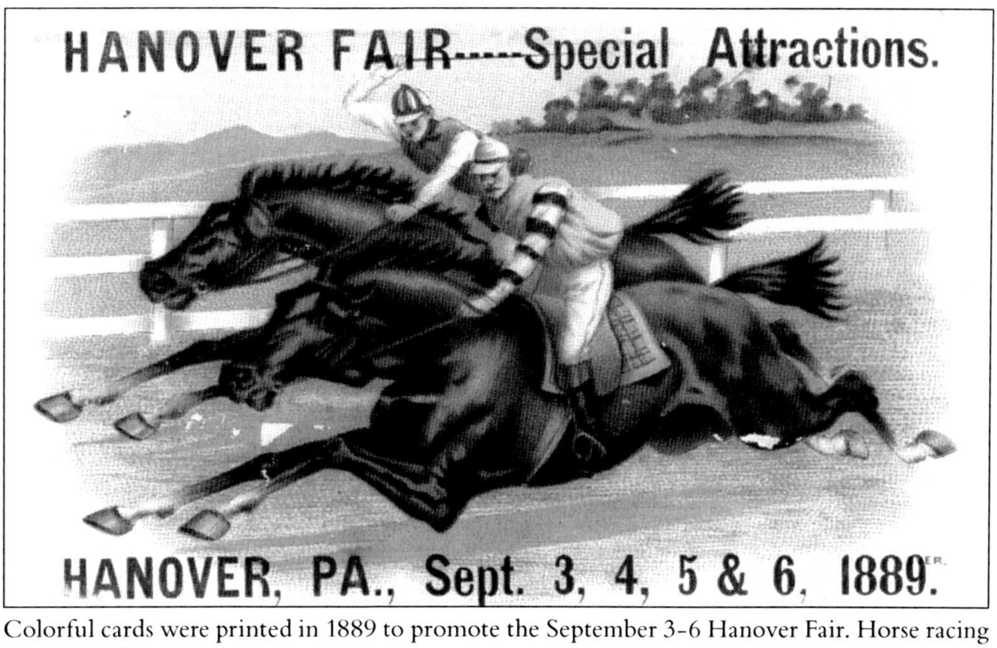

Colorful cards were printed in 1889 to promote the September 3-6 Hanover Fair. Horse racing was a popular event.

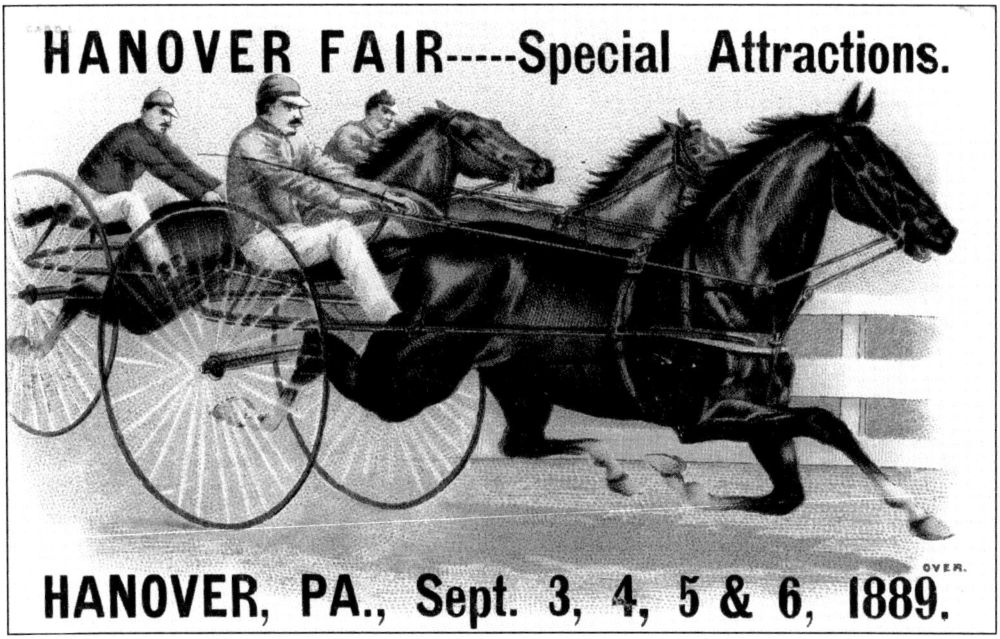

The Hanover Fair races were referred to as "trials of speed." Trotting races were held on Wednesday through Friday and paid purses of up to $350 per race.

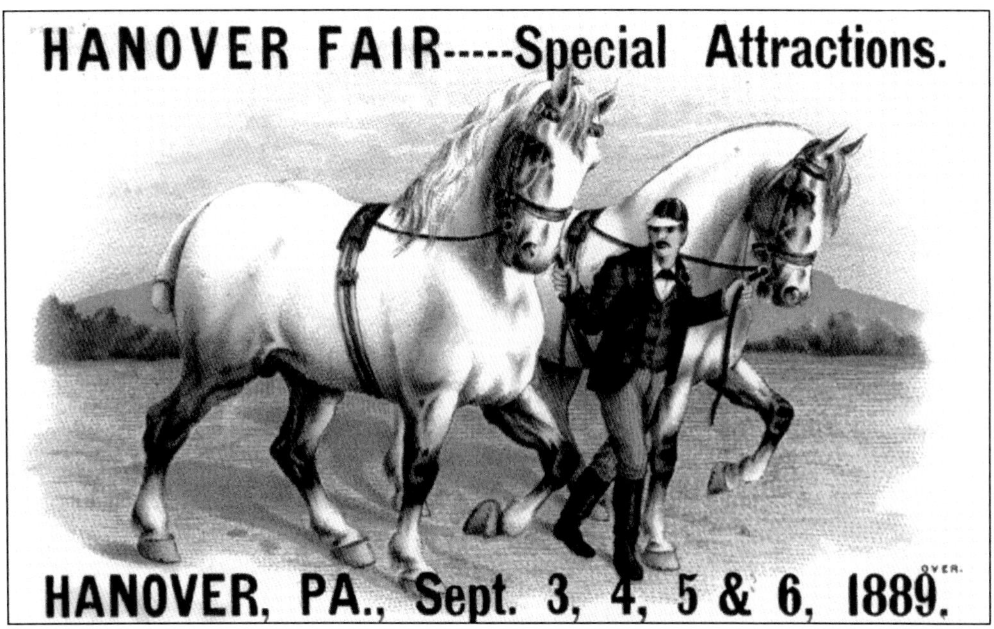

The judging of livestock was an important element of each fair, as was entrance in categories such as cakes and bread, preserves and jellies, canned fruits, and flowers and plants.

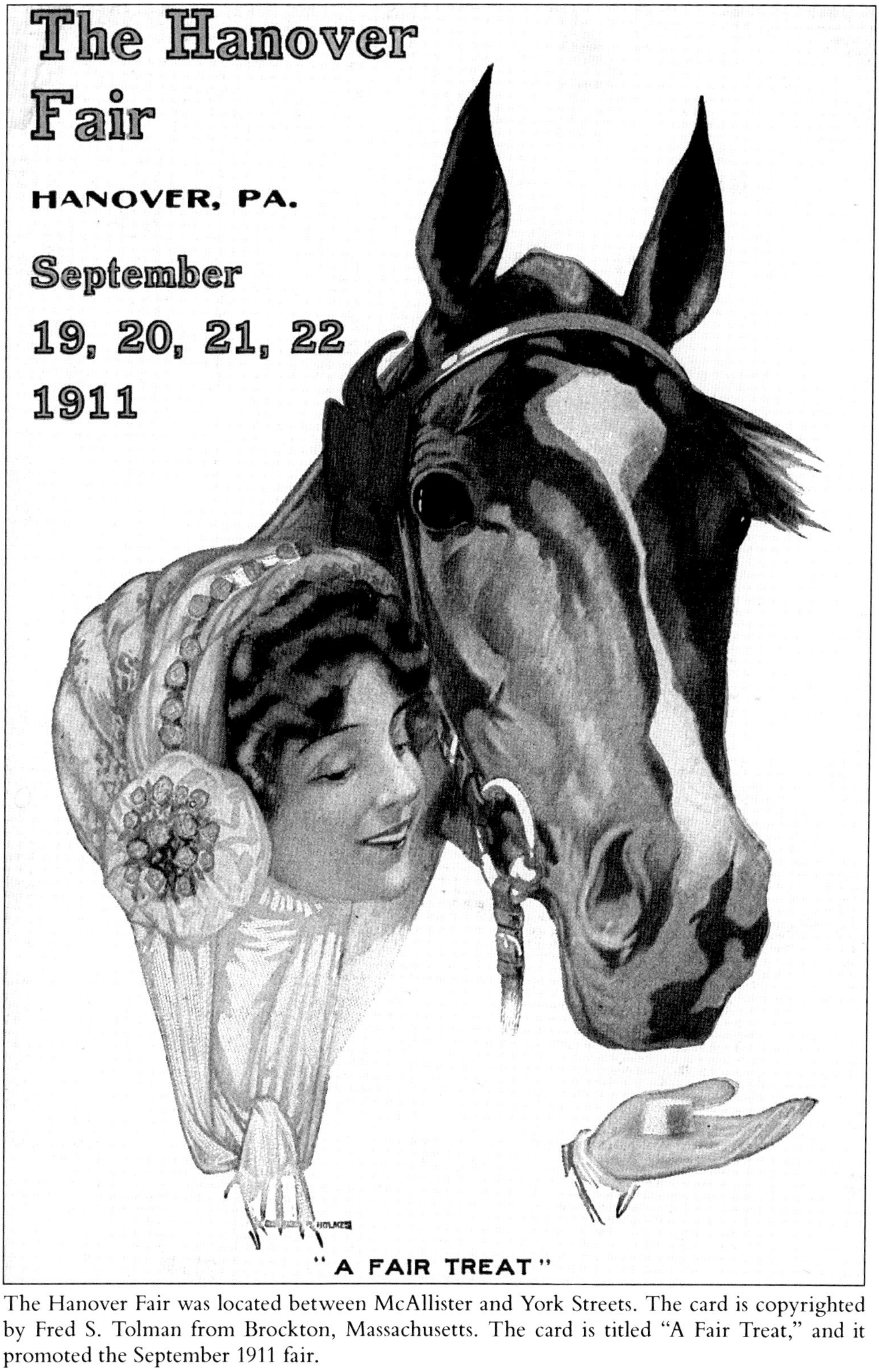

The Hanover Fair was located between McAllister and York Streets. The card is copyrighted by Fred S. Tolman from Brockton, Massachusetts. The card is titled "A Fair Treat," and it promoted the September 1911 fair.

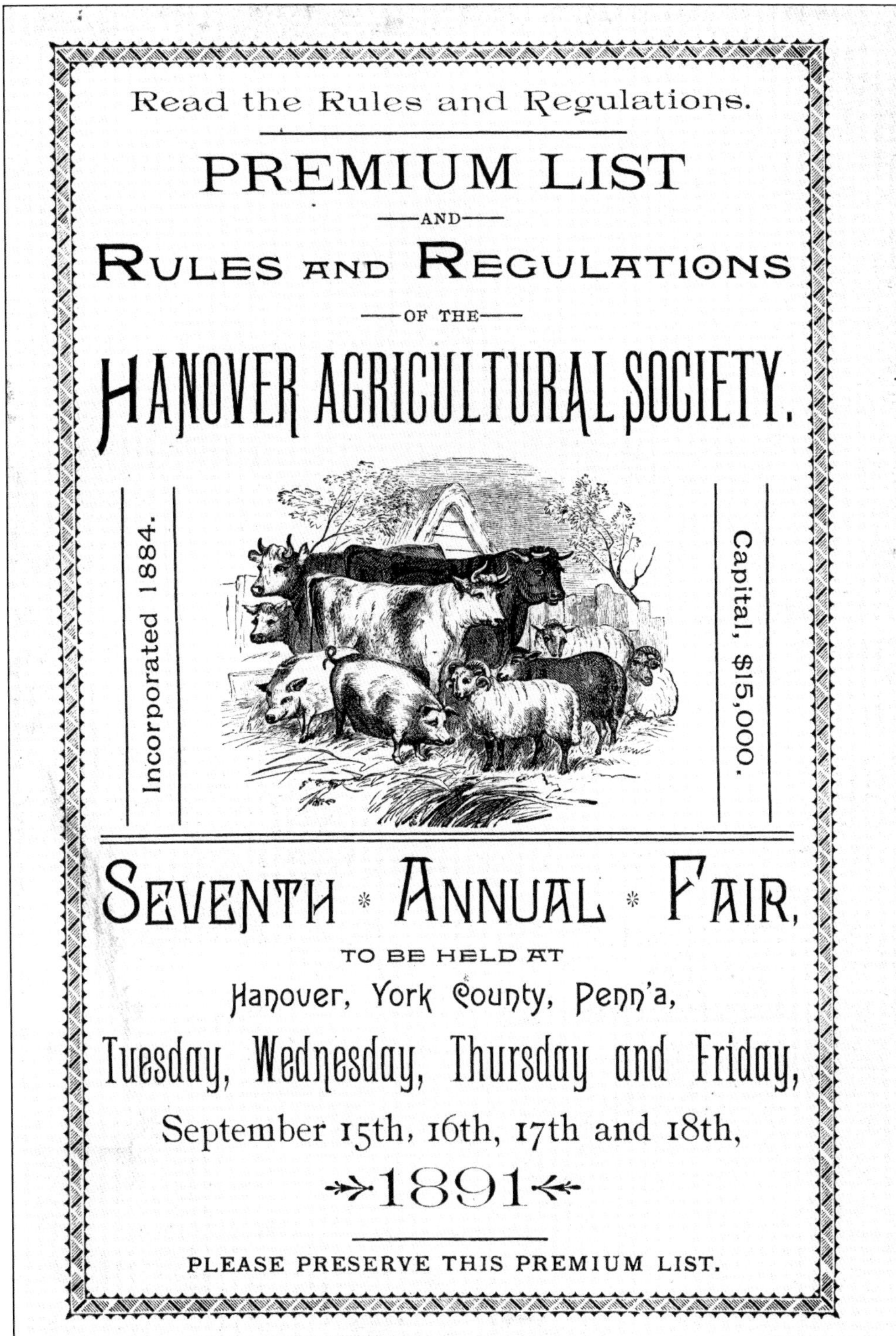

Read the Rules and Regulations.

PREMIUM LIST

—AND—

RULES AND REGULATIONS

—OF THE—

HANOVER AGRICULTURAL SOCIETY.

Incorporated 1884.

Capital, $15,000.

SEVENTH * ANNUAL * FAIR,

TO BE HELD AT

Hanover, York County, Penn'a,

Tuesday, Wednesday, Thursday and Friday,

September 15th, 16th, 17th and 18th,

1891

PLEASE PRESERVE THIS PREMIUM LIST.

The 1891 Hanover Fair was held September 15–18 and represented the seventh annual fair. The premium list and rules and regulations program encompassed 16 pages.

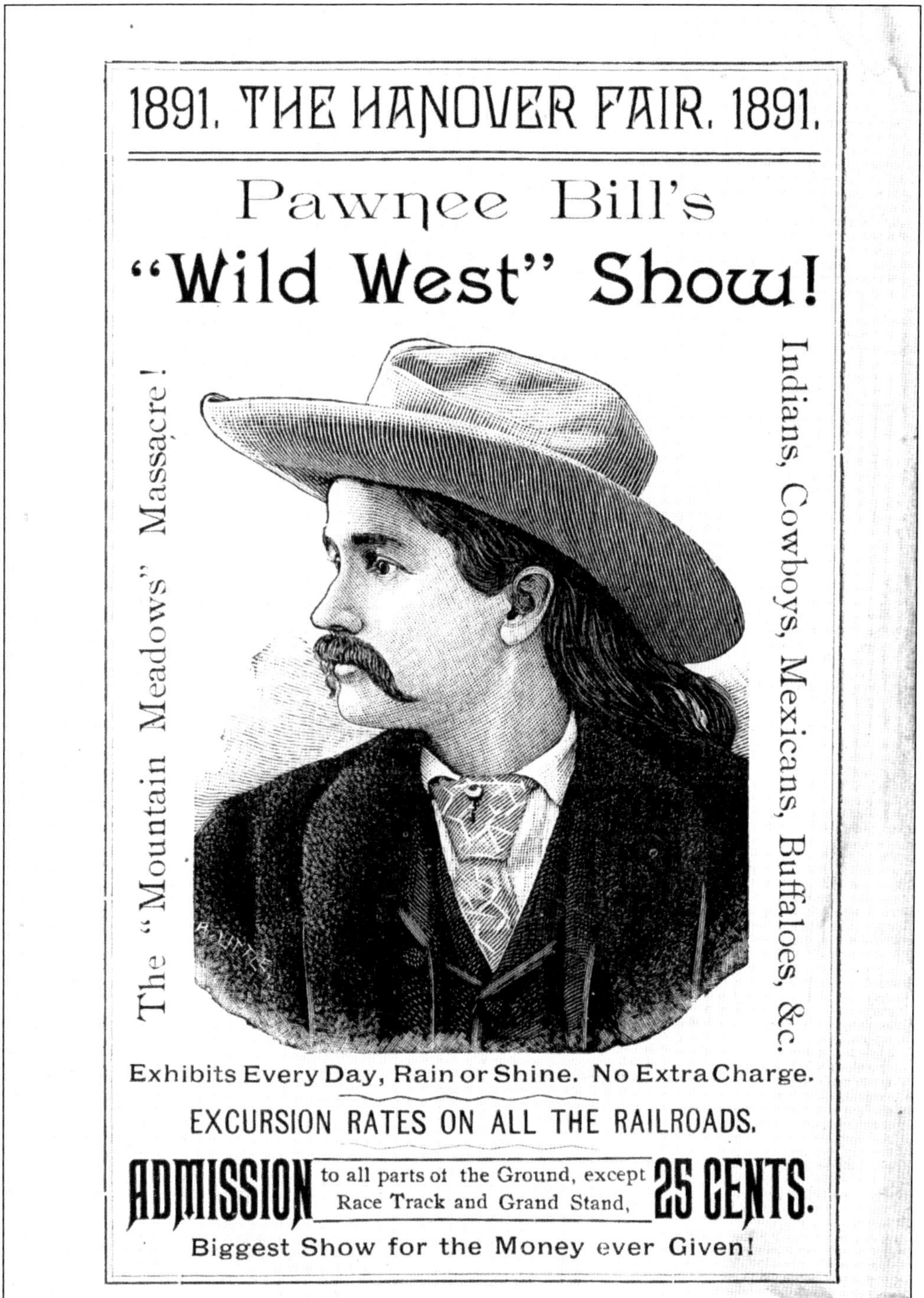

The rear of the program rules book advertised the feature attraction for 1891, Pawnee Bill's Wild West Show. The show advertised American Indians, cowboys, Mexicans, Texas steers, and buffalo as well as shooting and riding exhibitions.

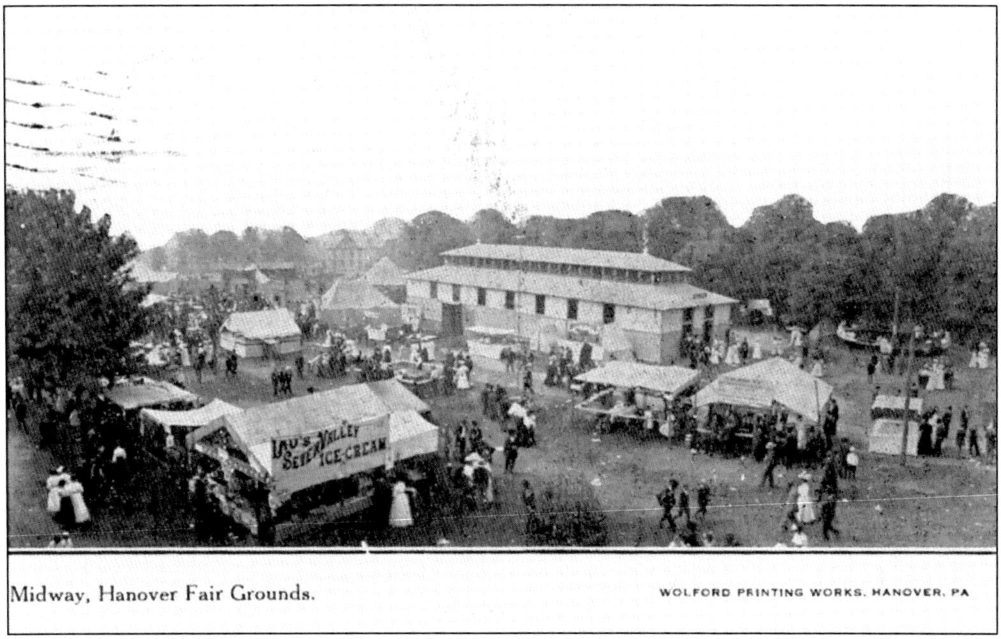

The midway at the Hanover Fairgrounds is shown. The card was postmarked 1912 and was printed by Wolford Printing Works, Hanover, Pennsylvania. The sign beside the tent reads Lau's Seven Valley Ice Cream.

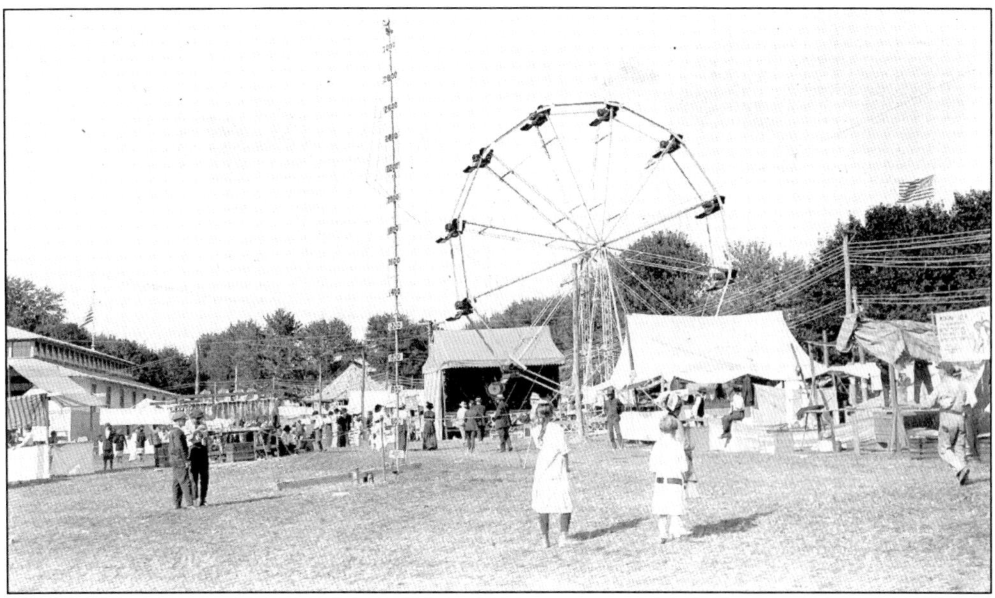

The midway and the Ferris wheel were part of the Hanover Fair, with agricultural display buildings to the left.

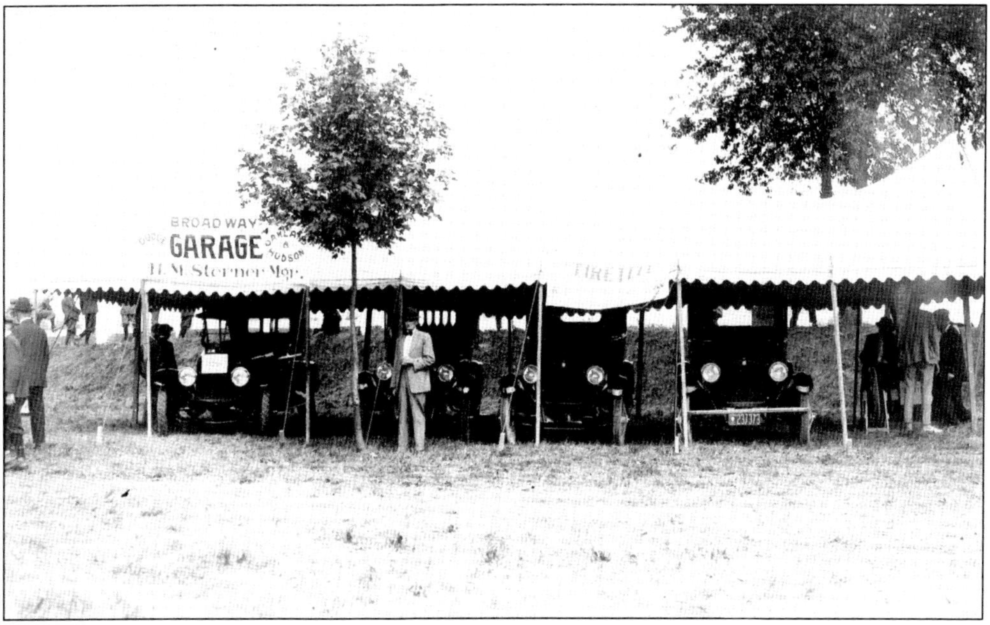

H. M. (Herb) Sterner, a Dodge dealer, had a vendor's tent at the Hanover Fair. Sterner also sold Hudson, Oakland, and Firestone tires.

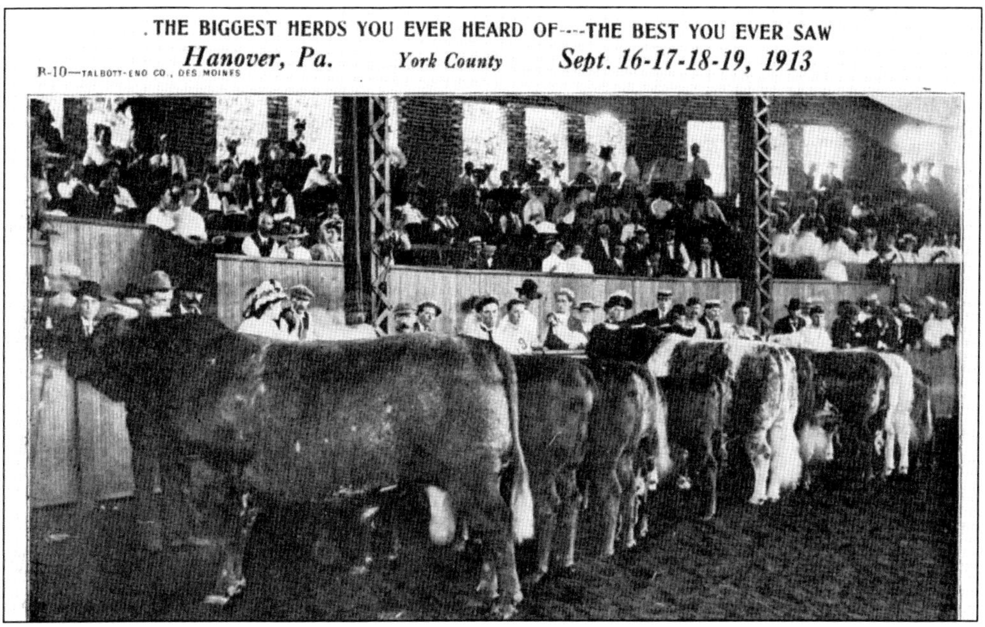

Cattle showing and judging was taking place in the arena when this 1913 Hanover Fair publicity card was photographed.

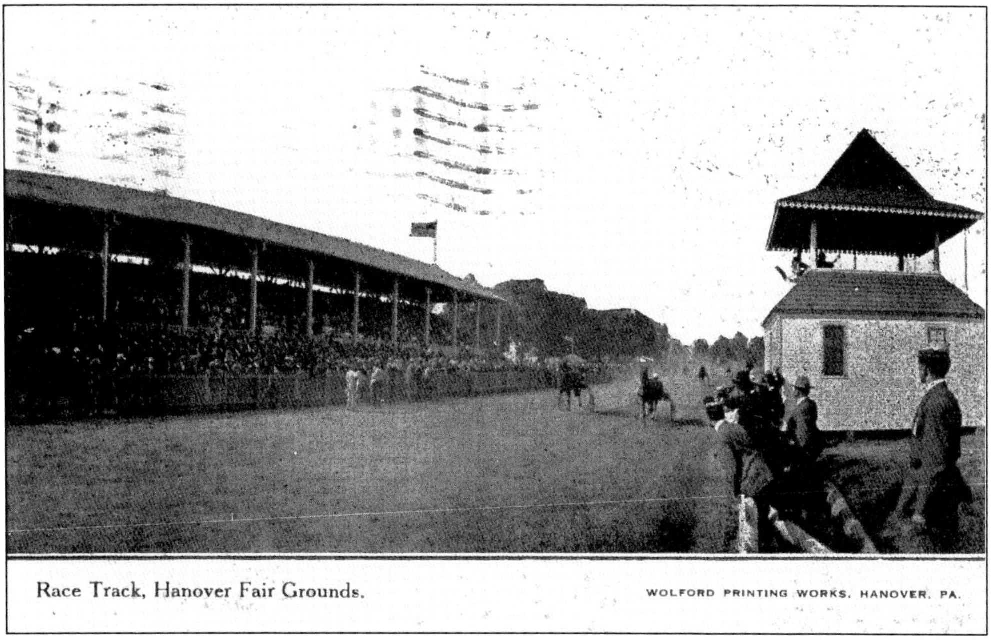

The racetrack at the Hanover Fairgrounds was printed by Wolford Printing Works, Hanover, Pennsylvania. The card was mailed in 1911.

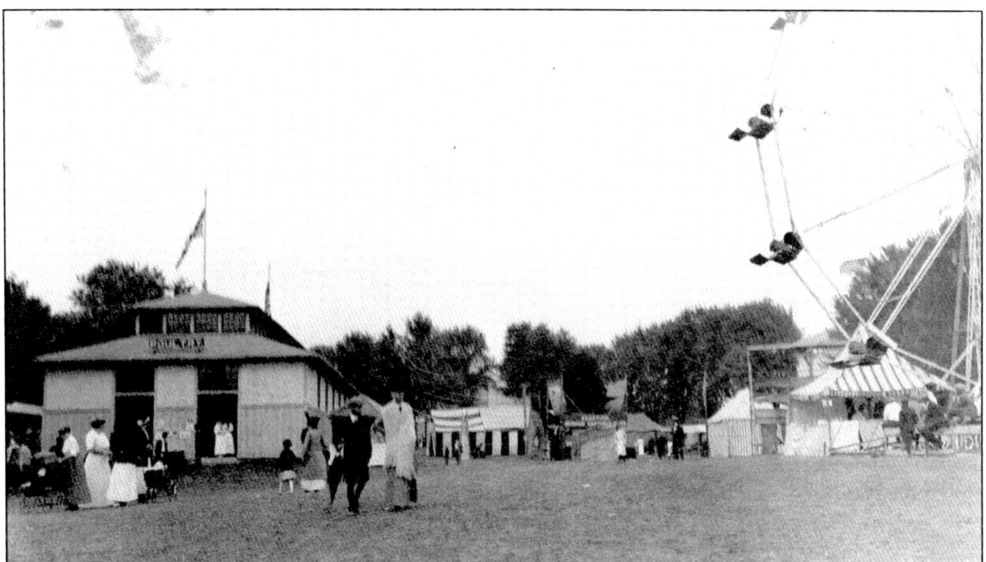

This is the midway at the Hanover Fair, with the poultry building to the left and the Ferris wheel on the right. The Hanover Fair held its last fair in 1930. The Hanover Agricultural Society disbanded in 1931 and sold the real estate to L. B. Sheppard to be used by the Hanover Shoe Farms.

Two

Industrial Fires

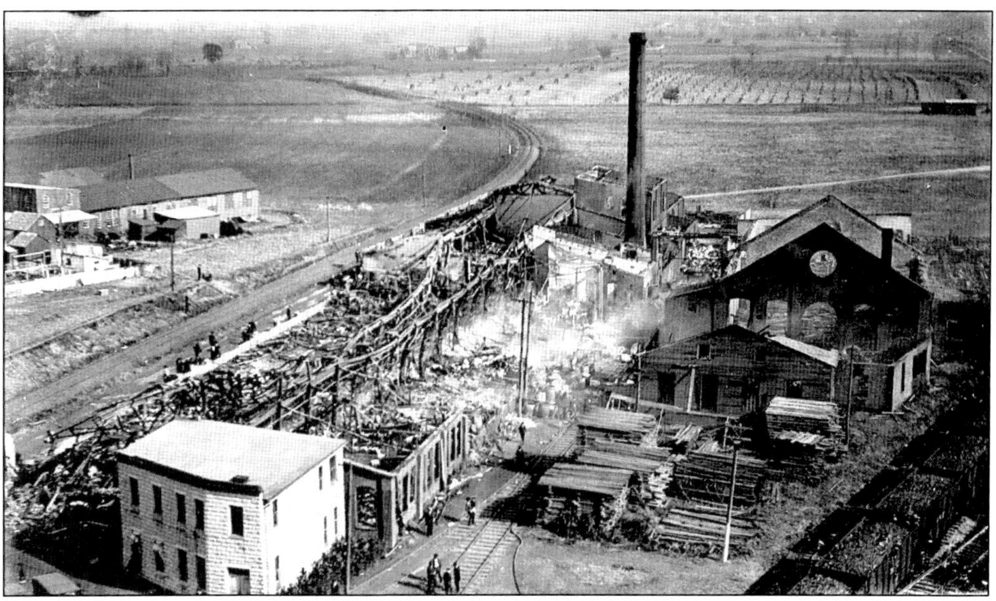

This is a picture of the GENCO fire. GENCO was the trade name for the General Gas and Electric Company, which manufactured gasoline-powered electric generating plants for rural use. The plant was located on East Middle Street between the Pennsylvania Railroad on the left and the Western Maryland Railroad on the right. Note the string of coal cars in the lower right corner.

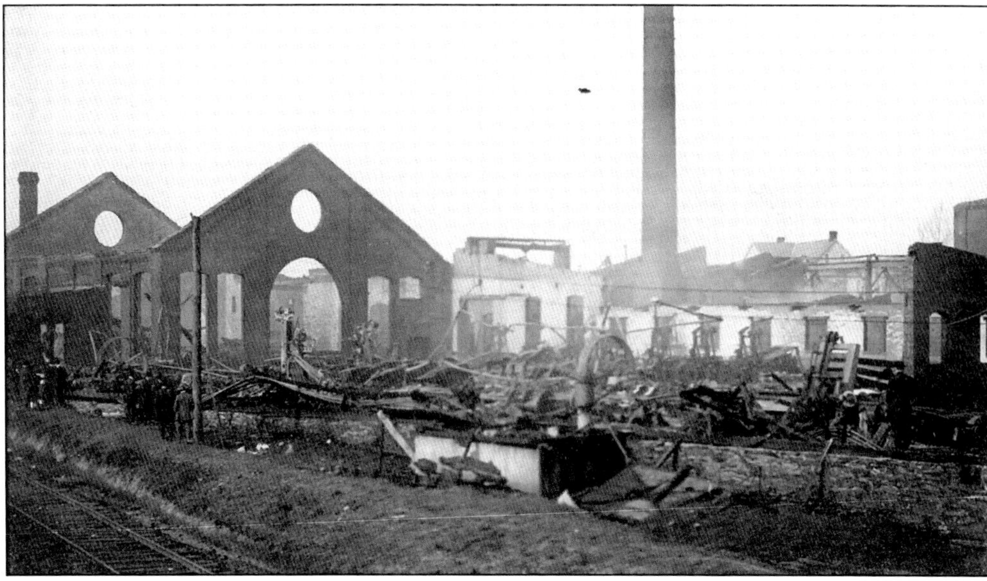

A view from the opposite side of the GENCO Plant is facing toward East Middle Street. Fire destroyed the building in October 1916.

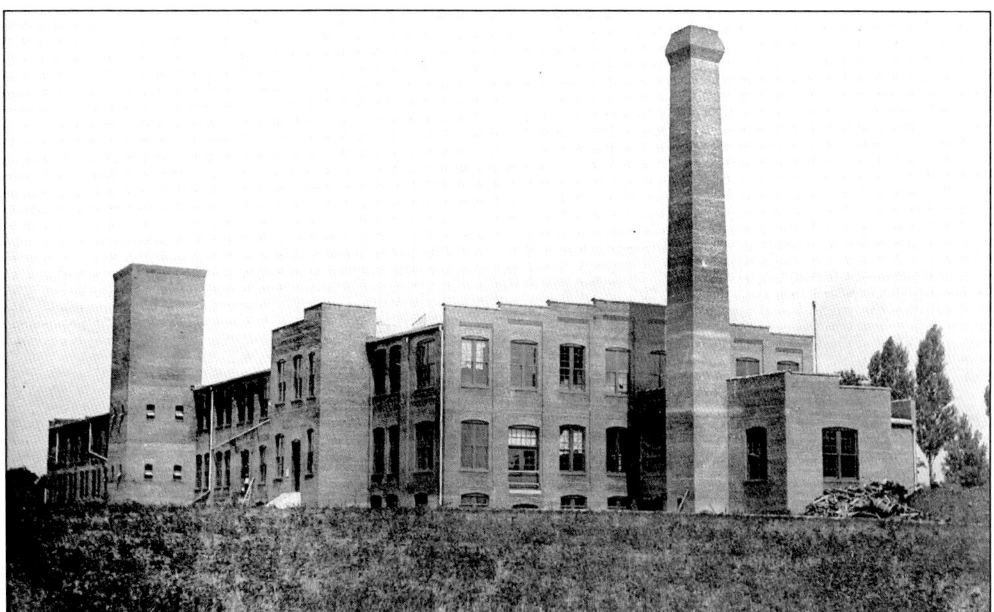

This is the E. R. Haffelfinger Wallpaper building, located on Pine Street in the northwest section of Hanover, viewed before a fire. The company was founded in 1910 on East Middle Street.

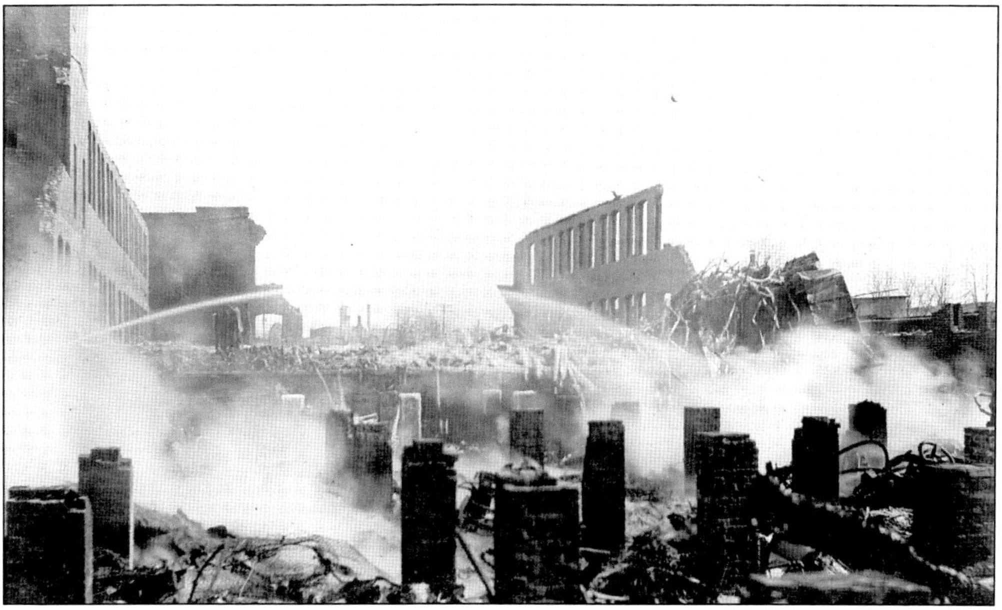

The Haffelfinger Wallpaper Company suffered a fire in 1916 when it was located on East Middle Street and this second devastating fire in 1920 after it moved to Pine Street. This scene is during the 1920 fire.

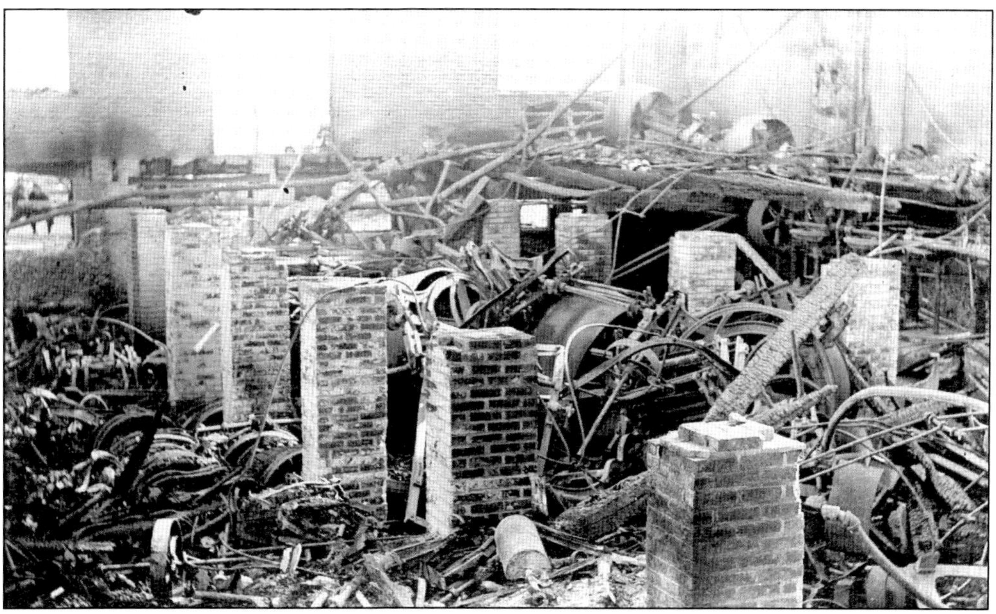

The close-up of the Haffelfinger Wallpaper Company fire from the prior postcard reveals the floor supports and the remains of machinery, which had fallen to the ground.

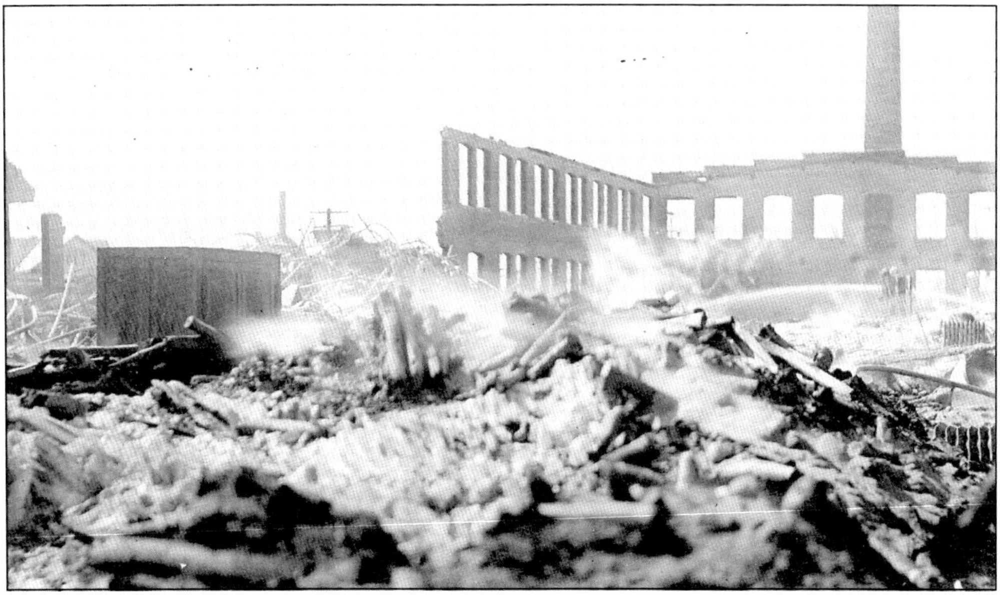

The Haffelfinger Wallpaper building shows the Pine Street plant destruction after the fire. Another plant was rebuilt on the site.

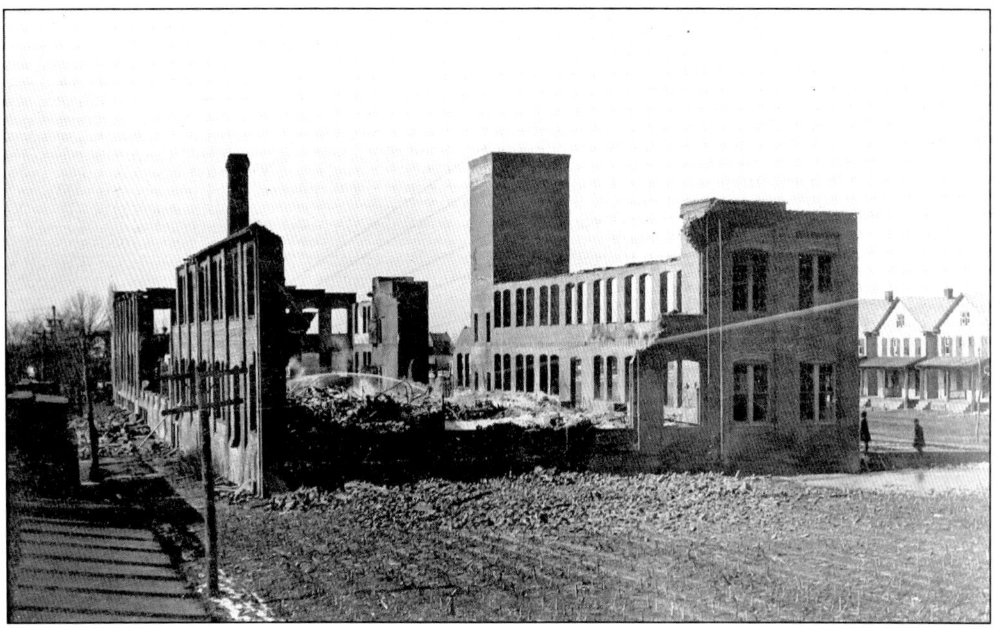

The Haffelfinger Wallpaper building is shown during cleanup, after the fire located on Pine Street, which is at the center right. Jacob C. Eisenhart acquired the 400 Pine Street plant in 1937, and production continues today. The current owner is S. Forry Eisenhart Jr., whose father purchased the business from his uncle Jacob in 1968.

Three

The 1915 Tornado

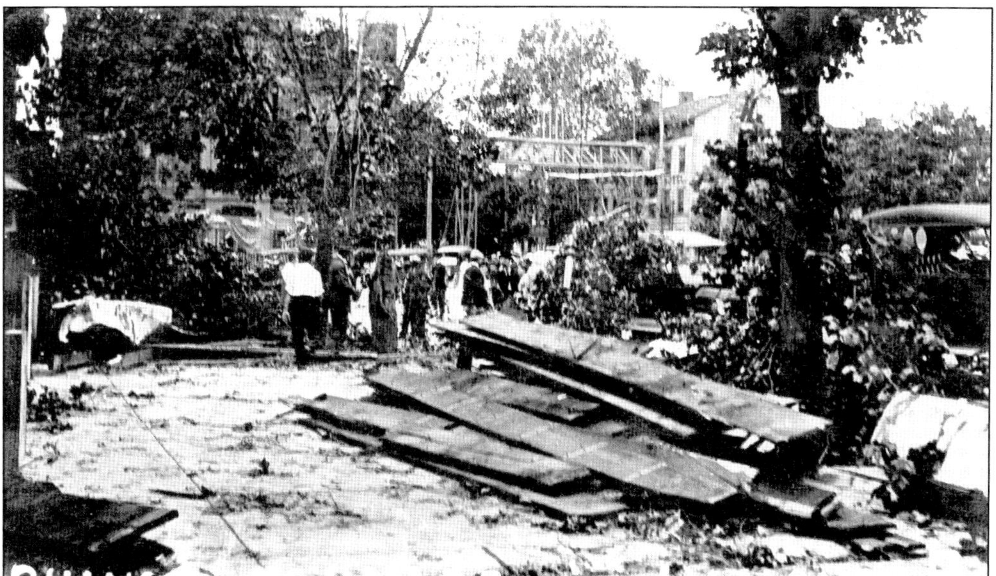

A violent tornado struck Hanover on Saturday evening, August 21, 1915, traversing from the southwest, destroying downtown buildings generally southwest of York Street and Center Square. This view from Center Square is facing Frederick Street. The Peoples Bank building is partially visible behind the trees to the left. The Central Hotel is to the right of the center of the card, with the framework of the arch erected over the Frederick Street entrance, to be used in the centennial celebration, which would commence just three weeks later. It is still standing undamaged.

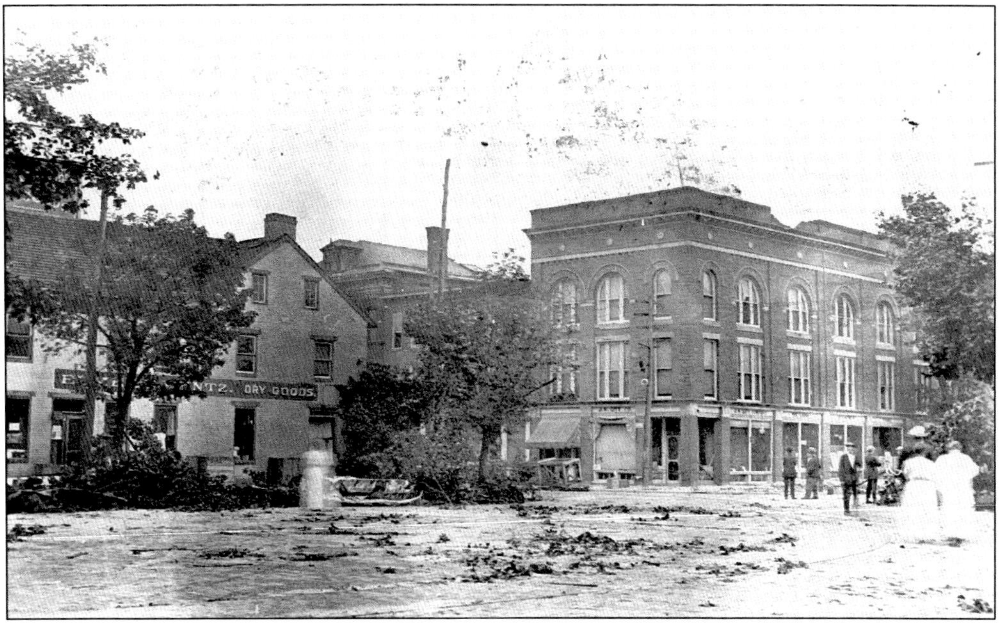

This card reveals the Baltimore Street entrance to the square in the center of the photograph. The Elmer E. Wentz dry goods store is on the left, and the J. W. Gitt department store is to the right, with what appears to be tornado damage to the cornice of the roof.

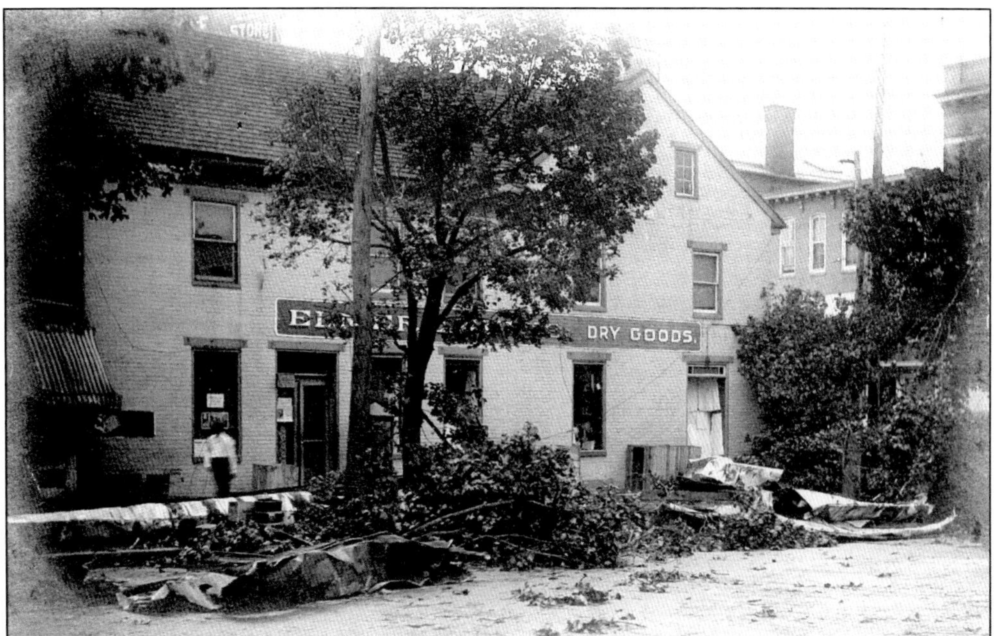

A close-up of the Elmer E. Wentz dry goods store in the southeast corner of Baltimore Street and Center Square depicts debris deposited in front of the store by the tornado.

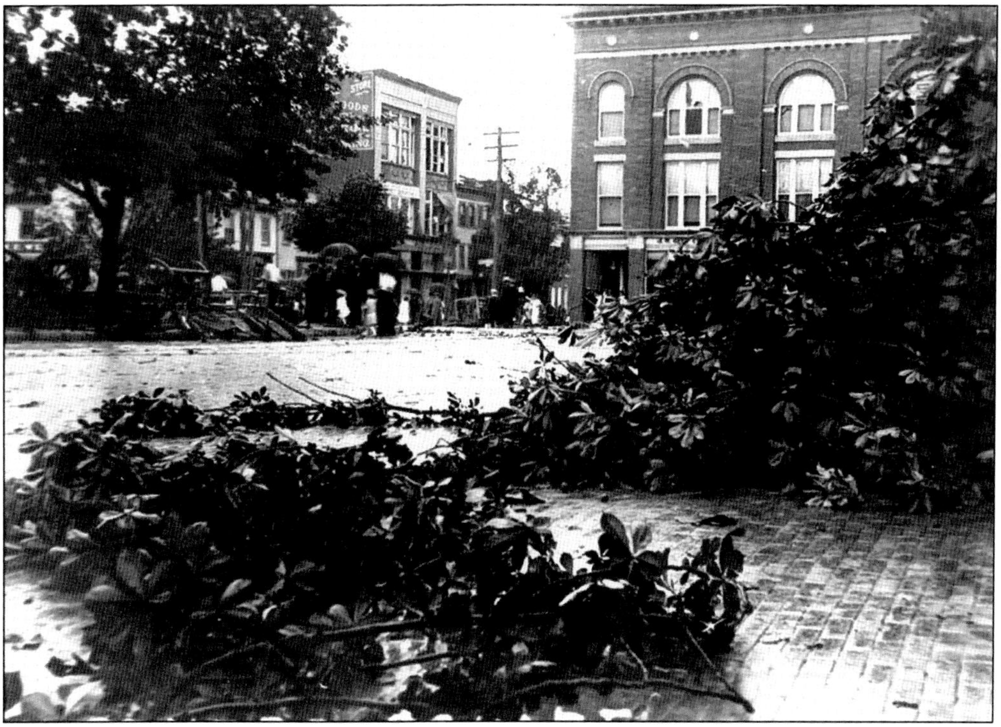

This scene from Center Square looking into Baltimore Street in the center of the view reveals fallen trees and the damaged upper cornice of the Gitt building at the right and, on the left, the N. B. Carver and Sons department store building, which lost half of its roof.

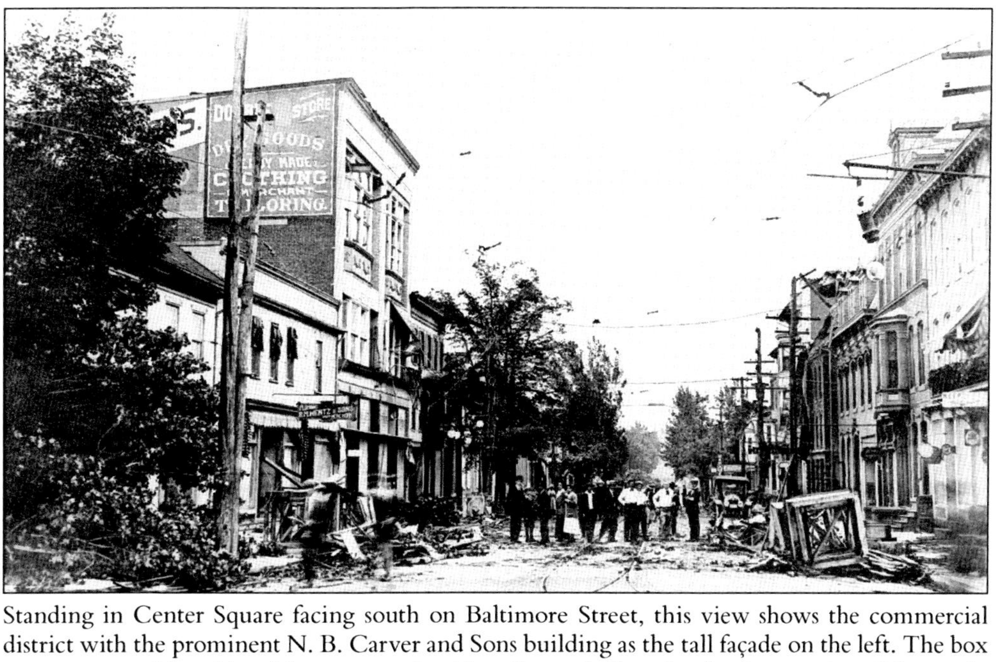

Standing in Center Square facing south on Baltimore Street, this view shows the commercial district with the prominent N. B. Carver and Sons building as the tall façade on the left. The box structures on either side of the street at the sidewalks are believed to be the remains of the nearly finished centennial arch, which was being erected for the celebration three weeks hence.

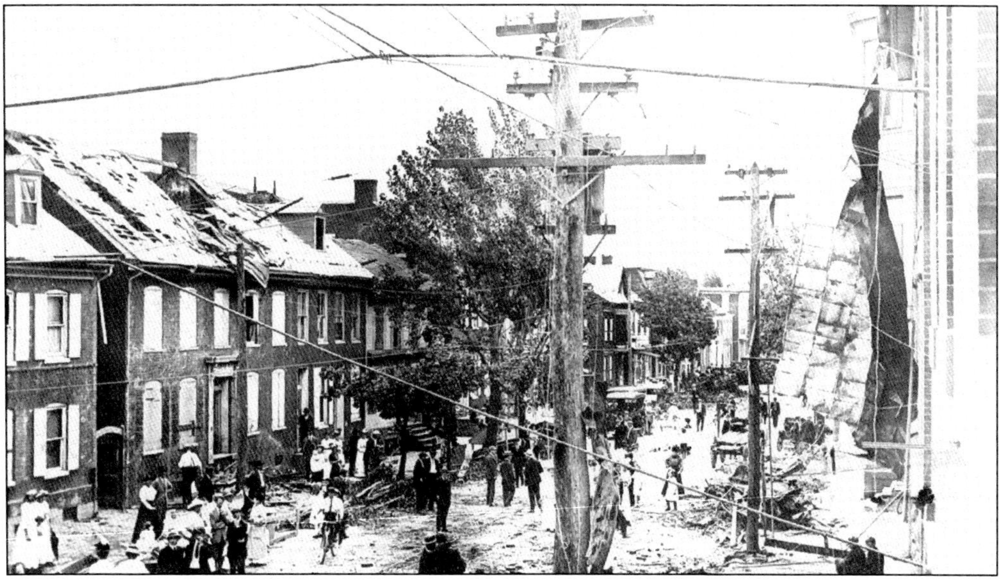

This is documentation of the damage to Baltimore Street from the southeast corner of the street and the square looking southeast to the east side of the first block of Baltimore Street. The second block of Baltimore Street begins to the right of the utility pole just right of center in the view. The second house from the left, with the damaged roof, was the Davis Garber home at 28 Baltimore Street.

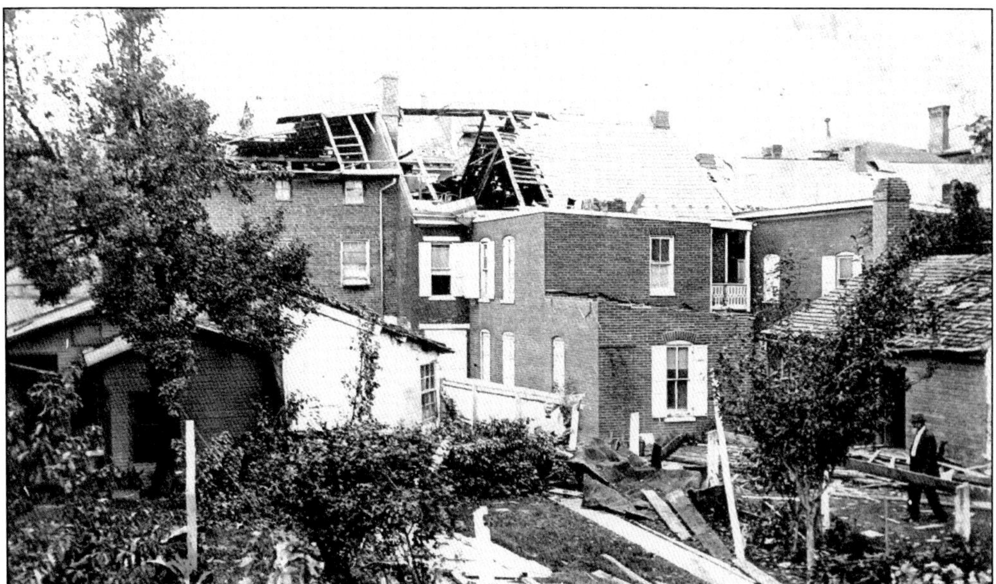

Taken from South Railroad Street looking west, this records the rear of 22–30 Baltimore Street with the Davis Garber rear roof damage at 28 Baltimore Street, the same home as on the previous card but shown from the front.

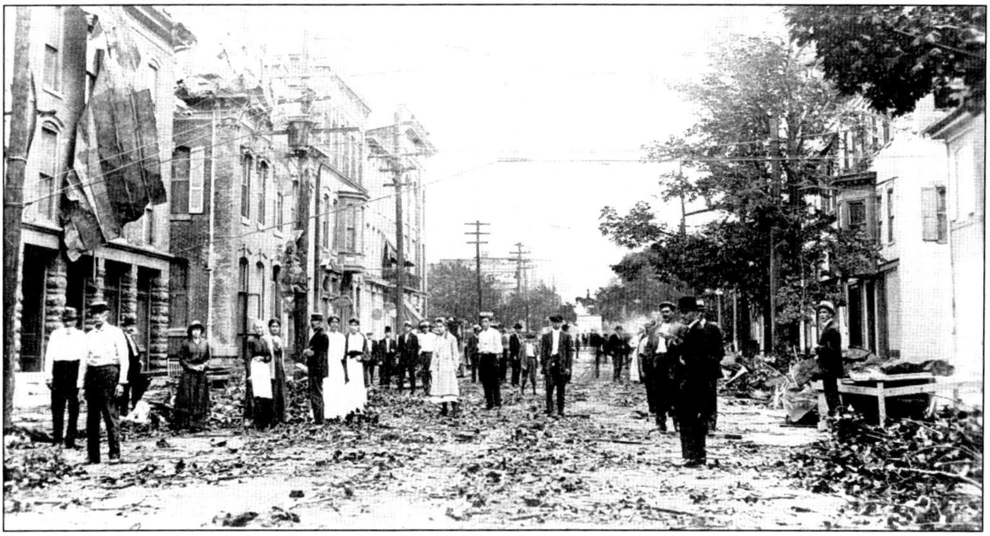

The west side of the first block of Baltimore Street appears on the left of the card. The Picket Statue on Center Square is evident just right of center above the heads of the onlookers. The Hanover post office was located at 23–27 Baltimore Street and Farmers State Bank at 21 Baltimore Street, just north of the Exchange Place alley. A horse that had been tied to a tree became alarmed by the tornado, broke loose, and darted down Baltimore Street. It soon tripped on a wire and broke its right foreleg. Night patrolman Jesse L. Crabbs was required to shoot the animal. A few years later, Crabbs became chief of police, then formed Crabbs Detective Agency, and ultimately a law firm.

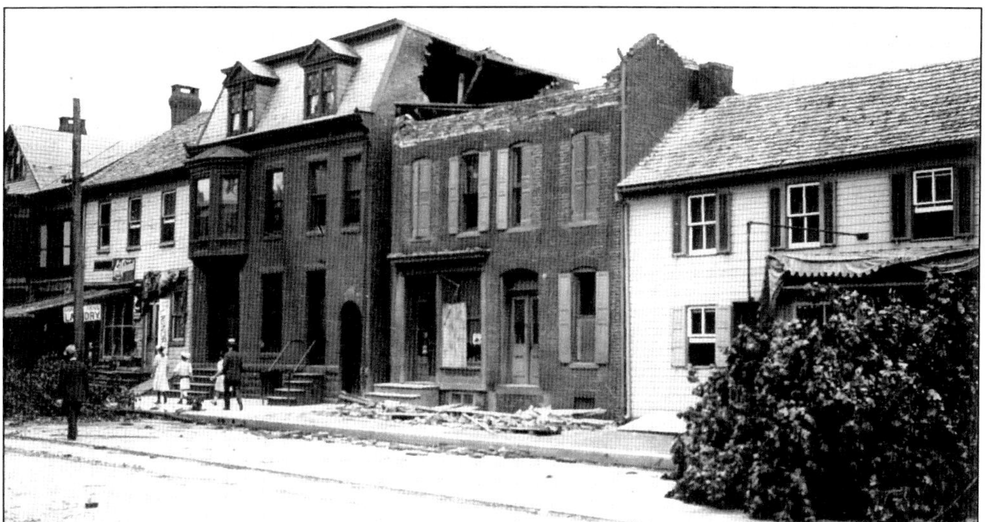

This is the east side of Baltimore Street, with Walnut Street to the left, just outside of the photograph. The Wortz and Fox fruit and meat stand was located at 104 Baltimore Street (the first building on the left), followed by the Charles Tang laundry at 106 Baltimore Street. The home and business of Wege Pretzel Company was located at 108 and 110 Baltimore Street. The gable end facing the adjoining home was smashed in by the neighbor's roof. Curtis Keefer's harness shop at 112 Baltimore Street and John Sterner's meat market at 118 Baltimore Street, in the white building, were located in the buildings from the center to the right of the photograph.

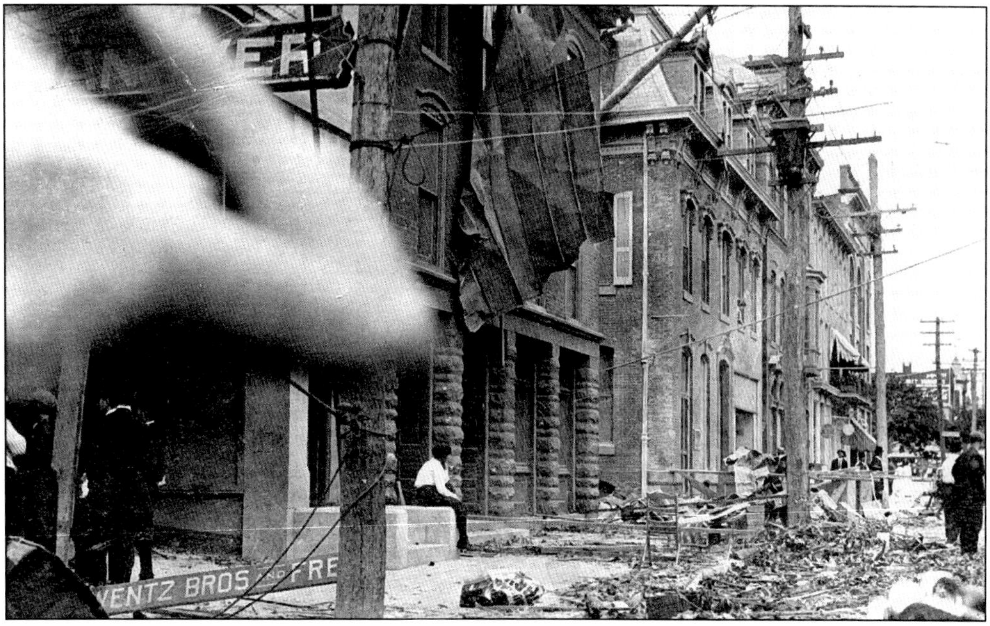

The west side of Baltimore Street approaching Center Square reveals the Wentz Brothers and Frey dry goods store sign at 33 Baltimore Street on the ground, the Hanover Theatre sign at 29 Baltimore Street, Hanover Trust Bank at 25, the Exchange Place alley, and the Farmers State Bank at 19 Baltimore Street in the Elks Club building.

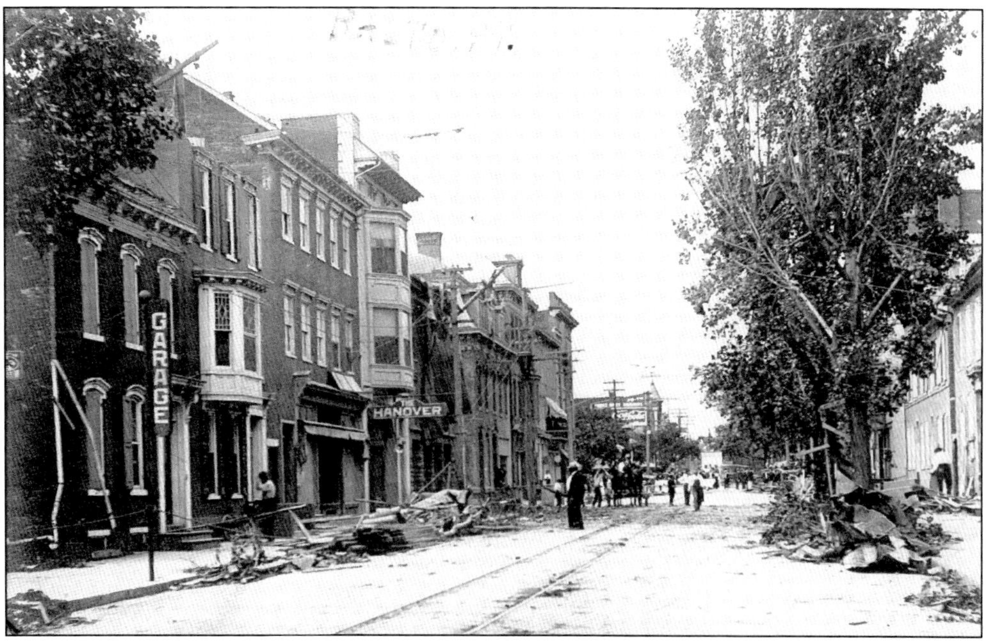

Farther out on Baltimore Street, the same buildings as in the previous card are evident. The Adams Sporting Goods House and Garage are reflected to the left at 43 Baltimore Street. The Picket statue is visible on Center Square.

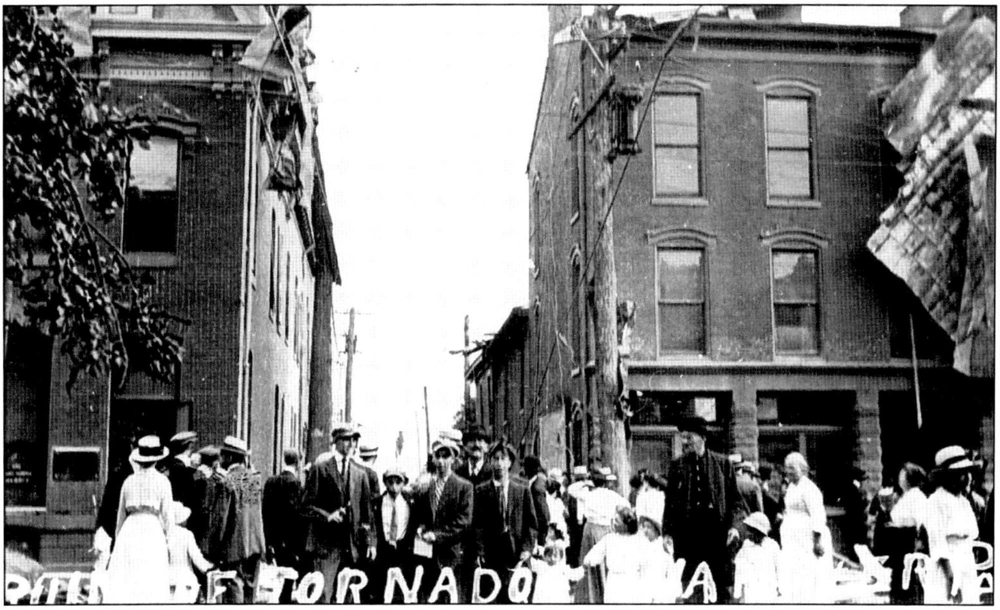

Facing west down Exchange Place from Baltimore Street is the Hanover Trust Company on the right at 25 Baltimore Street and the Elks Club building on the left at 19 Baltimore Street, with Exchange Place alley between them. If the image seems confusing, that is understandable. It is believed that, when printed, the negative was reversed, reflecting the two buildings in reverse order.

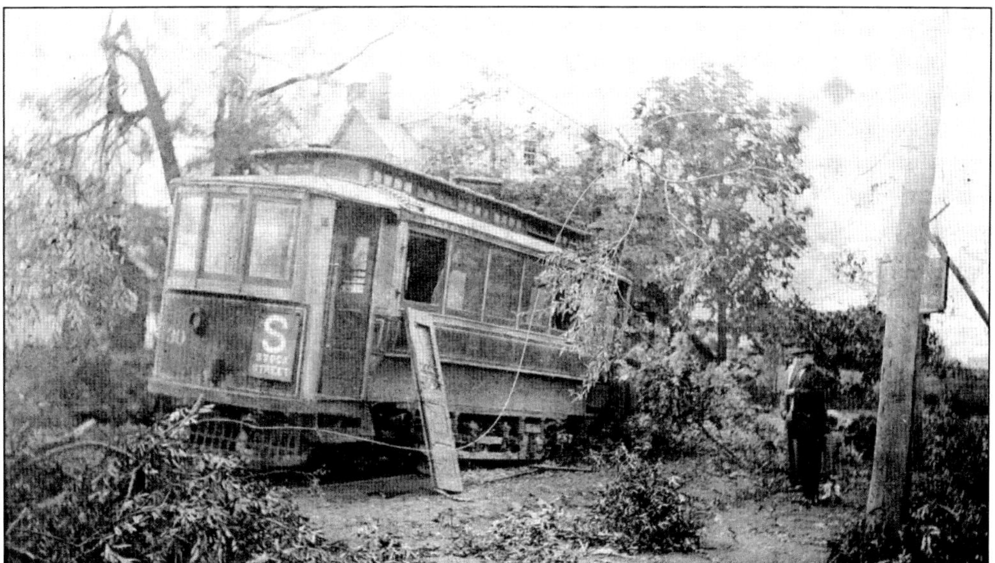

Approaching from Westminster Road into the Frederick Street area, the tornado found one of its first victims to be a Frederick Street trolley car operated by conductor Monroe Hildebrand and motorman Horatio Black. It was blown from the track near the current intersection of Frederick Street and Forney Avenue. The trolley passengers at the time were George W. Van Hise, the trolley company's chief lineman, and sisters Pauline and Margaret Hildebrand, daughters of the conductor. Pauline required five stitches to close a cut on her arm from falling glass.

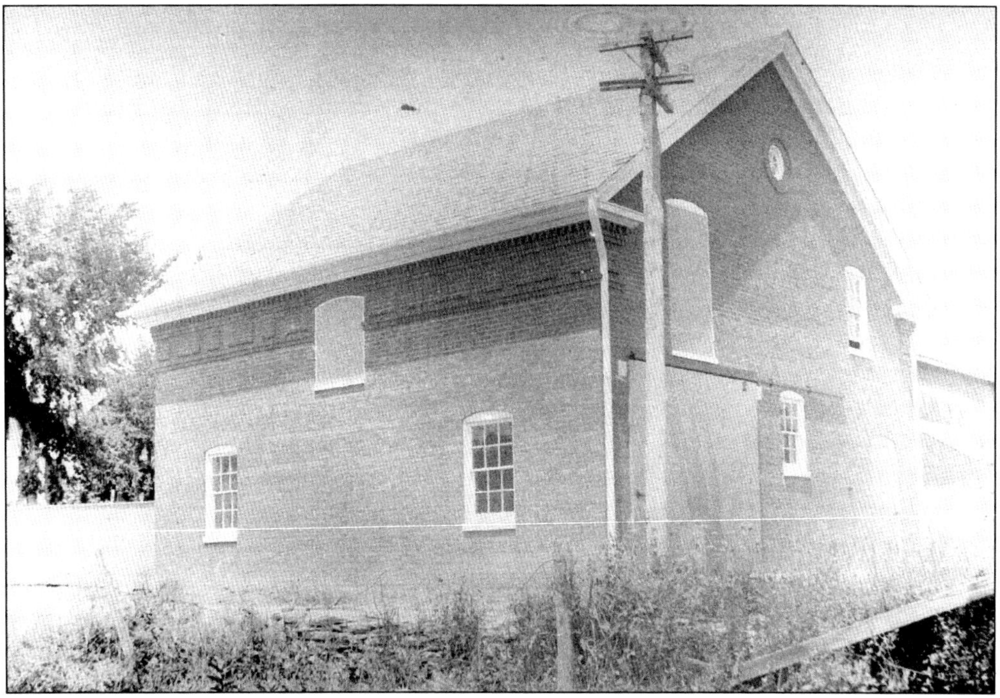

These two photographs are before and after images, reflecting massive damage to a sturdy, 10-year-old structure. This is the brick carriage house at the rear of 252 Frederick Street, in the rear alley of Exchange Place.

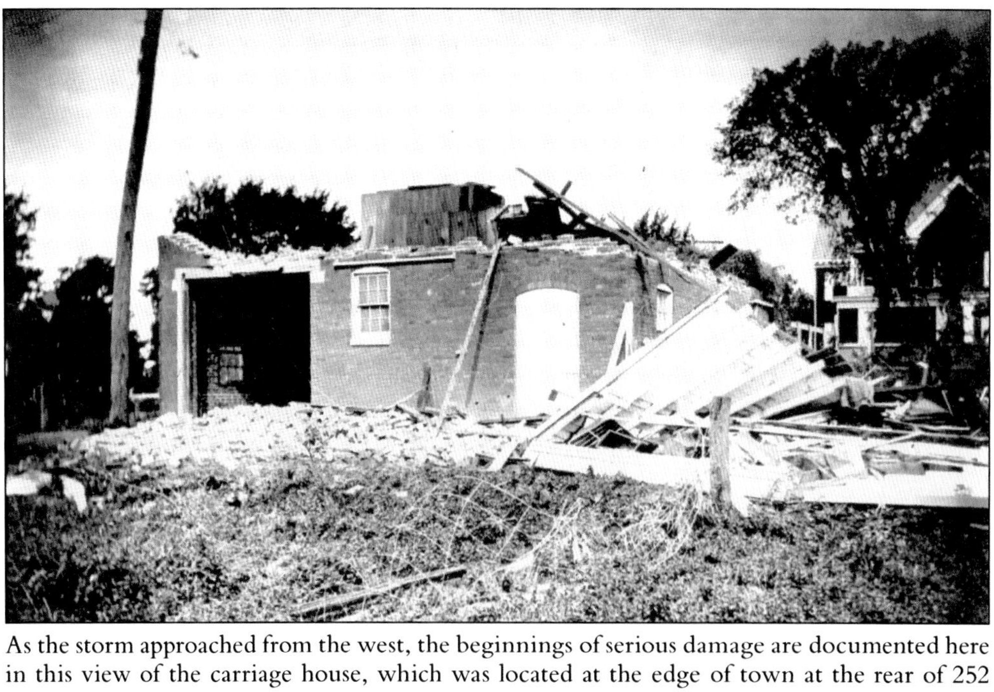

As the storm approached from the west, the beginnings of serious damage are documented here in this view of the carriage house, which was located at the edge of town at the rear of 252 Frederick Street and the southwest corner of Meade Avenue. The property, owned by David P. Forney, was rebuilt similar to its 1905 original construction.

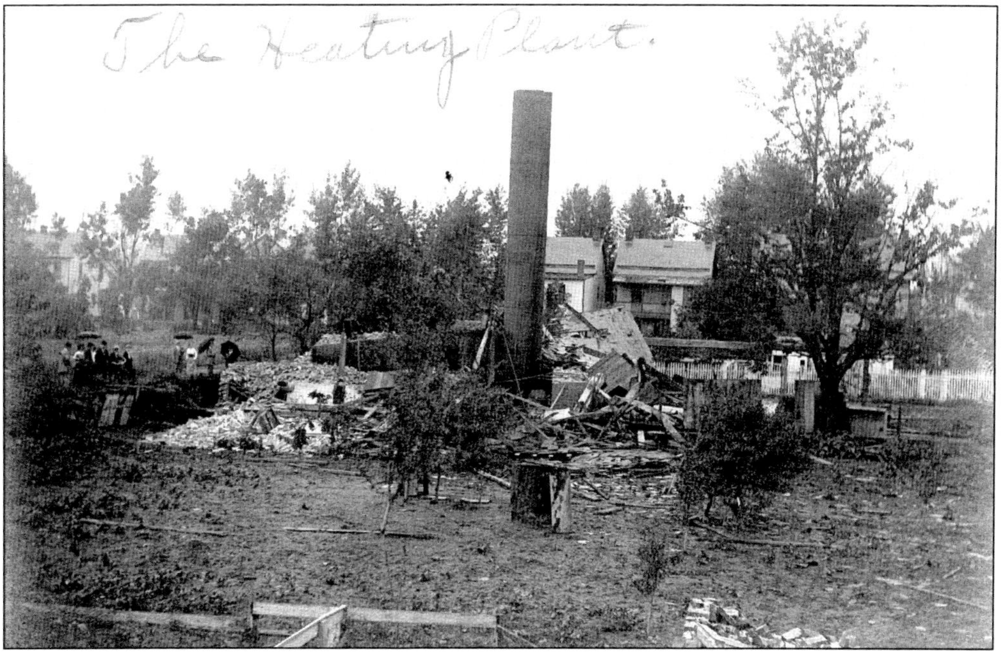

The view of the Hanover Electric Power Steam plant on Walnut Street was taken from Dr. Franklin F. Shue's veterinarian building on Eichelberger Alley, facing west toward Centennial Avenue. The homes behind the smokestack are the rear of 28 and 30 Centennial Avenue.

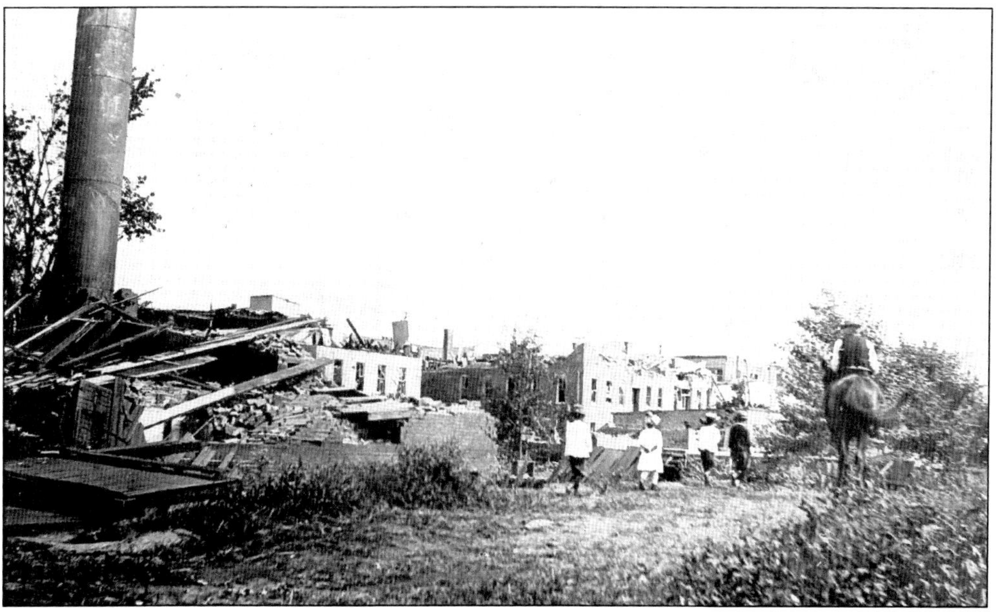

The rubble of the Hanover Electric Light, Heat, and Power Company steam-heating plant at West Walnut Street is on the left with only the smokestack remaining. This is looking north with, from left to right, the Keystone Variety Works and Hanover Glove Factory buildings.

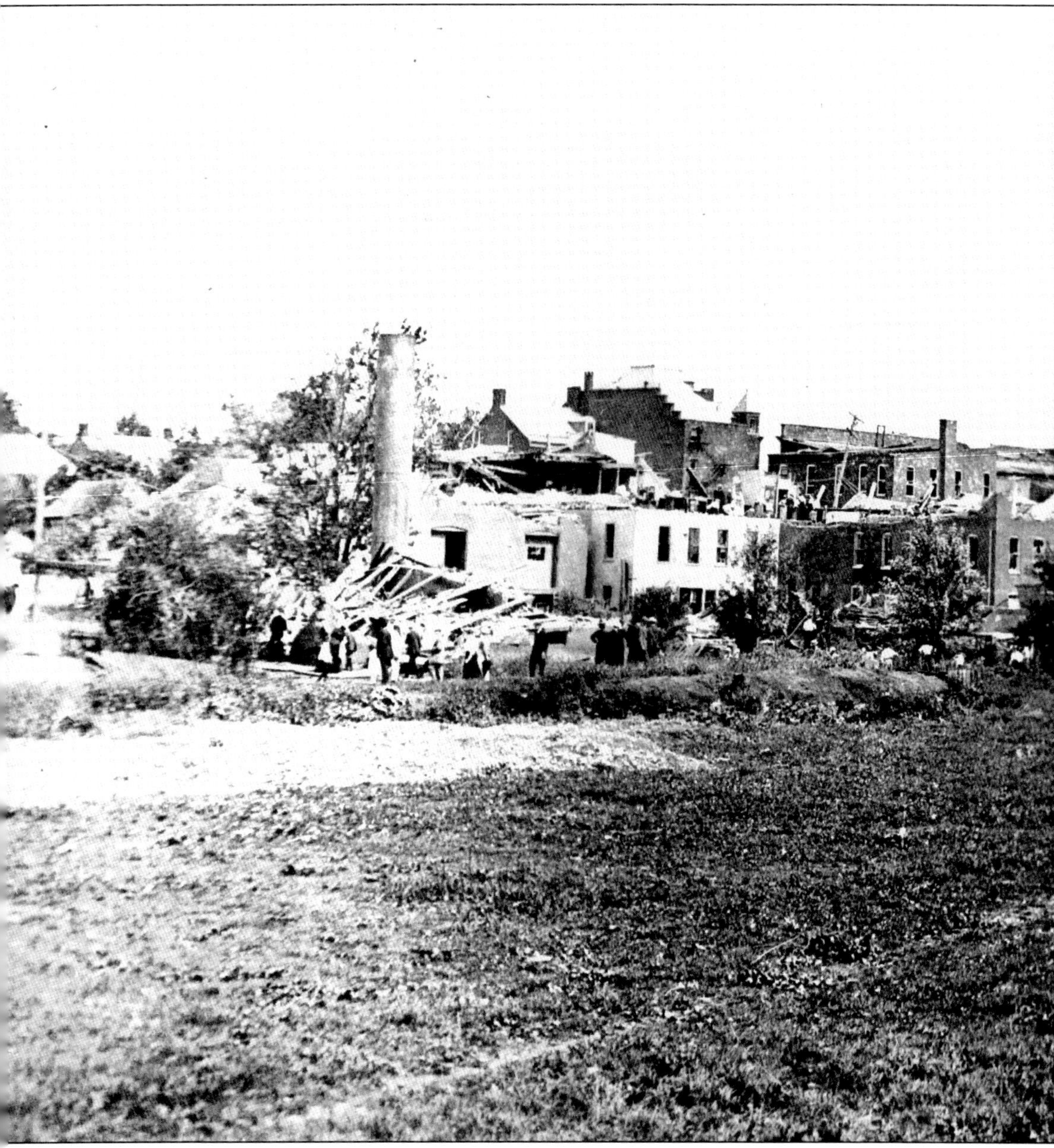

Much of the destruction occurred west of Baltimore Street in an area generally bounded by West Middle Street and Centennial Avenue. This photograph was taken just southeast of the not-yet-built West Walnut Street School (in 2005 the yellow brick apartment building at Centennial Avenue and West Walnut Street) looking northeast with the buildings on the horizon representing Carlisle Street on the left side, buildings on Center Square left of the center of the photograph, and Baltimore Street buildings from center to right of the photograph. This view is the rear of those buildings. At first glance, it almost represents a bombed-out World War II town. The spire on the horizon to the left is St. Mark's Church, 107 Carlisle Street,

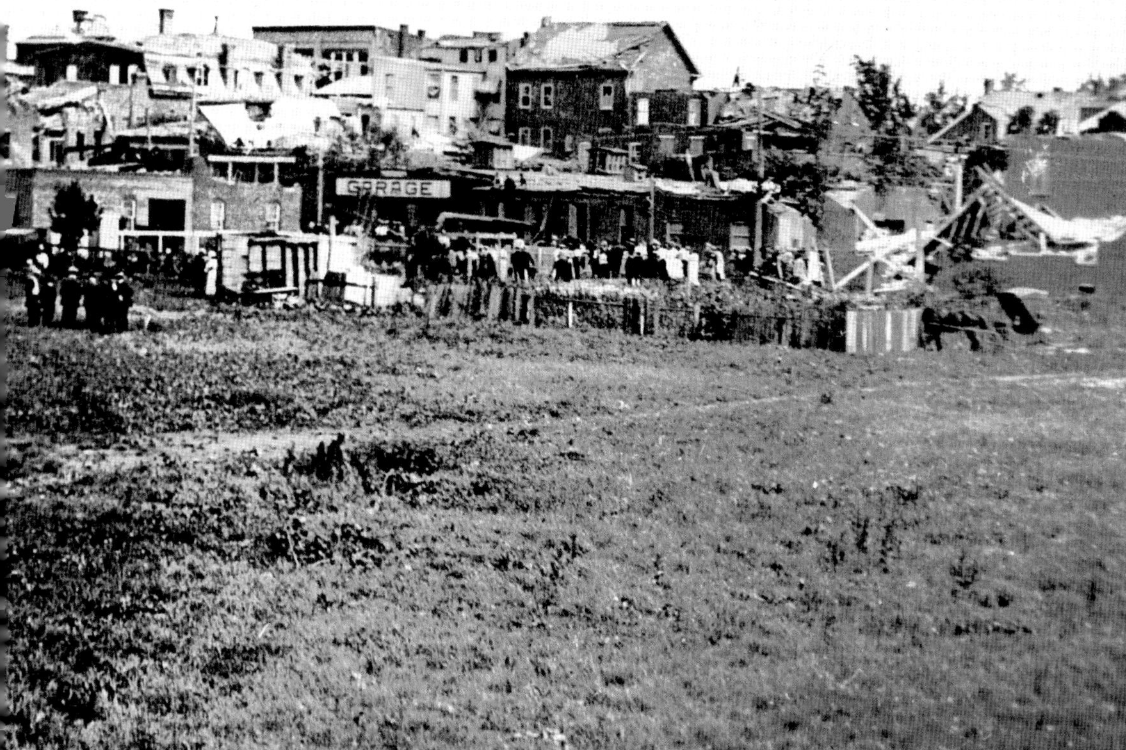

the smokestack fifth from the left is the remains of the Hanover Steam Heating plant on West Walnut Street. The unmistakable towers of the Peoples Bank building on Center Square are visible about a third of the card's length from the left. In the foreground to the right of the steam plant smokestack are the industrial plants of Center Shaft Penholder Company, Keystone Variety Works (printers and manufacturers of boxes at Exchange Place), and the Hanover Glove Company at Exchange Place, all located to the left of the group of men standing in the center of the photograph. Directly to their right is the veterinary hospital of Dr. Franklin F. Shue, followed by the rear of the Adams Garage at 43 Baltimore Street.

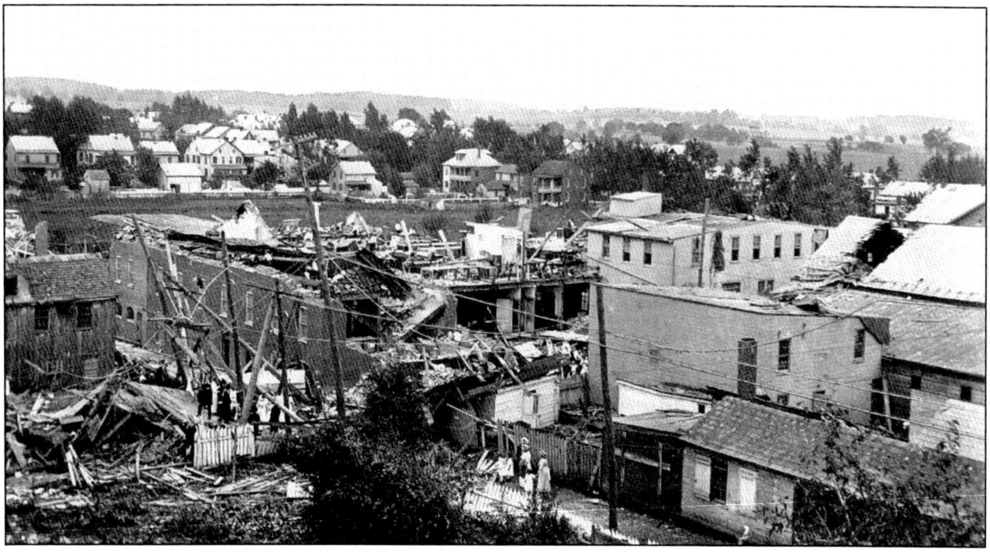

This scene is taken from the Center Square area looking southwest over the destruction, with West Middle Street homes in the top beyond an open field. The brick building to the left of center is the Hanover Glove Factory on Exchange Place. The corner of the building at the leaning utility pole left of center is the corner of Exchange Place and Eichelberger Alley. Eichelberger Alley is to the left of the building with Exchange Place barely visible to the right of the utility pole.

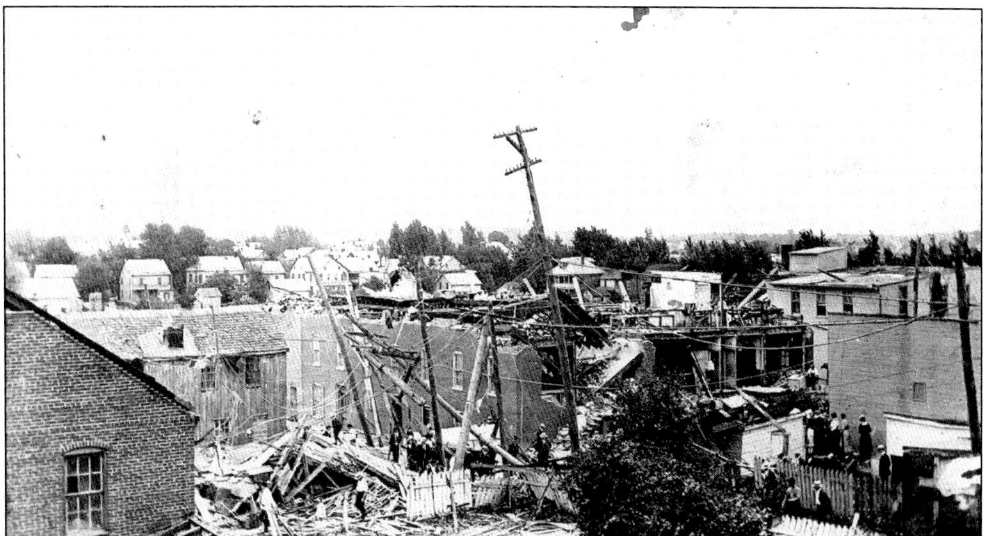

The same homes in the last postcard along West Middle Street are in the background of this view, but they are shown at a slightly lower height and a bit more southerly. The Hanover Glove Factory remains are the brick building in the center. This is the east side of Hanover Glove Factory on Eichelberger Alley, looking from Walnut Street north toward Frederick Street. This same side of the building is visible in the previous photograph to the left of the leaning utility pole, which is left of center. The first brick building on the left edge is the garage at the rear of 28 Frederick Street on the north side of Exchange Place. The frame building to its right was the rear of 25 Baltimore Street at the corner of Exchange Place and Eichelberger Alley.

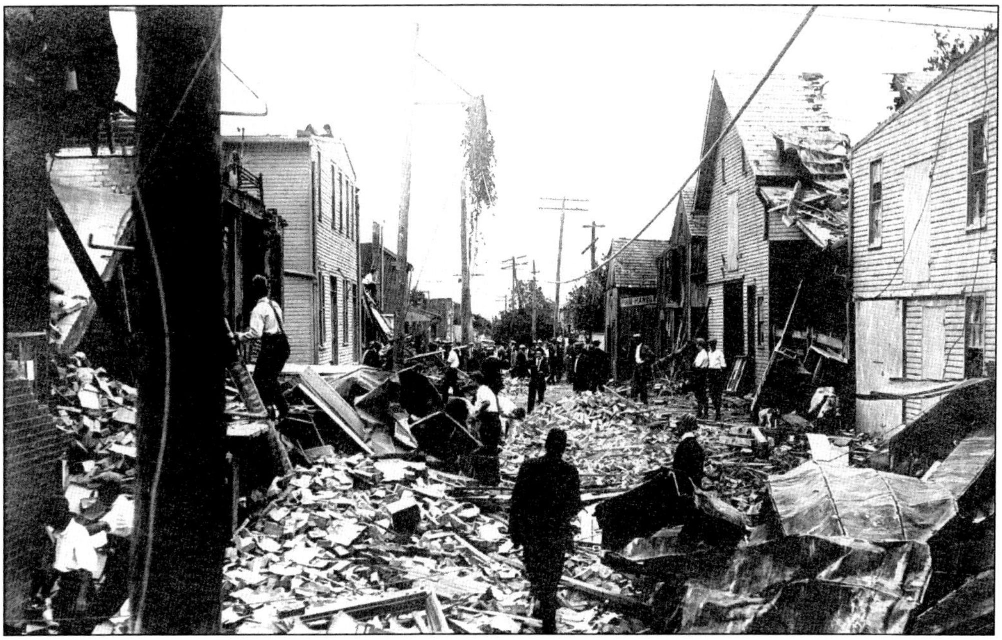

Exchange Place facing west runs down the center of the card. The Hanover Glove Factory is to the immediate left. It is difficult to comprehend when viewing this level of destruction that not one death or serious injury occurred, although a few minor injuries are recorded in this chapter. On Saturday night, it was the custom for large crowds to gather downtown to do their shopping. August 21 was no different. Thankfully, however, the tornado was preceded by a heavy downpour of rain, which emptied the streets and sent the crowd into stores, movie theaters, and other establishments. It is likely that this prevented any deaths or serious injuries.

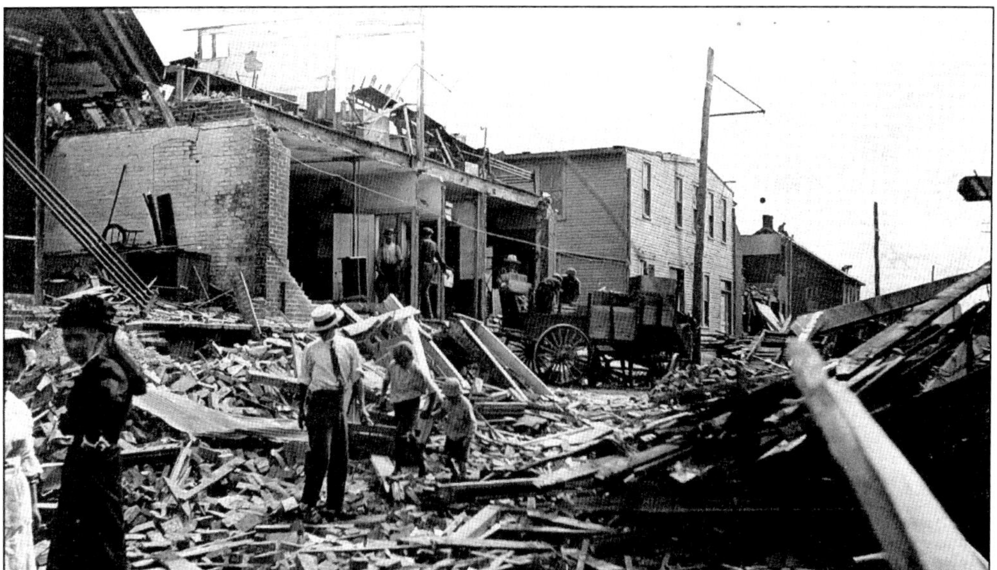

A different view of the same area of Exchange Place, but more oriented toward the south side of the alley, shows the Hanover Glove Factory with a wagon being loaded with salvageable goods, and the Keystone Variety Works to the right.

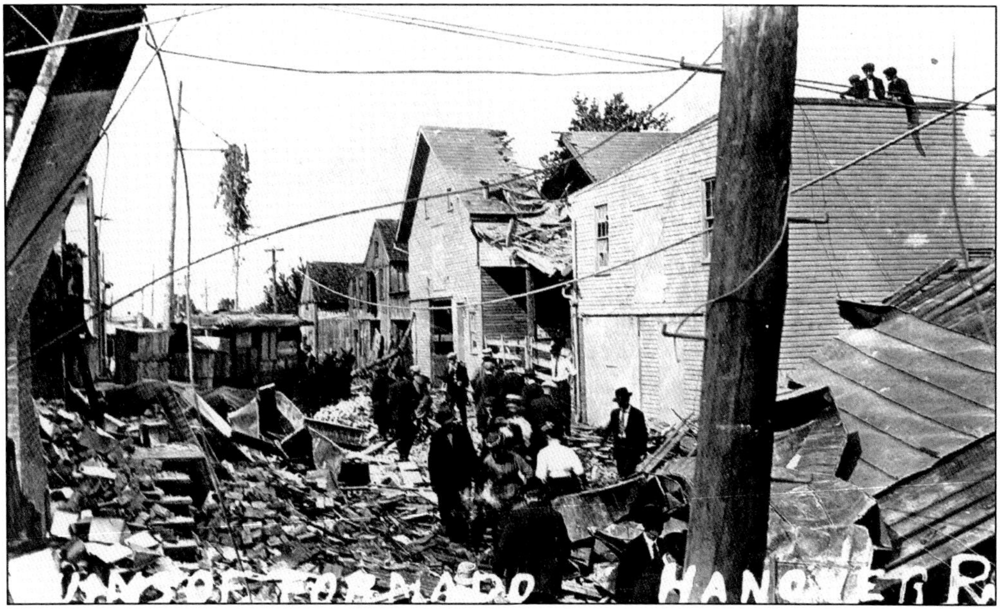

This is the north side of Exchange Place in the same area as the prior photograph across from the glove factory. Many of these postcards indicate a significant number of spectators. Crowds of visitors came from all directions after hearing of the destruction. In fact, the Hanover newspaper reported on Monday, August 23, that the influx of tourists was so great that restaurants ran out of food on Sunday and turned away hungry customers. Automobile parties were reported in town on Sunday from Maryland, Delaware, New Jersey, New York, and the District of Columbia. The York newspaper reported that on Sunday morning at 7:00, crowds had gathered in the York square waiting for trolley transportation. The regular two cars were not adequate, and two trains were brought into service. There were seven cars in total, and still service was not prompt. By 4:00 p.m., it was reported that the trolley had transferred 3,000 passengers from York and was unable to bring them back from Hanover even by 10:00 p.m.

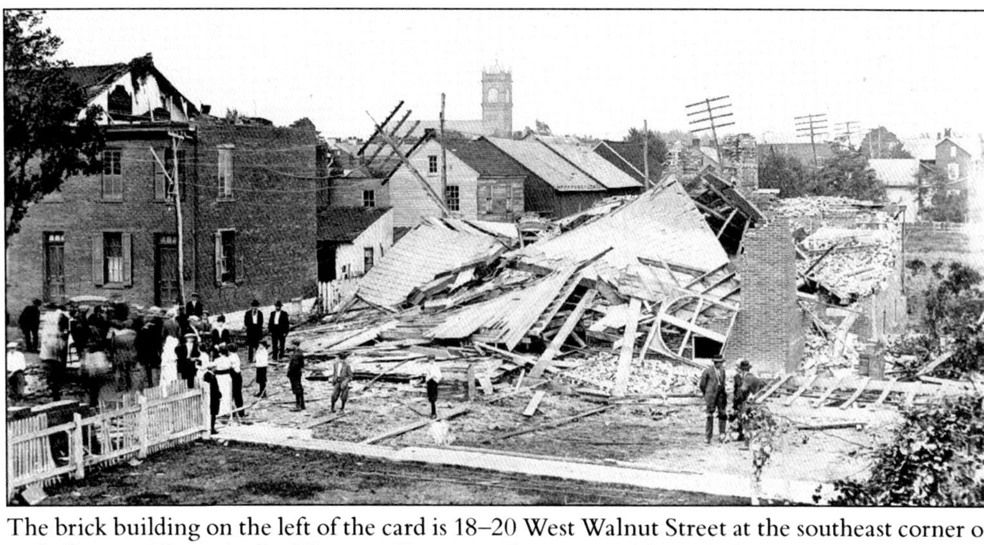

The brick building on the left of the card is 18–20 West Walnut Street at the southeast corner of Eichelberger Alley. The building is still in use. The St. Joseph's Catholic Church steeple at 240 Baltimore Street can be seen in the rear center of the postcard photograph.

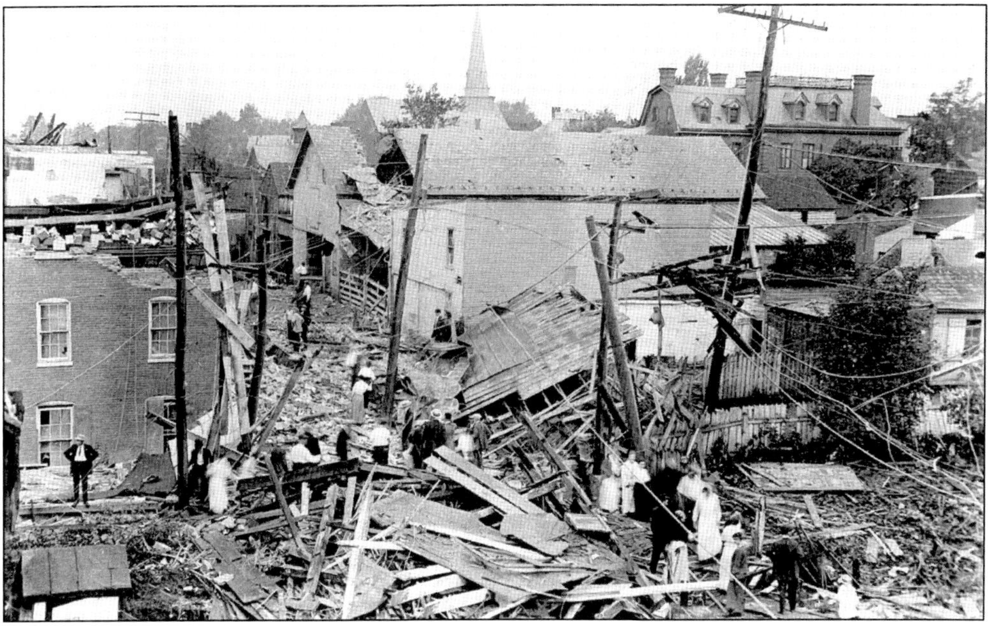

This view from the rear of the Gitt garden (see page 56) is looking west, with the Methodist church steeple at the corner of Frederick Street and Centennial Avenue in the center background. The large distinctive building in the right rear is the east side of the Louis B. Hafer residence at 54 Frederick Street.

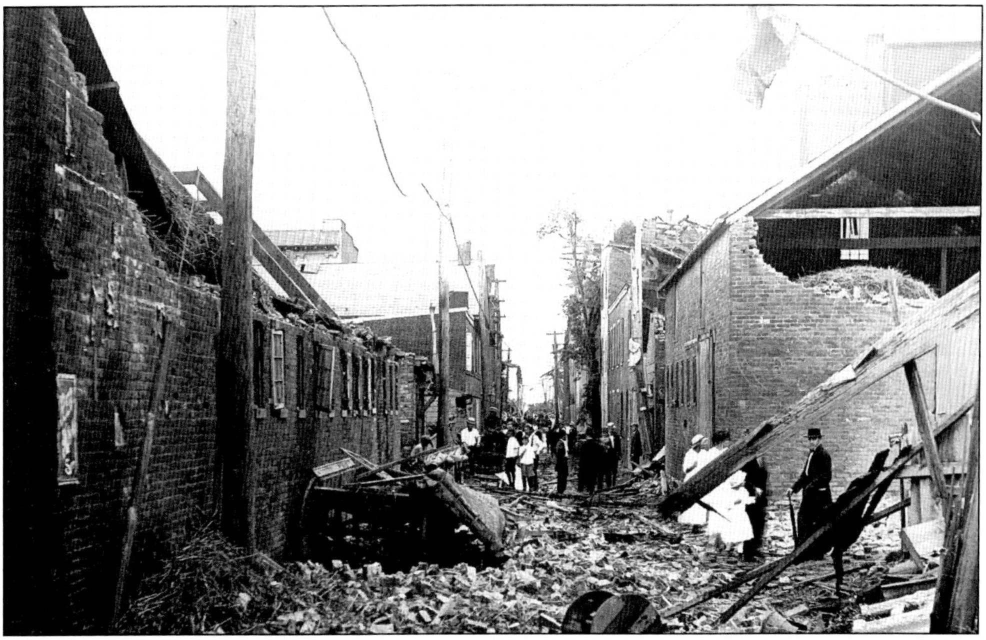

This view looking west on Bixler Alley, the first alley to the east of Baltimore Street from the square, looks from Railroad Street toward Baltimore Street and into Exchange Place in the distance. The first building to the right is the horse stable of the Hotel O'Bold, which fronted on Broadway and Center Square. The Newman Livery stable is on the left forefront extending nearly halfway up to Baltimore Street.

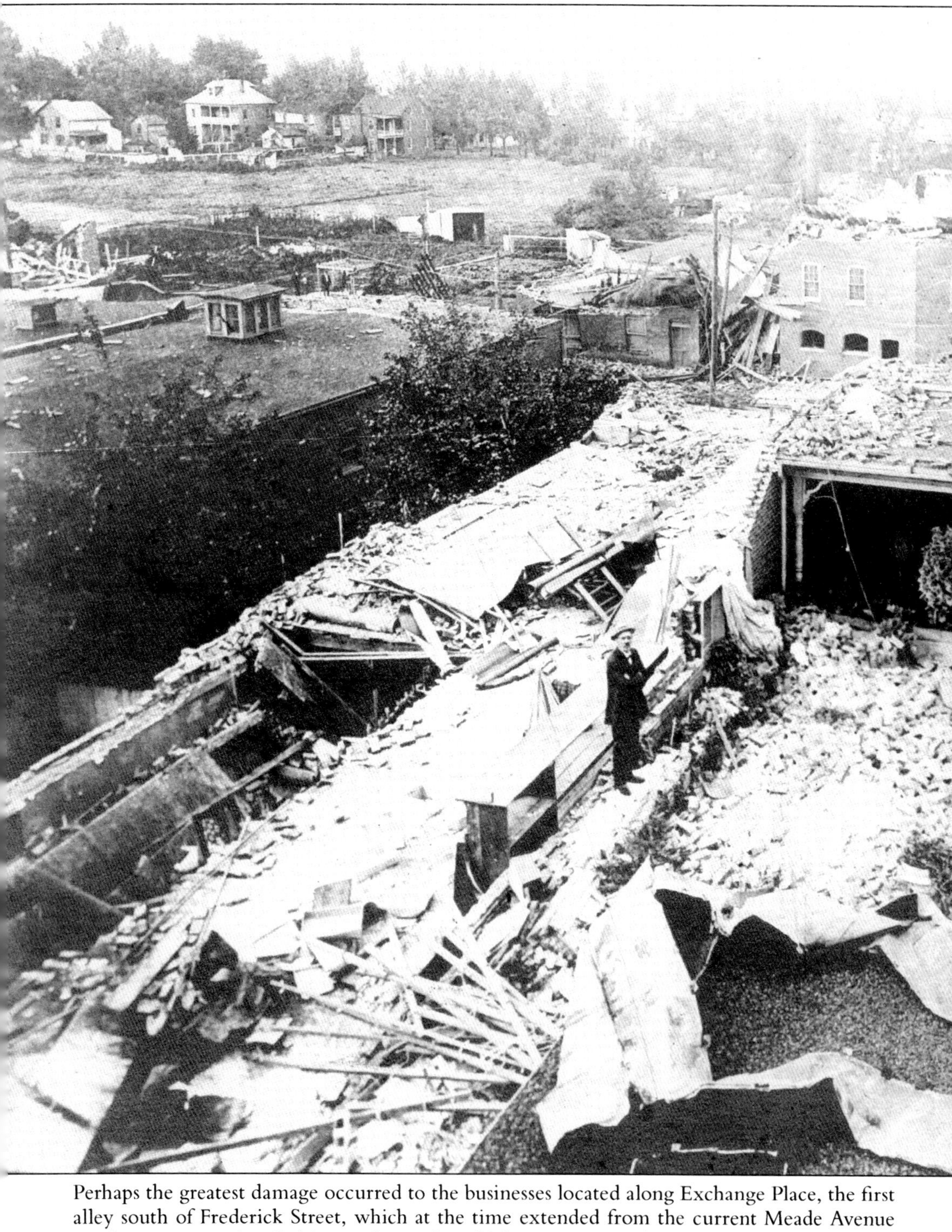

Perhaps the greatest damage occurred to the businesses located along Exchange Place, the first alley south of Frederick Street, which at the time extended from the current Meade Avenue on the west, crossing Baltimore Street (at which point it was known as Bixler Alley) and terminating at Railroad Street on the east. This dramatic view shows the destruction along Exchange Place. The homes in the upper left corner are on West Middle Street and can also be

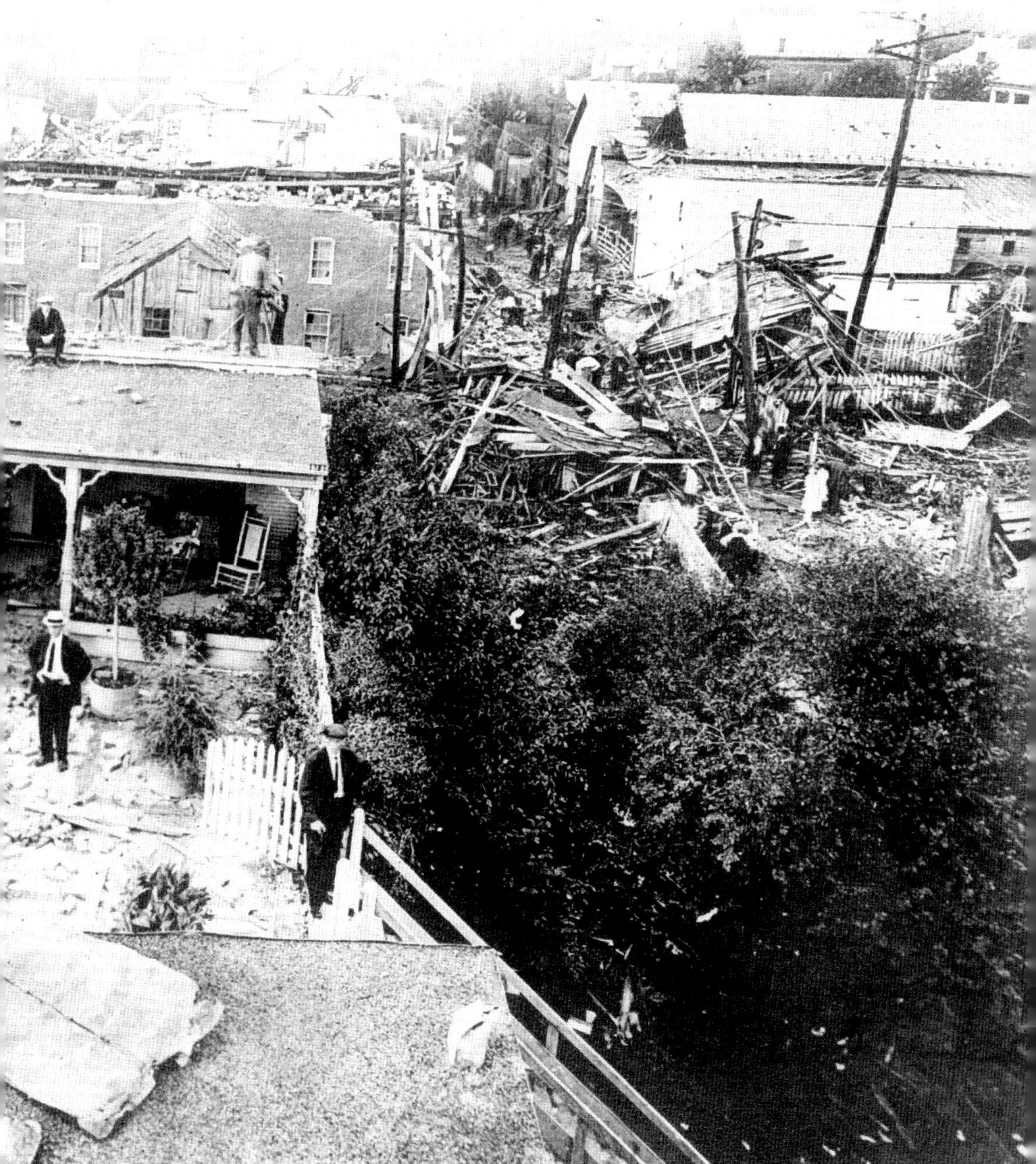

seen on page 52. The far upper right corner steeple is the original Methodist church at Frederick Street and Centennial Avenue. The property in the center is the roof garden of the George N. Gitt residence at 29 Baltimore Street, facing west from Baltimore Street. The Hanover Glove Factory buildings are behind this across Exchange Place. This photograph was on the front page of the August 23, 1915, edition of the *Evening Sun*.

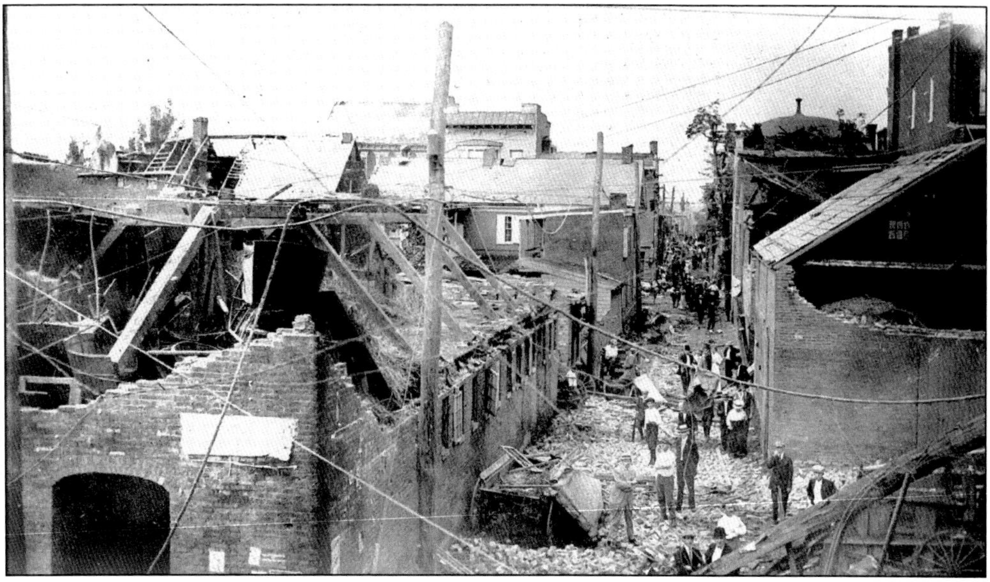

Another view of the same area as the page 55 photograph, taken from Railroad Street looking west on Bixler Alley across Baltimore Street to Exchange Place, reveals more of the damage to the area roofs. The large, brick livery stable of C. N. Newman, on the left, was totally destroyed. It housed 21 horses at the time, and all escaped uninjured, although one was caught beneath the debris for several hours before being freed.

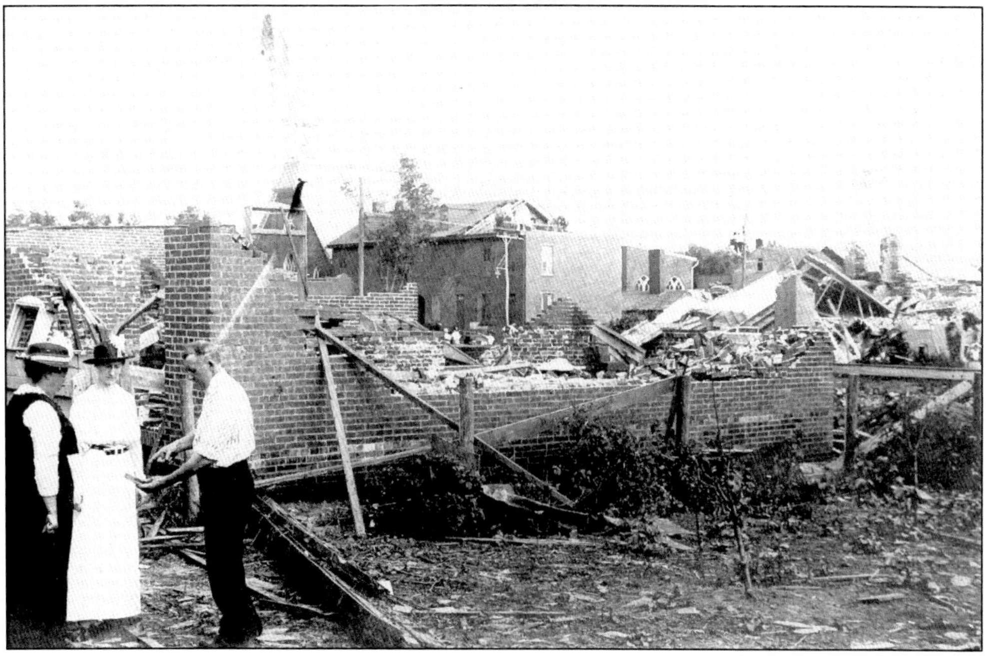

A slightly different view of the same location of the postcard on the bottom of page 54 again shows the corner of West Walnut Street and the southeast corner of Eichelberger Alley in the center. Right of center are the tops of arched windows, located in the social hall of St. Paul's Lutheran Church, with the church front façade and steeple evident in the middle of the left half of the card, which, at the time, was located on West Walnut Street.

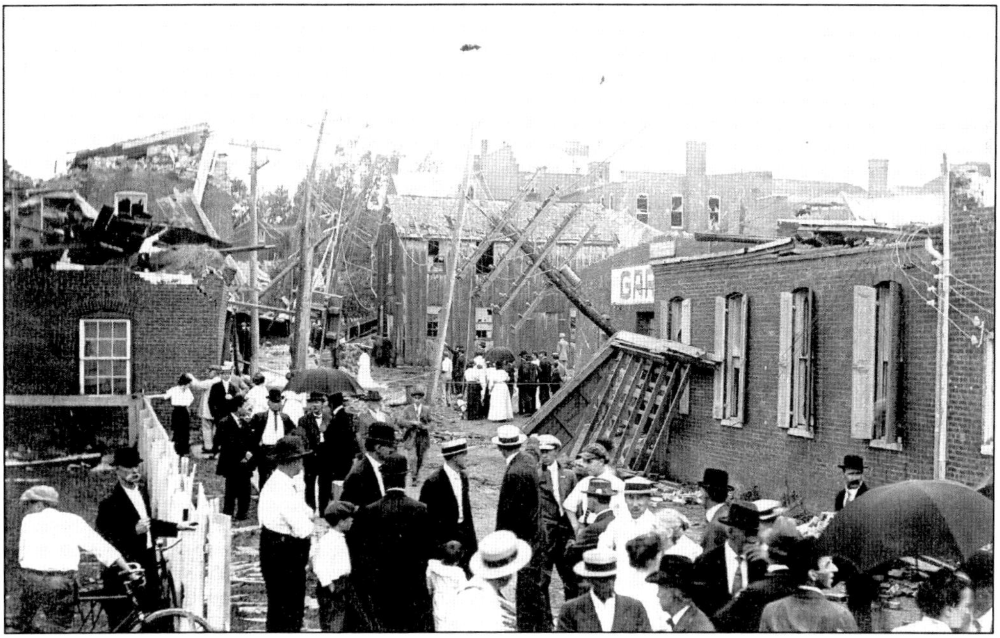

Looking from the corner of West Walnut Street and Eichelberger Alley, toward Frederick Street, Exchange Place crosses in the center of the photograph. The Peoples Bank building on the southwest corner of Frederick Street and Center Square is just evident on the right, to the top center of the image, and is distinguishable because of its corner turret.

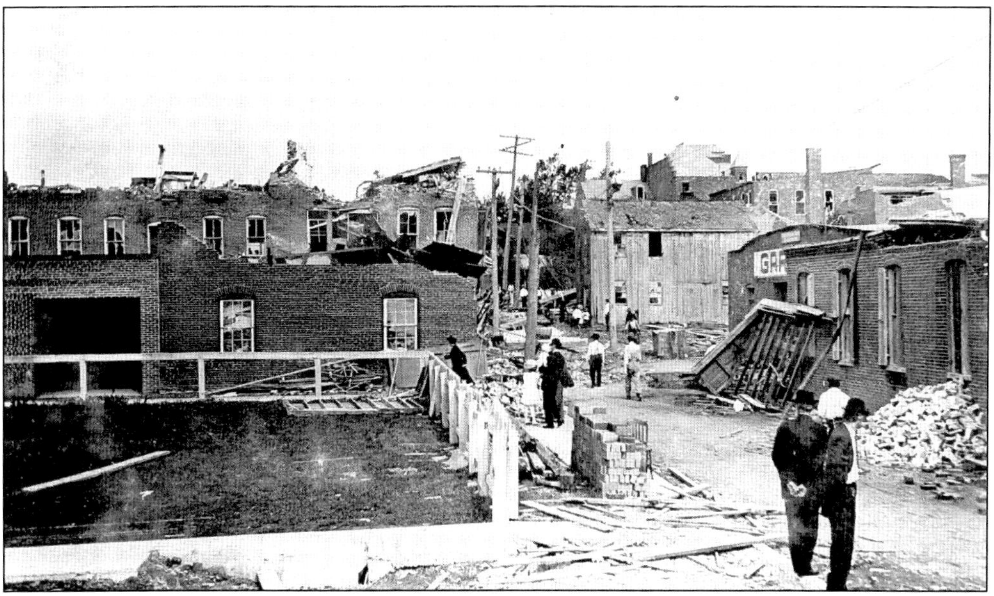

A wider-angle view of the previous postcard was taken from West Walnut Street looking north down the first alley (Eichelberger) to the rear of the first block of Baltimore Street. The first buildings on the right are the service garages for the Adams Sporting Goods House and Adams Motor Company, owned by William J. Adams, which was located on 43–47 Baltimore Street. On the left, after the fence, is Dr. Franklin Shue's veterinary building and, behind that, the rear of the Hanover Glove Factory, which fronted on Exchange Place.

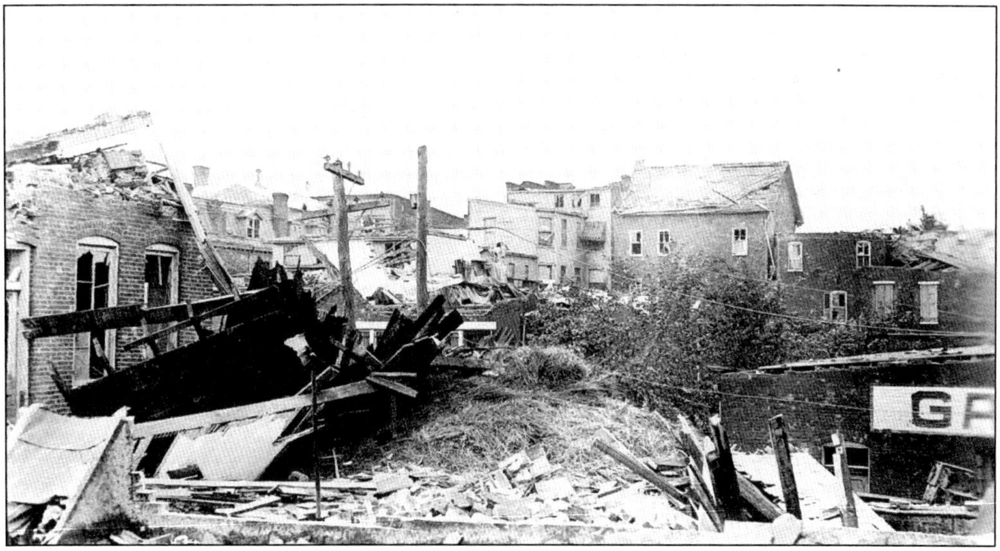

Eichelberger Alley is in the foreground, and the buildings in the background are the rear of the first block of Baltimore Street. The building in the left foreground is the south side of the Hanover Glove Factory, with the rear of the Adams Motor Company garage on the right foreground. The south side of the mansard roof Elks Club building at 19 Baltimore Street is visible to the right of the glove factory.

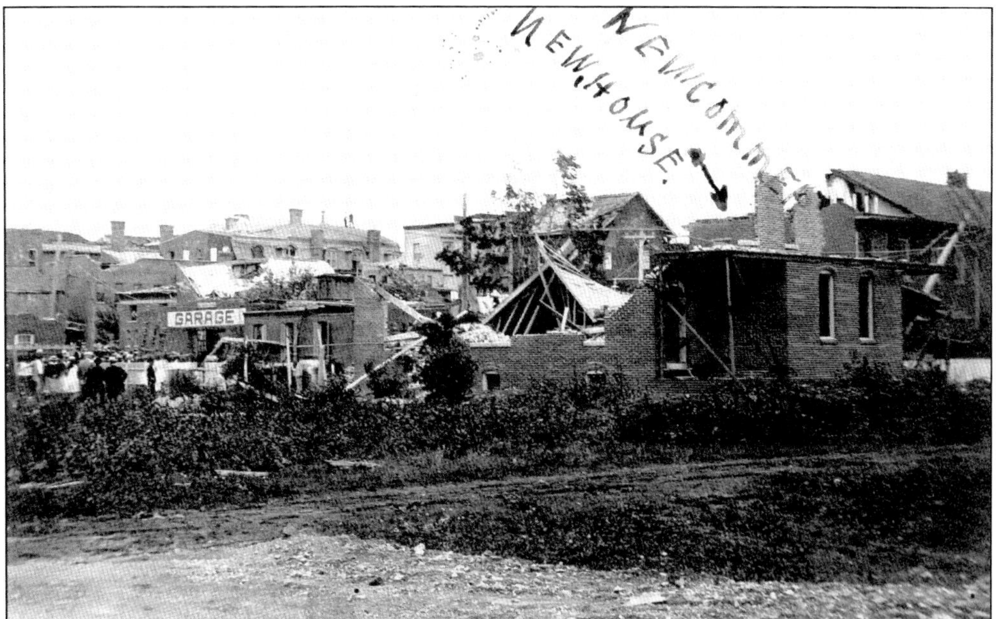

As a former owner wrote on the card, the property in the right forefront was the under-construction home of David Newcomer. This scene was photographed looking north from vacant land west of Ruth Avenue and south of West Walnut Street. Eichelberger Alley ran horizontally across the middle of the card, from the light area on the right middle edge, in front of the garage sign building (Adams Garage). The Elks Club on the corner of Baltimore Street and the Exchange Place alley is visible on the horizon, just left of the upper center, with several individuals standing on the roof.

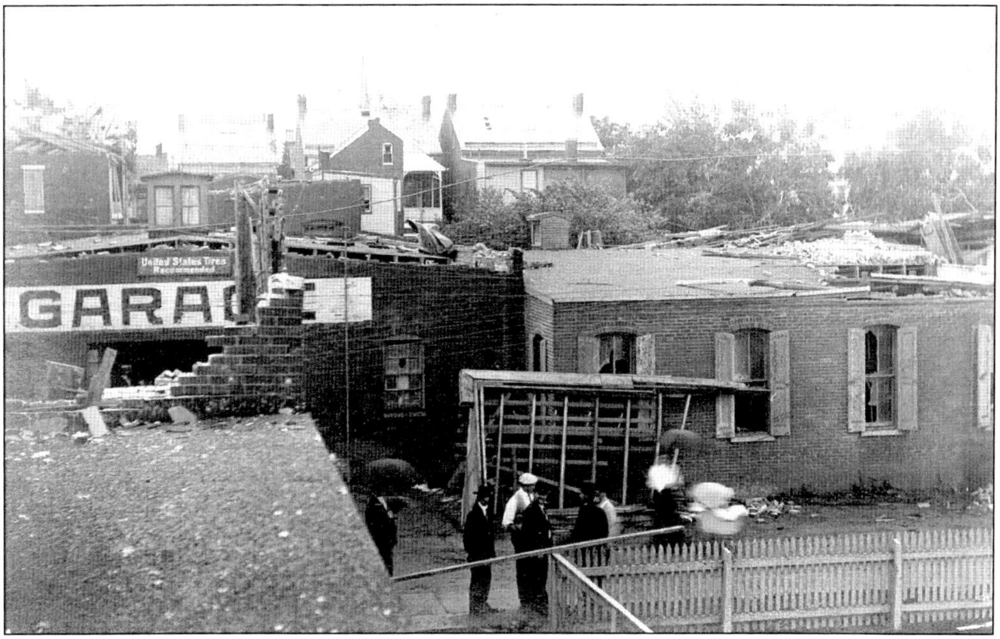

Taken from the Dr. Franklin Shue veterinary building, looking east northeast, this photograph reveals the rear of houses located, from left to right, at 39–45 Baltimore Street. The Trinity Reformed Church spire at 116–118 York Street is evident on the horizon left of center. Both buildings in the foreground were part of the Adams Garage complex. Just to the right of this on West Walnut Street would have been St. Paul's Lutheran Church.

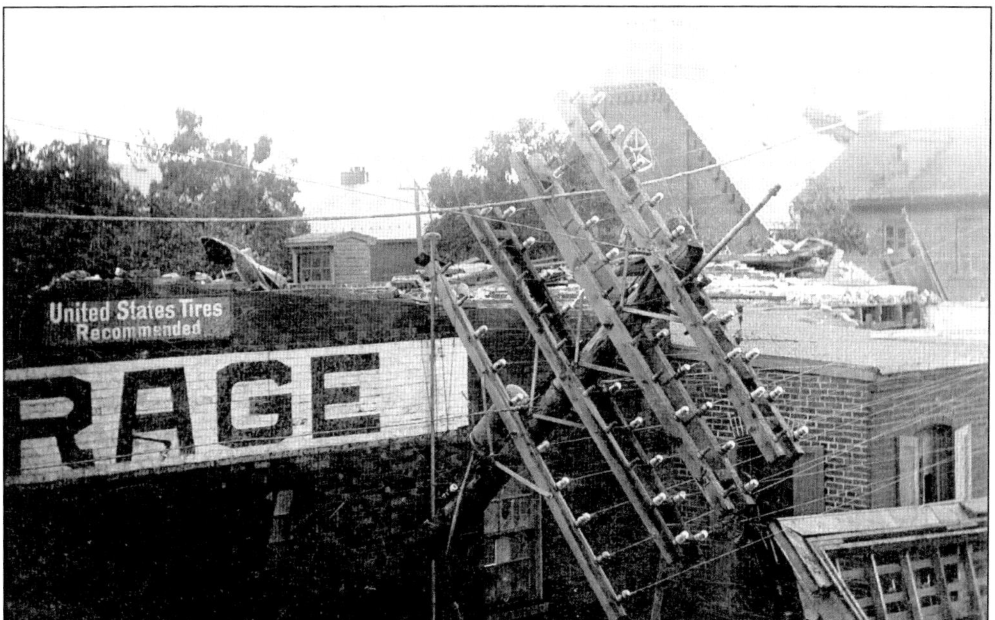

This scene of the same buildings in the forefront of the previous card clearly shows the St. Paul's Lutheran Church on West Walnut Street, with residences to its right at 14–16 West Walnut Street. This was taken from the veterinary office facing east.

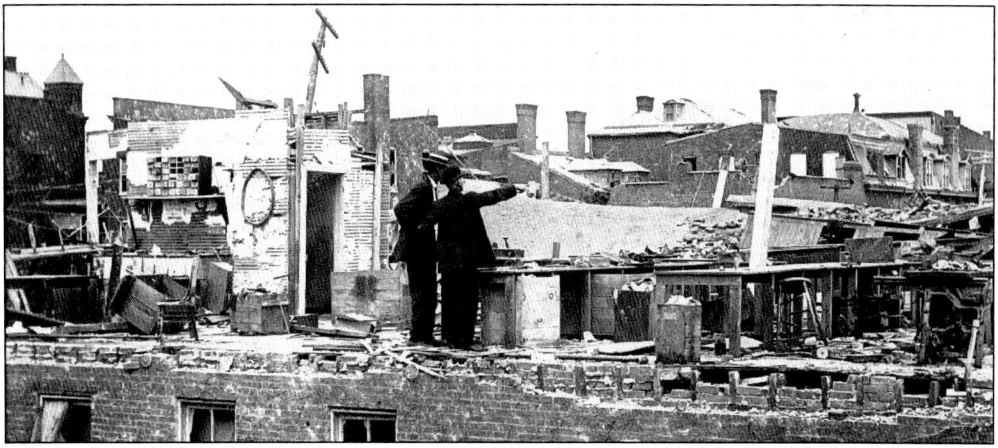

The remains of the Hanover Glove Factory are shown. The far left edge from the center up clearly reveals the Peoples Bank building on Center Square at Frederick Street. The upper right edge reflects the distinctive architecture of the Elks Club building at 19 Baltimore Street. Hanover Glove Company had no cyclone insurance, nor did the nearby Keystone Variety Works. To allow for recovery, the glove business stock was moved to the Hanover Shoe Company on Park Avenue. The inventory of gloves was carried far and wide by the tornado. After the storm subsided, gloves were found along Penn Street, and two pairs were found in a cornfield a mile away. A *Record-Herald* article of August 25, 1915, stated, "John Auchey, a fruit grower, residing beyond the Pigeon Hills about five miles from town, reported finding a number of glove boxes on his property from the Hanover Glove Factory." As if the storm damage was not enough, the previous day's *Record-Herald* newspaper ran a request by the company that parties known to them had removed quantities of gloves from the wrecked factory. The company said that if the gloves were voluntarily returned, no questions would be asked.

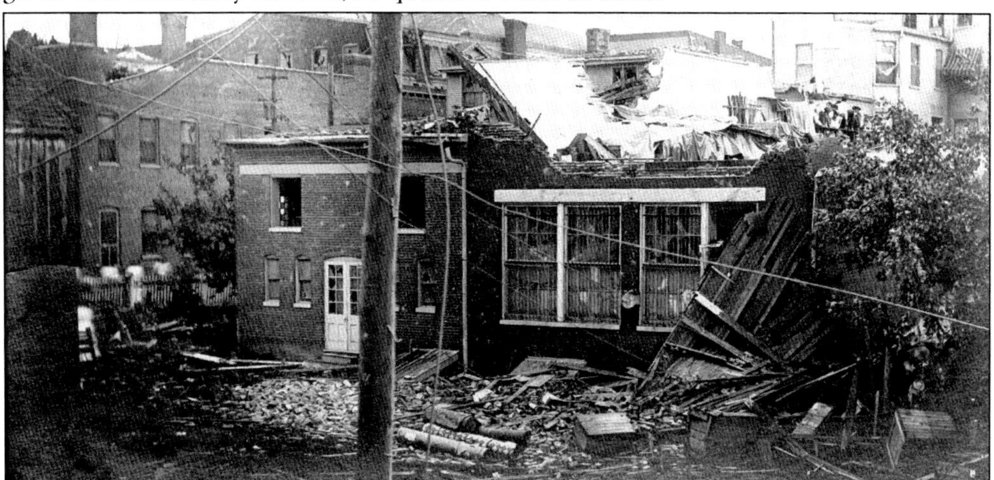

Taken northeast across Eichelberger Alley, this image reflects the rear of the buildings from 19–33 Baltimore Street. The four windows just right of the photograph's center are Wentz Brothers and Fry dry goods store at 33 Baltimore Street, with the rear of the Hanover Electric Theater and its double doors to the left. The rear of the upper floor of this building was the location of George Gitt's roof garden, which can be seen on pages 56–57. The next open space is the rear of 25 Baltimore Street, followed by Exchange Place, and the Elks Club building at 19 Baltimore Street with its mansard-style roof.

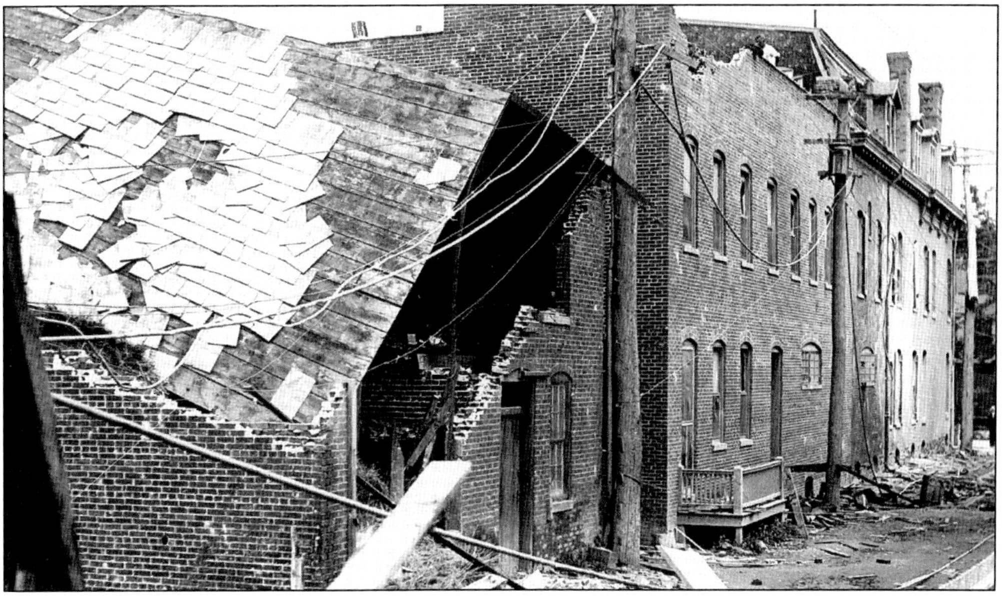

Looking east on Exchange Place toward Baltimore Street, the building on the left with the roof sliding off was the garage at the rear of 28 Frederick Street, the first building after the Peoples Bank building. The remainder of the buildings, from the card's center to its right, are the Elks Club, which fronted on 17-19 Baltimore Street. The steps and porch in the center forefront were the rear entrance to the Elks Club.

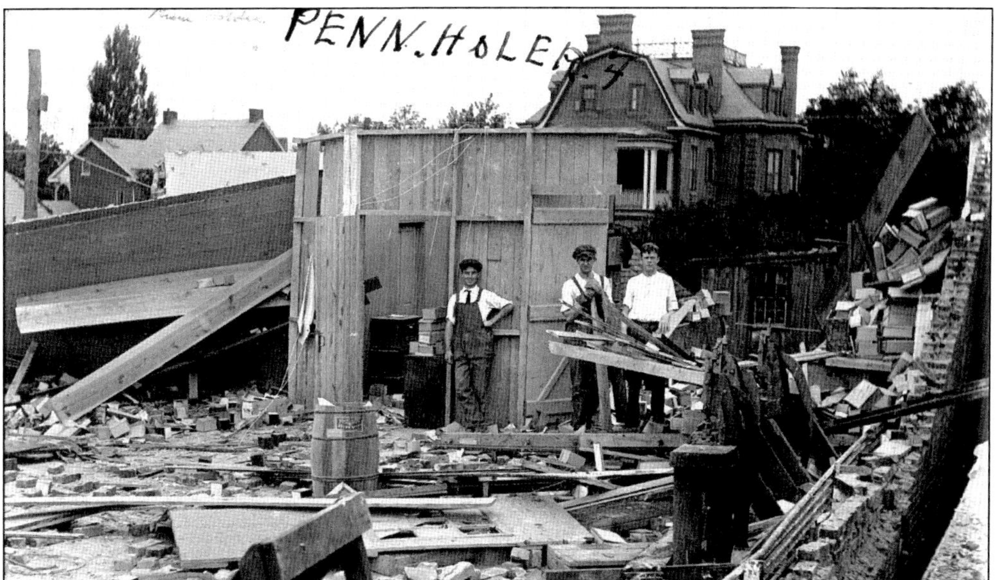

Perhaps the company that suffered the most crippling destruction during the tornado was the Center Shaft Penholder Company, owned by Harry E. Hoke, the inventor of the penholder. Not only did the storm bring almost total destruction to the plant, but according to the newspaper, its former factory had burned to the ground in the early spring of the same year. Samuel Bixler was the recent building's owner. To the right of center behind the rubble is the Louis B. Hafer house, which still exists today, at 54 Frederick Street, and 106 Frederick Street, to the left.

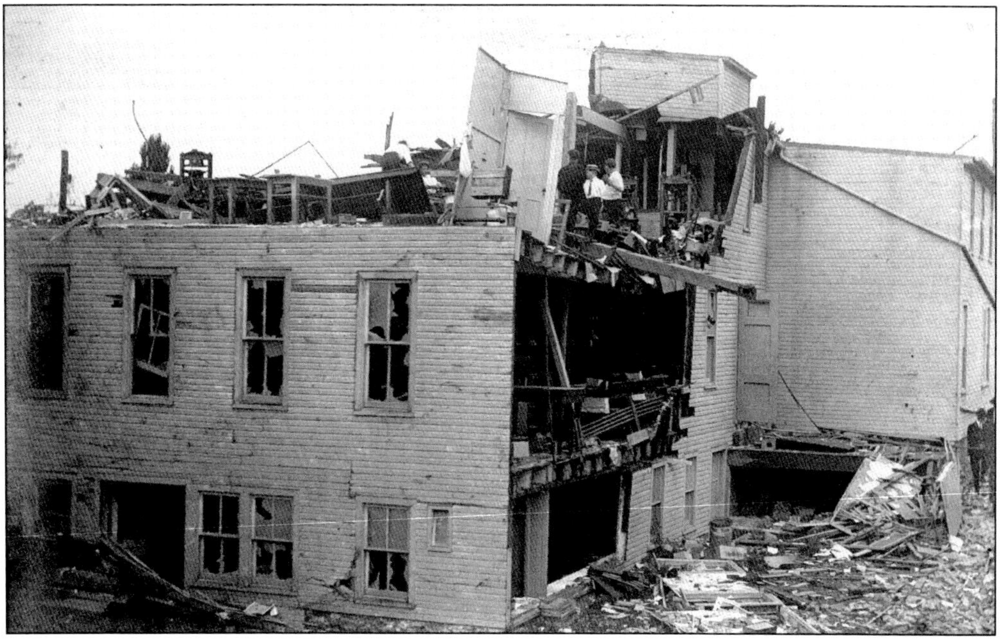

Facing northwest, the rear of the Keystone Variety Works building on the south side of Exchange Place reflects massive damage. Notice the sightseers who are shown standing precariously on the leaning beam on the third floor.

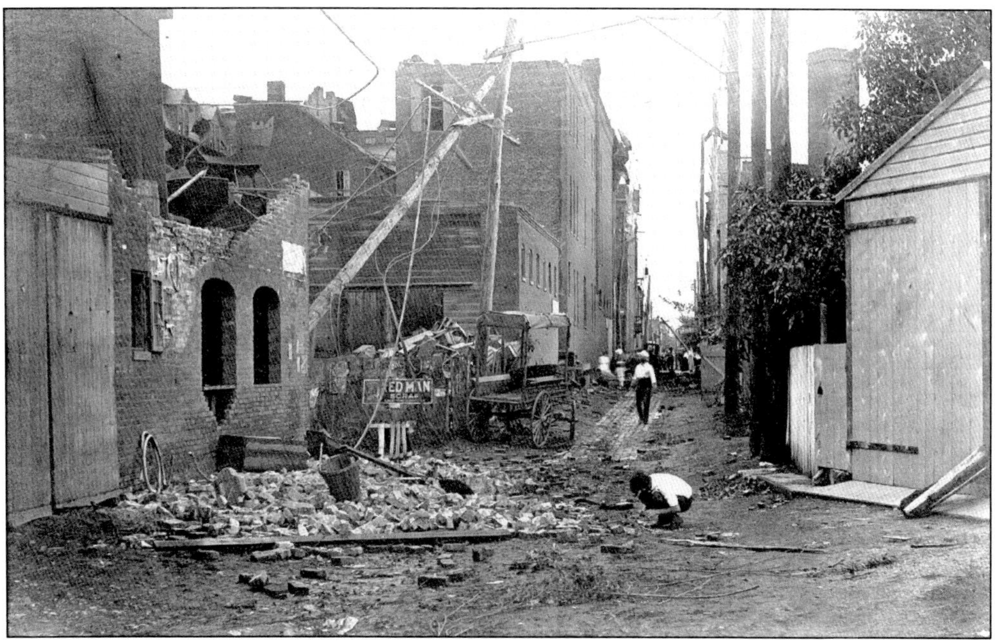

Looking north along the east side of the Tanger building, which fronts on 37 Broadway, this alley becomes Railroad Street north of Broadway. The main J. C. Tanger building roof was blown off onto the Smith and Jenkins awning across the street at 100 Broadway. The building left of center is the O'Bold Hotel, which was reported to have been completely unroofed.

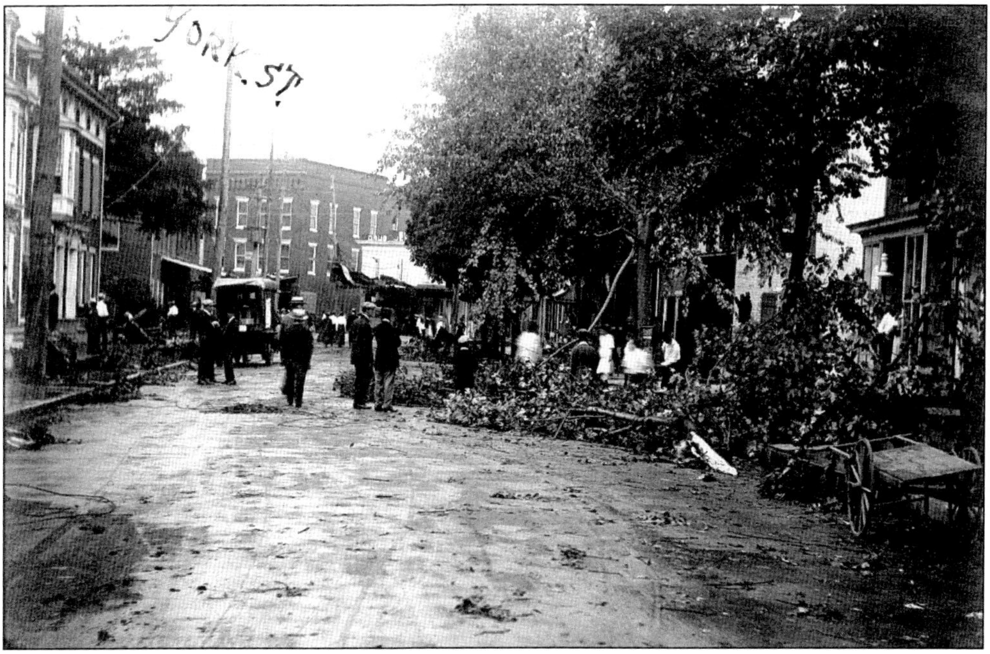

York Street looking north into the intersection of Broadway shows the Shirks Hardware store at 40 Broadway and the Smith and Jenkins Drug Store, which was later removed to widen Railroad Alley into Railroad Street.

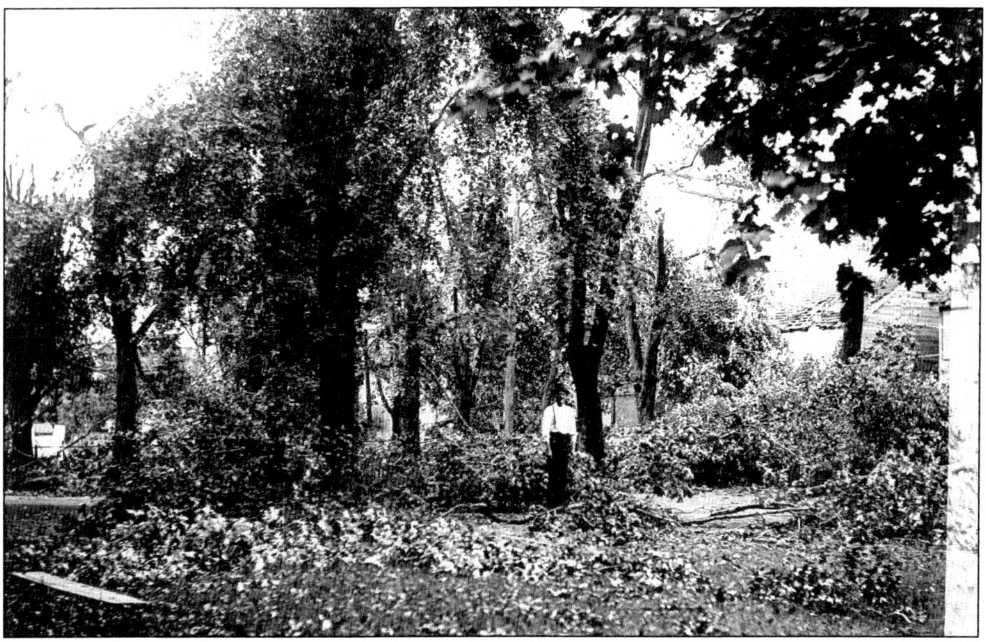

After leaving downtown and crossing York Street, East Walnut Street became a target for the tornado. Robert W. "Bones" Hawthorne, janitor of the East Walnut Street School, is surveying the damage to the schoolyard. At this point, he is probably considering either calling in sick or realizing that all his winter firewood needs have just been met.

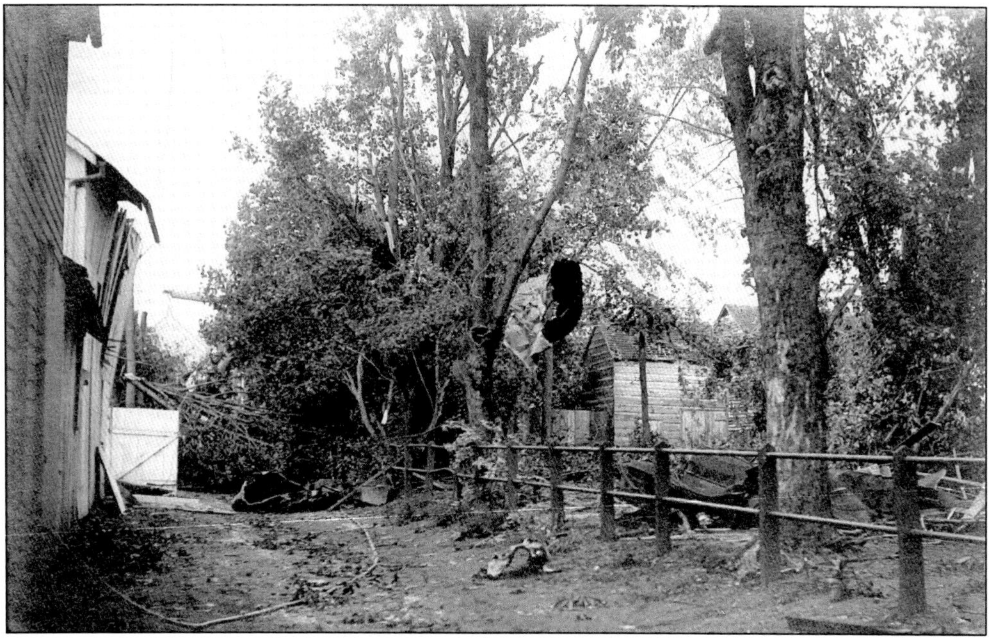

Additional schoolyard damage to the East Walnut Street School is evident, surrounded by the school's fencing.

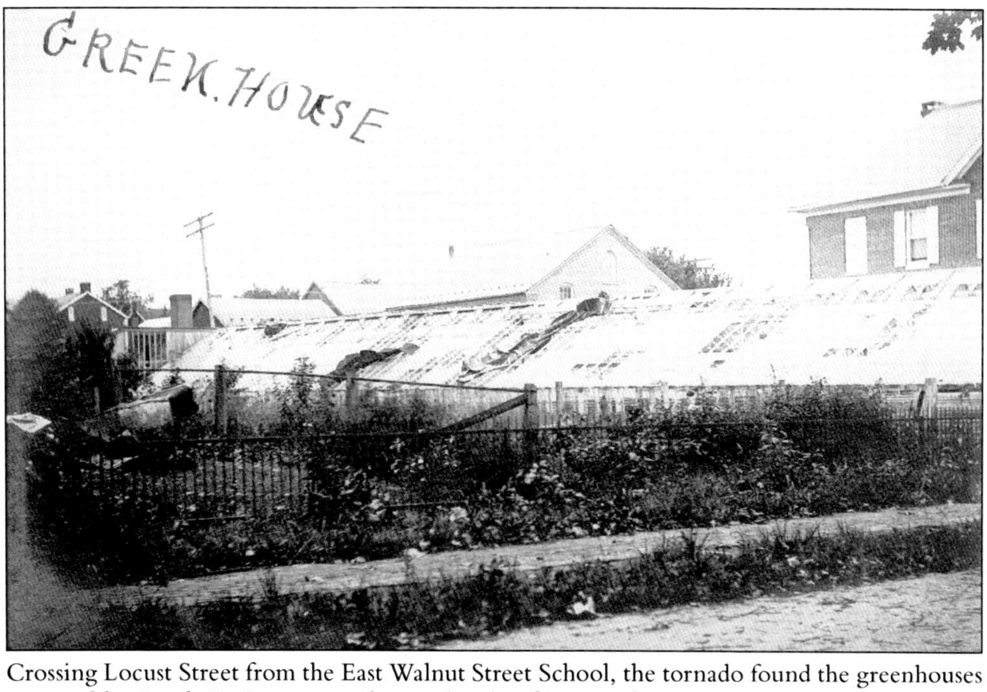

Crossing Locust Street from the East Walnut Street School, the tornado found the greenhouses operated by Frank E. Cremer on the north side of East Walnut Street. Several hundred glass panes were broken, in addition to damage to the plants. Total damage was estimated at $800. The brick home behind the greenhouse to the right is 214 East Walnut Street with the brick garage behind it. The brick building on the left edge is 215 Broadway.

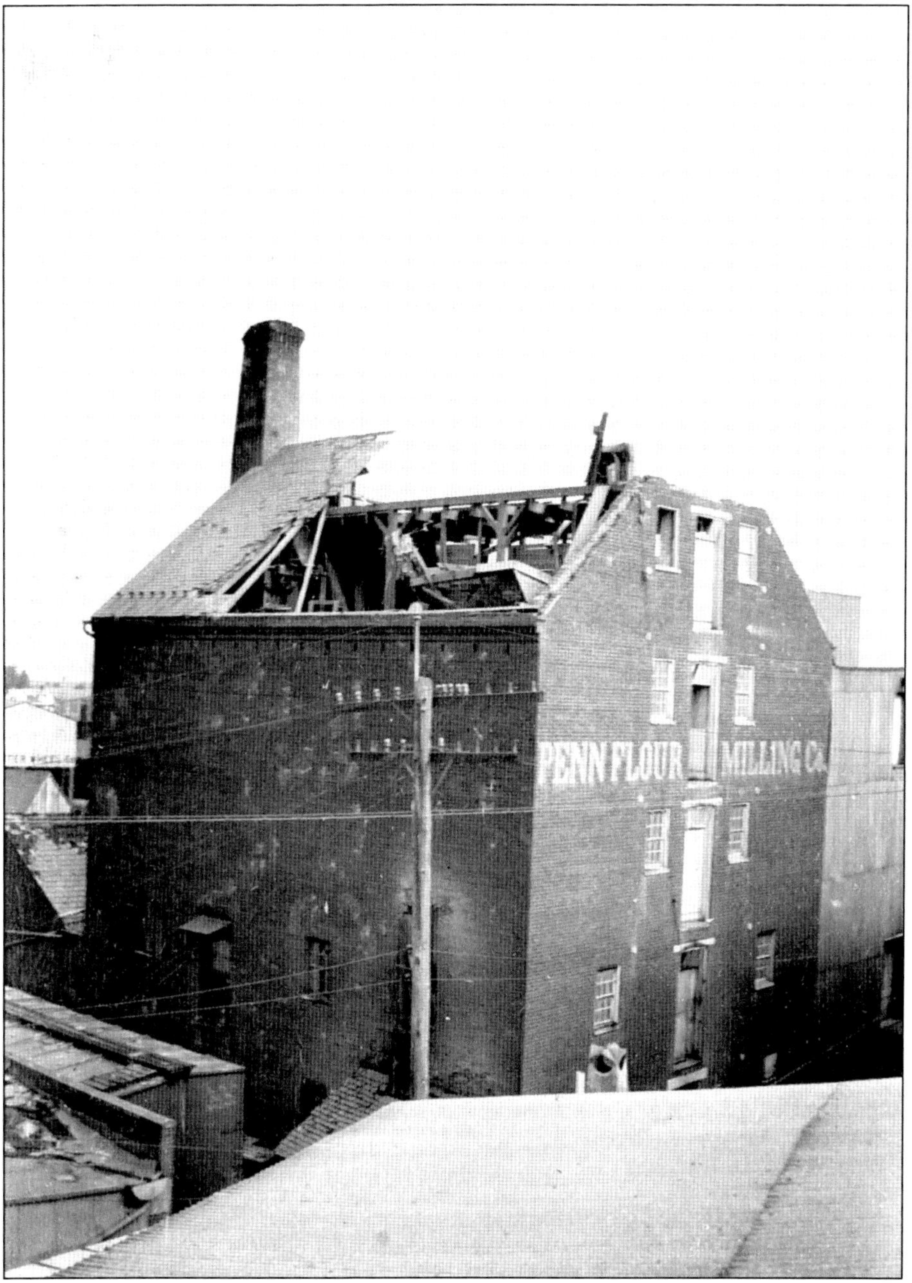

The tornado caused serious damage starting on the 400 block of Broadway. It crossed over the Fitz Water Wheel Company between the railroads and Penn Street, venturing down Penn Street until eventually reaching the J. F. Rohrbaugh Planing Mills and Lumber Yard. Located on the northwest side of the very beginning of East Chestnut Street, just off Broadway, the Penn Flour Milling Company experienced substantial damage to the fifth floor and roof. Notice the rail boxcar in the lower left, which is on a rail siding to the southwest of the building abutting East Chestnut Street that ran directly in front of the side of the building with the name painted on it. Another rail siding existed on the far side, beyond the frame structure, on the right of the view. The frame building was also part of the mill and served as a warehouse.

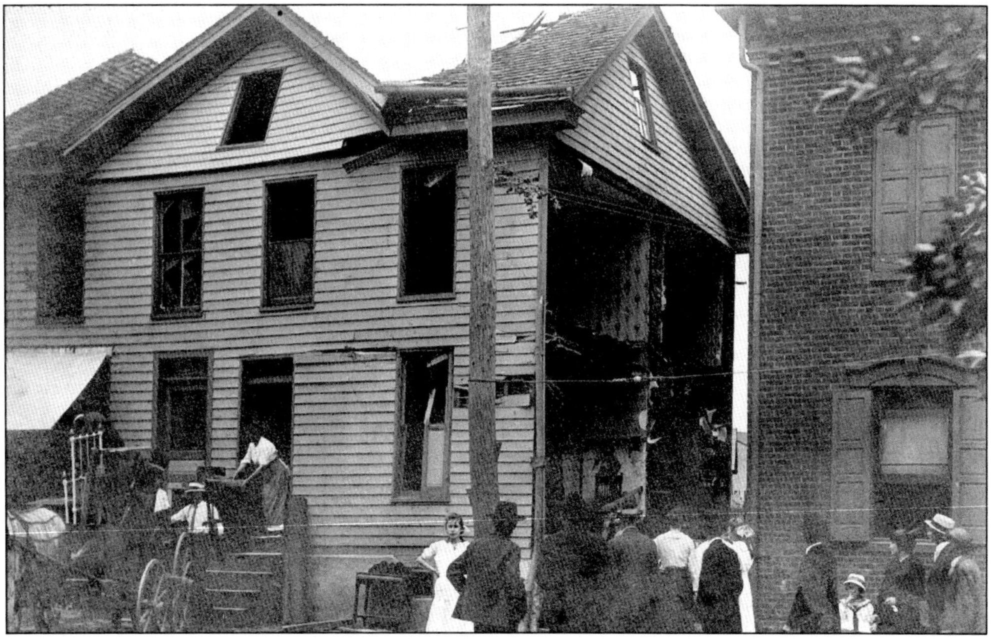

This card reveals the damage to the east side of the home of Harry Kuhn, located at 412 Broadway. The building to the right is the City Hotel, which extended east to the railroad crossing on Broadway. Residents commented that the home reminded them of a dollhouse after the tornado's destruction. The entire roof of the City Hotel was torn off, and the barn to the rear was demolished with the loss of life of one pig.

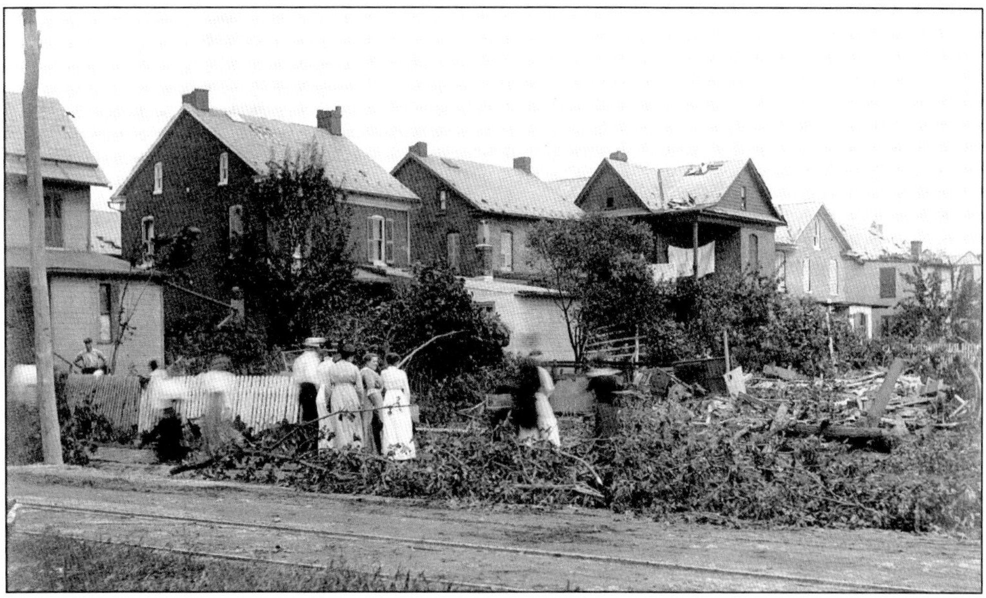

Taken from Stock Street at the first alley to the rear of Broadway looking north, the rear yards of the homes on the southeast side of Penn Street are visible. Shown are the entire Jacob Ernst home on the left at 7 Penn Street, followed by the homes of Charles Lorey, Marie Stambaugh, and Mrs. George Reed at 13 Penn Street. Note the trolley tracks on Stock Street in the foreground.

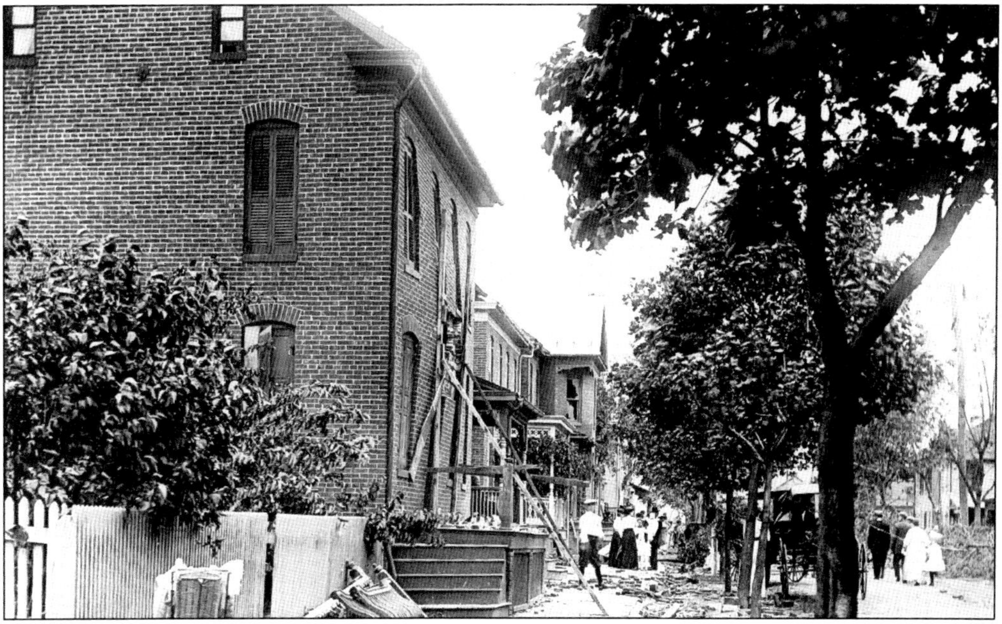

Across the street at 8 Penn Street, the first home on the northwest side of Penn Street, north of Stock Street is the brick residence of Edward O. and Lucy Snyder, which suffered front wall damage, as shown in this photograph looking northeast on Penn Street. Repairs were made, and the home still exists today.

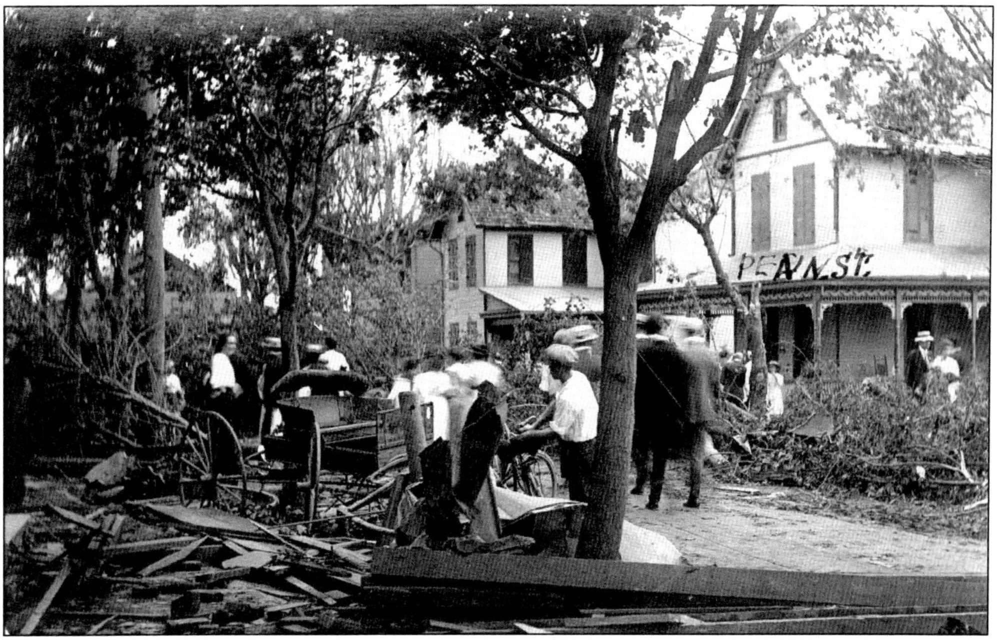

The southeast side of Penn Street includes 15 Penn Street, the residence on the right, which was the home of Isaac Witmer. At this house, the roof was lost, the interior walls cracked, and the windows, fences, and fruit trees were damaged. To the left is 19 Penn Street, which was occupied by Alice Bauserman. This residence suffered little damage. The J. F. Rohrbaugh lumber business was just down the street.

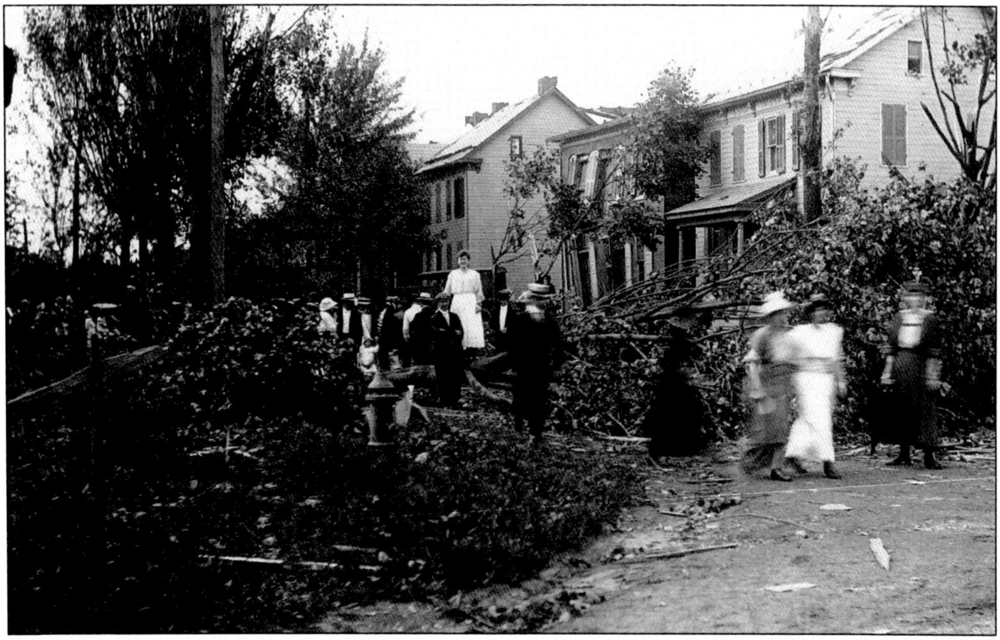

Further damage to the northeast side of Penn Street is evident looking southwest toward Stock Street. The first home on the right was the residence of Ruel Diller. The following home to the left was 20 Penn Street, which suffered severe damage, as shown in detail in the following cards.

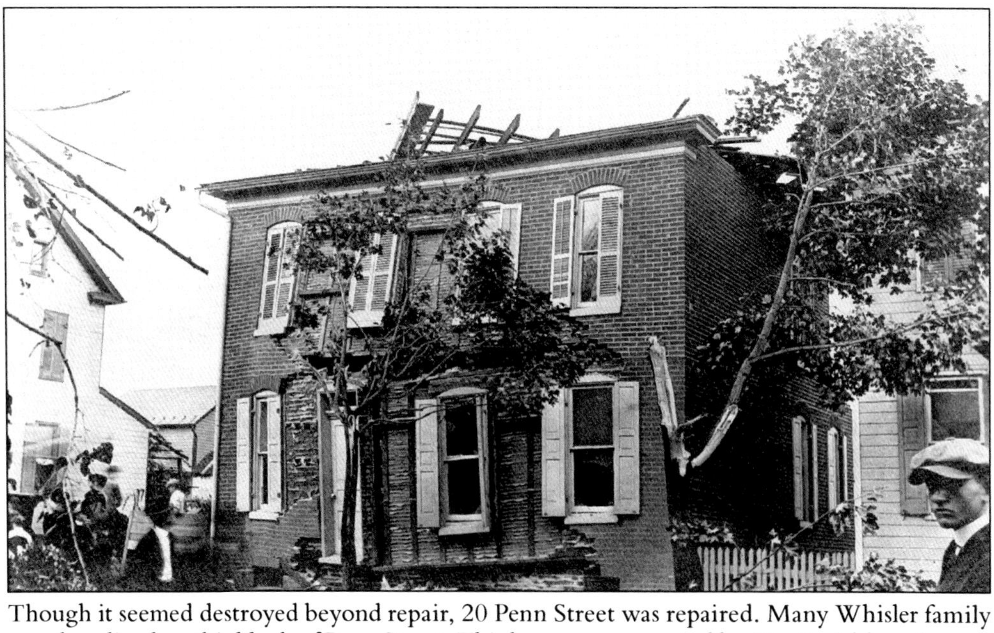

Though it seemed destroyed beyond repair, 20 Penn Street was repaired. Many Whisler family members lived on this block of Penn Street. This house was occupied by Martin (although some newspaper reports say Mark) Whisler at the time of the tornado.

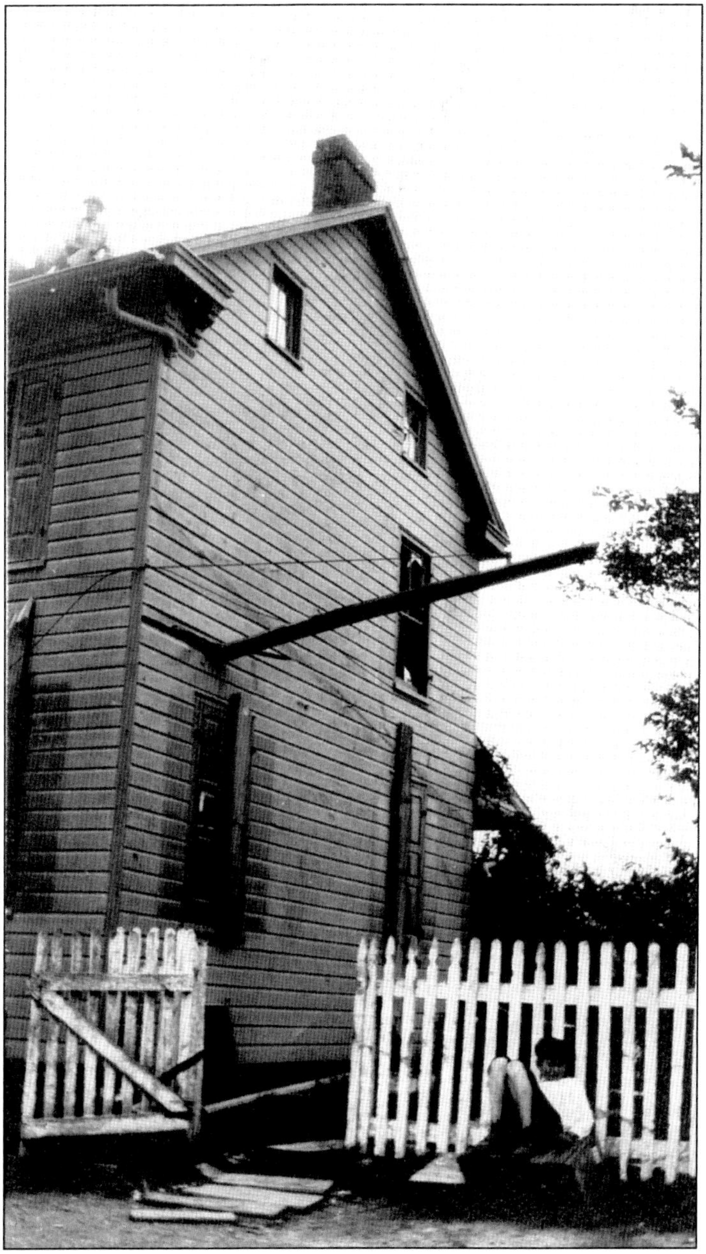

The force of the tornado is evident in this photograph of 133 Penn Street, a tenant house owned by John Rohrbaugh, and the residence of Albert Garman. Note the lumber plank, claimed by reporters to be 14 feet in length, that was thrust nearly horizontally into the home's weatherboarding. Note also the man on the roof surveying roof damage. The Garmans' son Milliard, 11 years old at the time, was in the alley near Rohrbaugh's Planing Mill, picking grass for his chickens, on the evening of Thursday, August 26, 1915, five days after the tornado. He came in contact with a live electric wire hanging from a tree, which the electric company overlooked when making repairs. He was burned on his left hand, ear, and leg so severely that finger amputation was considered, according to a report by the *Record-Herald* on August 27, 1915.

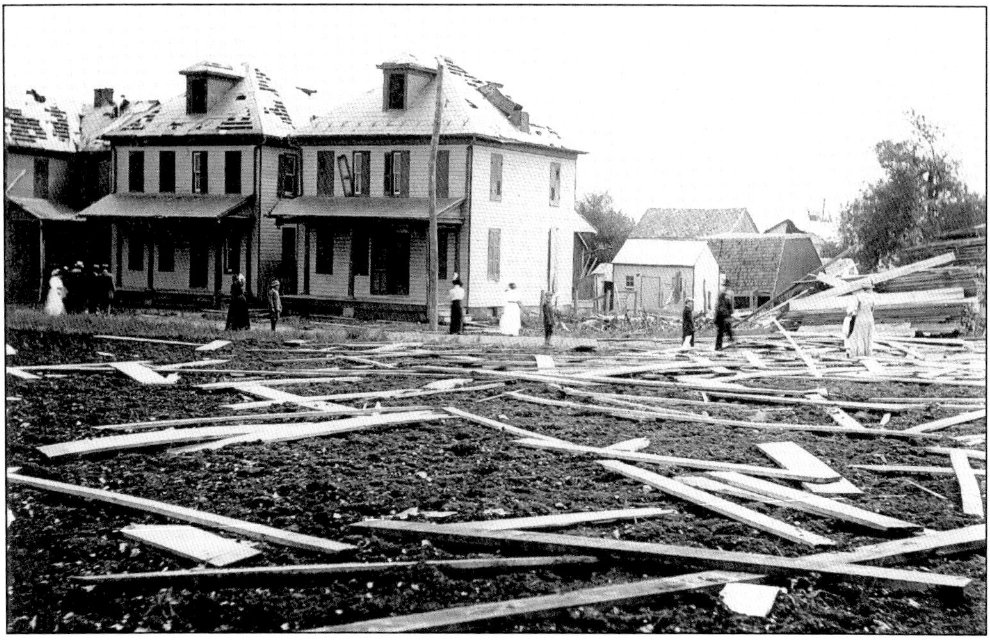

These homes at 141–145 Penn Street were across the street from the previous photograph and, as in the prior card, were located near the site of the J. F. Rohrbaugh Lumber Yard. Stacks of lumber, which were the source of all the debris in the street, can be seen to the right center of the card. Notice the amount of slate missing from the roofs of these homes.

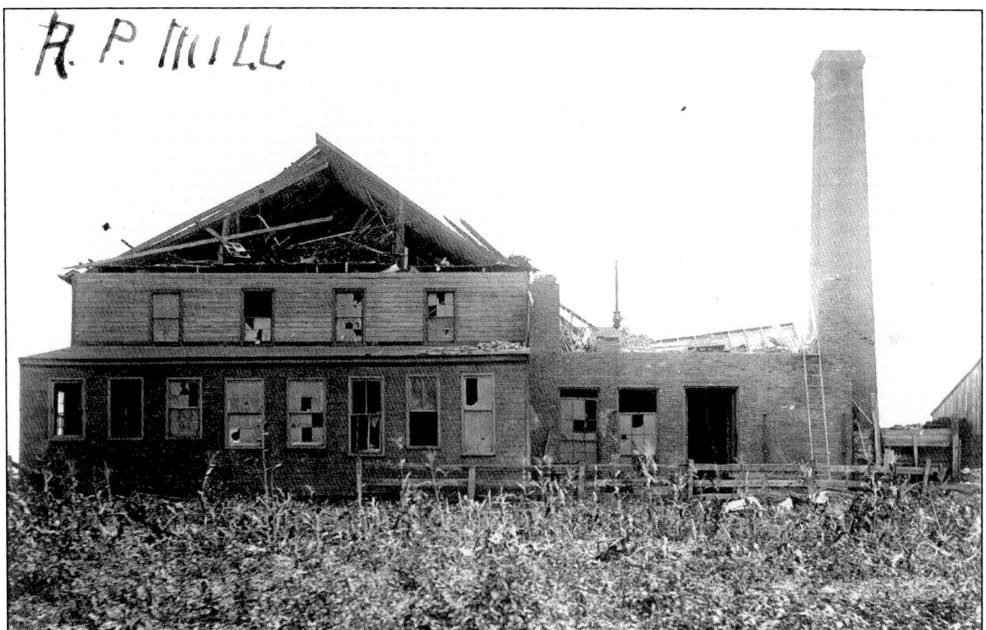

The J. F. Rohrbaugh and Company Planning Mill operated at the end of the 100 block of Penn Street and suffered major building damage and the loss of stacked lumber. This has been the site of plumbing distributors for a number of recent years and is now renumbered the 500 block of Penn Street.

Four

THE 1915 CENTENNIAL CELEBRATION

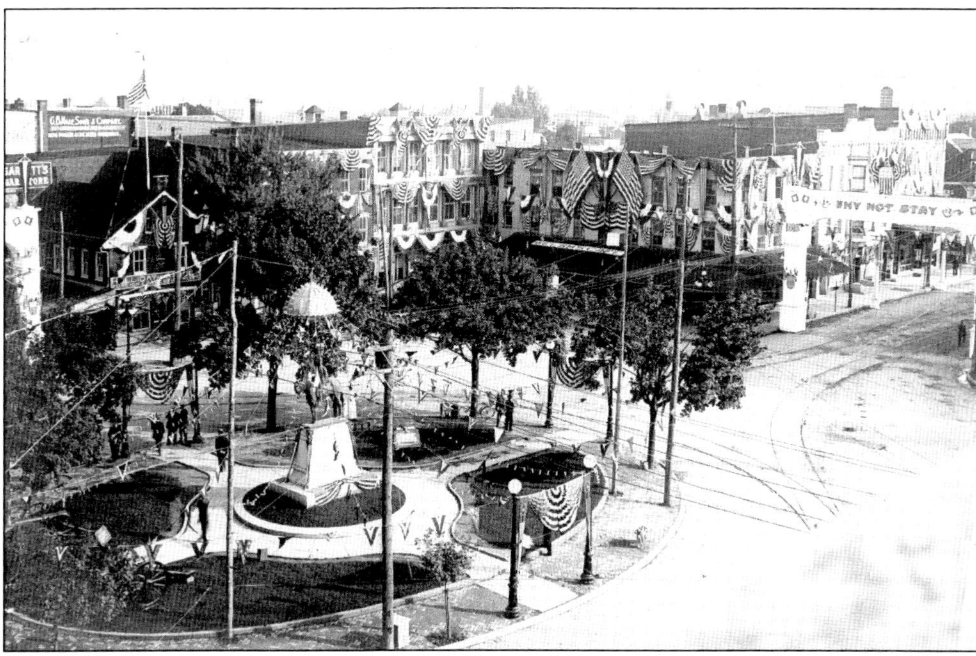

Hanover was incorporated as a borough on March 4, 1815. Since 1884, the Hanover Agricultural Society held their fair week the third week in September. This week had become regarded as a homecoming week for former Hanover residents. Therefore, the centennial celebration was planned for September 12–18, 1915. Center Square was decorated profusely, as evident from this card, which also shows the arch constructed over the Broadway entrance into town as well as, on the left edge, a portion of the Carlisle Street arch.

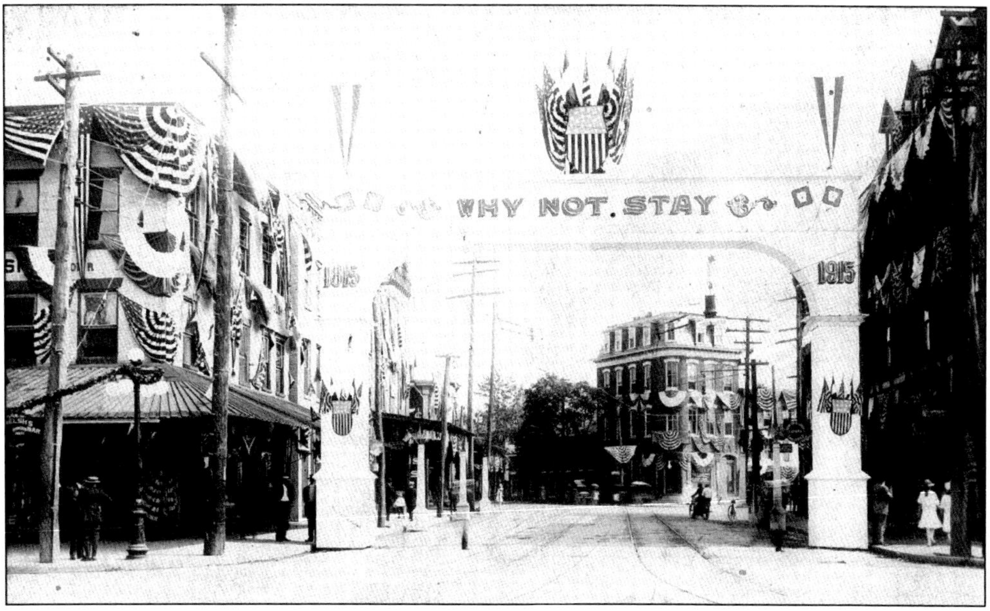

The general Hanover Centennial Committee was headed by Harry S. Ehrhart, secretary of the Ehrhart and Conrad Company wholesale grocers. The vice president was Clinton N. Myers, an owner of the Sheppard and Myers Company. Paul Winebrenner was selected as treasurer, a position he also held with the Hanover Saving Fund Society, and the secretary was Thomas J. O'Neill, a Hanover silk manufacturer. This view through the Broadway arch reveals the Mansion House to the left and Hotel O'Bold on the right.

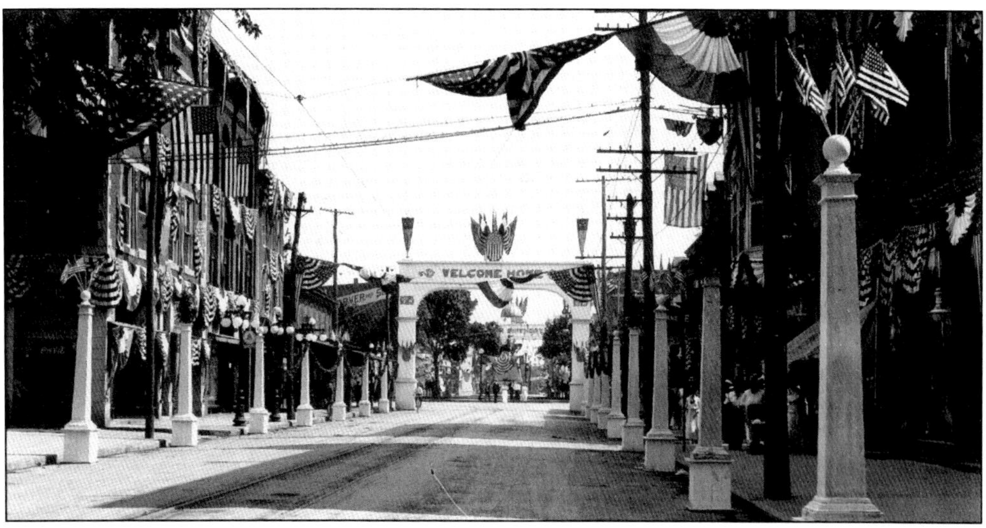

Prizes for decorations were awards of $25 for the best-decorated business building and $10 for the best-decorated private residence as well as smaller awards for second place. Further, Burgess H. M Stokes requested that on September 11, owners of all delivery wagons, including butchers, bakers, milk, and grocery wagons, decorate the carts for the centennial week. Carlisle Street facing Center Square beyond the arch reflects a series of pillars in the foreground. The August 24, 1915, *Record-Herald* reported the acquisition of 80 columns from Baltimore. The reverse side of the Carlisle Street arch had "Come Again" on the Center Square side.

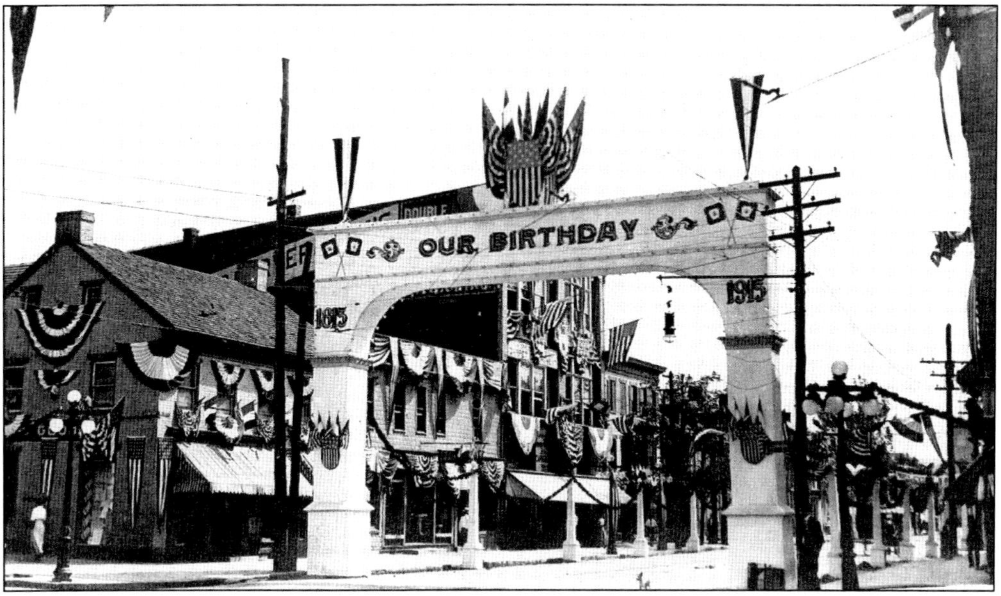

Sunday, September 12, 1915, began with a special centennial observance in all churches and a 2:00 p.m. general religious service in Wirt Park, with music by a community choir of 150 voices. That evening at 8:00, there was a band concert at Wirt Park and an electrical fountain display. The slogan over Baltimore Street's arch was "Our Birthday," as seen in this scene. The arches were wooden frames with canvas stretched over them and painted white.

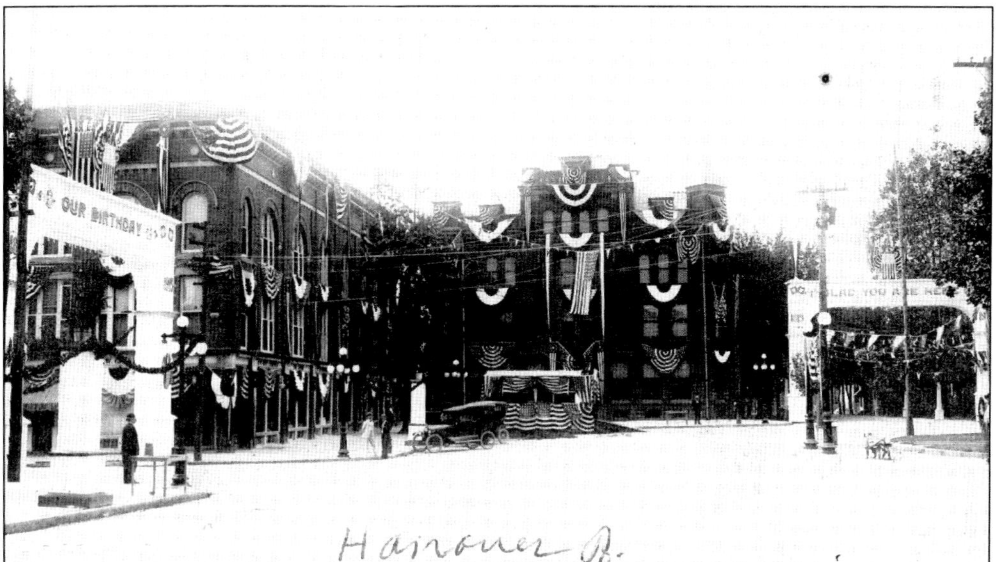

Monday morning, September 13, began at 9:00 with the ringing of all church bells and fire alarms, as well as the blowing of factory whistles for five minutes. Opening ceremonies were conducted at Wirt Park at 9:30 a.m. At 2:00 p.m., "old homers," as former residents were referred to, were treated to an automobile tour of the decorated town, starting from centennial headquarters at the Elk's Home at 19 Baltimore Street. That evening, another band concert and fountain display were held at Wirt Park. The southwest quadrant of Center Square in this image includes Gitt's department store to the left and the Peoples Bank of Hanover in the center.

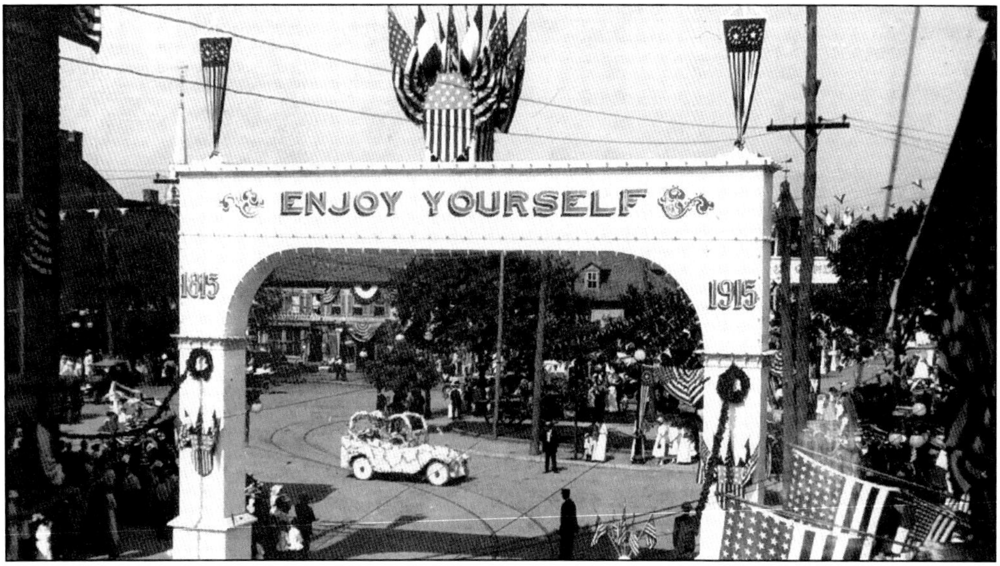

Seven parades were held from Tuesday, September 14 to Saturday, September 18, culminating with a fantastic parade and carnival. On the morning of September 14, a parade was held of civic and fraternal orders and schools from Hanover and the immediate vicinity. Prizes were presented to the groups based upon the largest number of participants. The Hanover Agricultural Society gave every parading student a free ticket to the Hanover Fair for Friday. If that was not encouragement enough, Baughman's Drug Store at 9 Carlisle Street provided each student with a ticket good for a glass of soda, redeemable, however, starting the week after the centennial celebration. The arch over the Baltimore Street entrance reveals the greeting to "enjoy yourself." Note the 48-star flag to the right, since Arizona and New Mexico joined the union in 1912. The decorated car under the arch looks deceptively like a modern-era dune buggy.

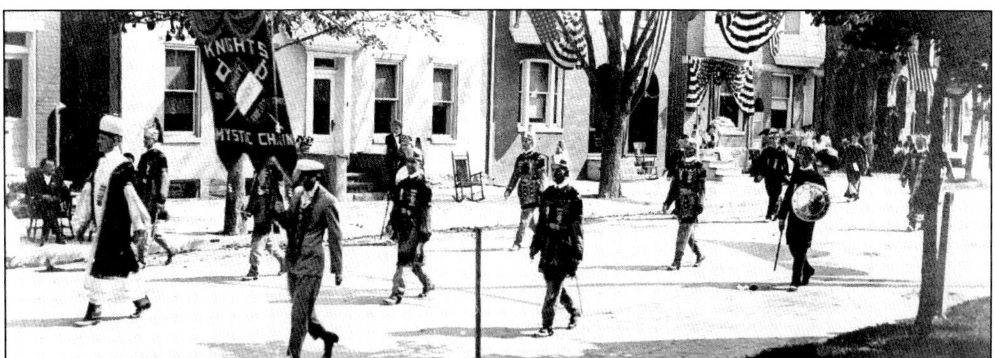

The second parade of the day occurred on the afternoon of Tuesday, September 14. This was the parade of the state convention of the Ancient Order of Knights of the Mystic Chain being held in Hanover. Horse races were held at the Hanover Fairgrounds the same day. That evening, Wirt Park was again the stage for a band and community choir concert, addresses by prominent Pennsylvanians, and a fountain display. The Knights of the Mystic Chain was listed under the category of secret society in the 1911 Polk Directory of Hanover, along with other organizations that are still recognized today, such as the Eagles, Knights of Columbus, and Moose. This photograph, taken on the first block, east side of York Street, memorializes one of the statewide groups participating in the Hanover convention that year.

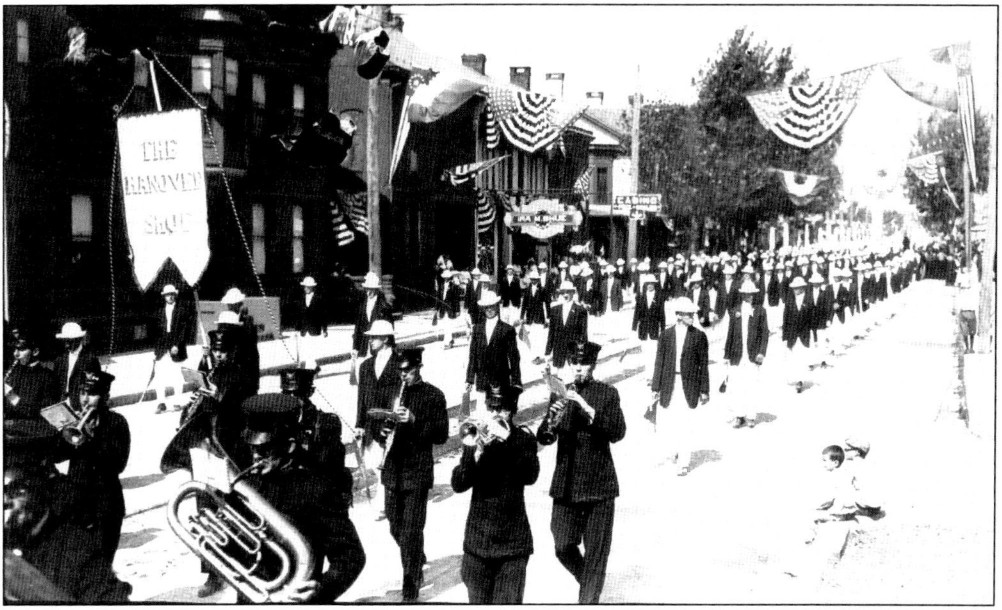

Wednesday, September 15 began at 9:30 a.m. with an industrial and trade display parade followed by Wirt Park addresses by dignitaries. The Hanover Fair held a grand procession of horses, carriages, and horned cattle at 10:00 a.m. on the race course. The afternoon began with horse races, followed by airplane flights at 2:00 and 4:00 by aviator John Richter. Acrobats, wire artists, and trained seals also performed. At 8:00 p.m., a fireworks display ensued. This industrial parade entry from the Hanover Shoe Company records the male workers marching in their company-provided uniforms. Trade signs of Ira M. Shue, a bicycle store at 113 Baltimore Street, and the Casino Theatre (a movie theater) at 111 Baltimore Street are evident in the background. Notice the two young boys in the right forefront, some of only a few spectators, who appear on numerous other photographs of the day's parade.

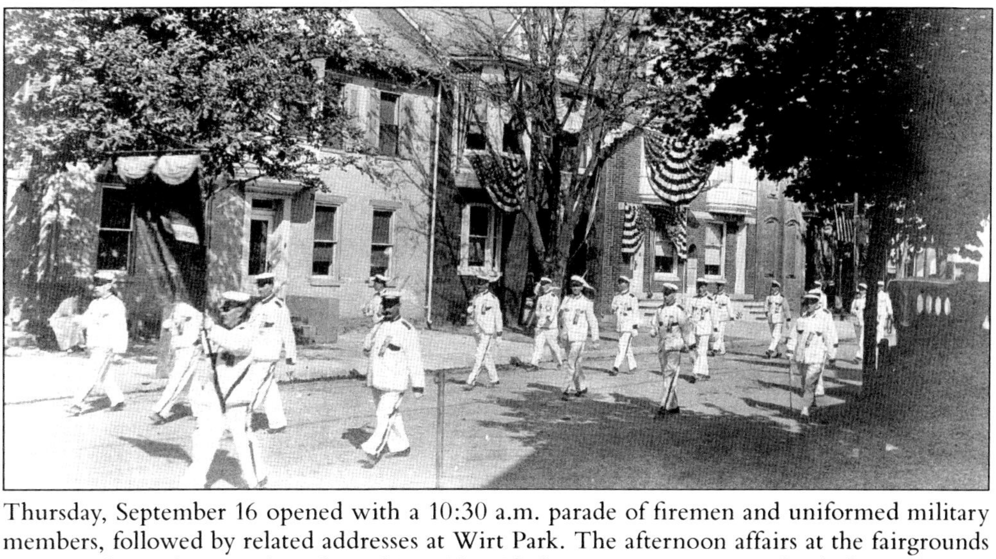

Thursday, September 16 opened with a 10:30 a.m. parade of firemen and uniformed military members, followed by related addresses at Wirt Park. The afternoon affairs at the fairgrounds were similar to the preceding day. This unidentified group participates in the day's parade with the east side of the first block of York Street in the background. Attendance evidently was not strong for the minor parades preceding the grand finale on Saturday.

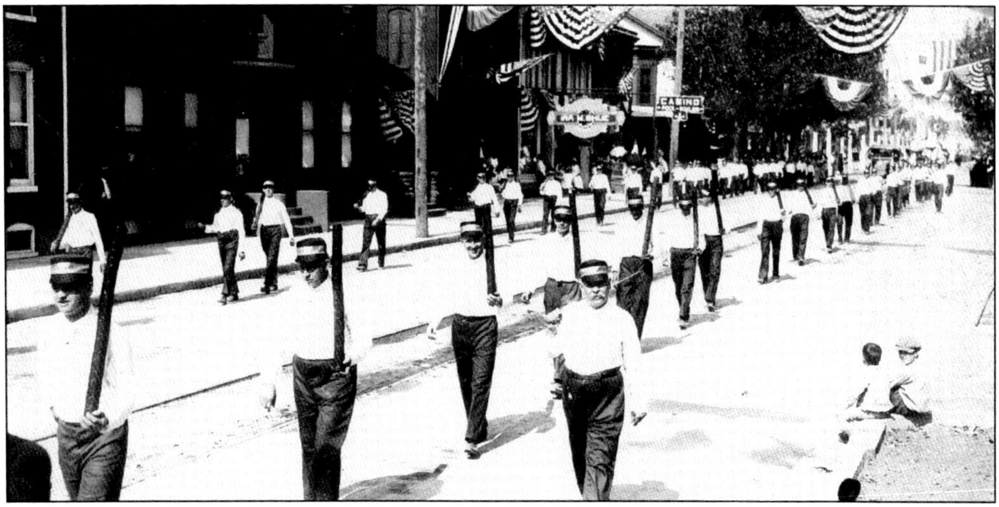

September 17, a Friday, included a 9:30 a.m. parade of decorated automobiles, motorcycles, and bicycles, as well as afternoon Hanover Fair activities comparable to the prior days. Postcards depicting decorated automobiles, motorcycles, and bicycles are not known to exist. This card is believed to be another entrant in the industrial and trade display parade of September 15. Marching south in the 100 block of Baltimore Street, it has been suggested that these individuals may be the employees of the Hanover Bending and Manufacturing Company that made plow handles at its plant located at Factory Street and the Western Maryland Railroad.

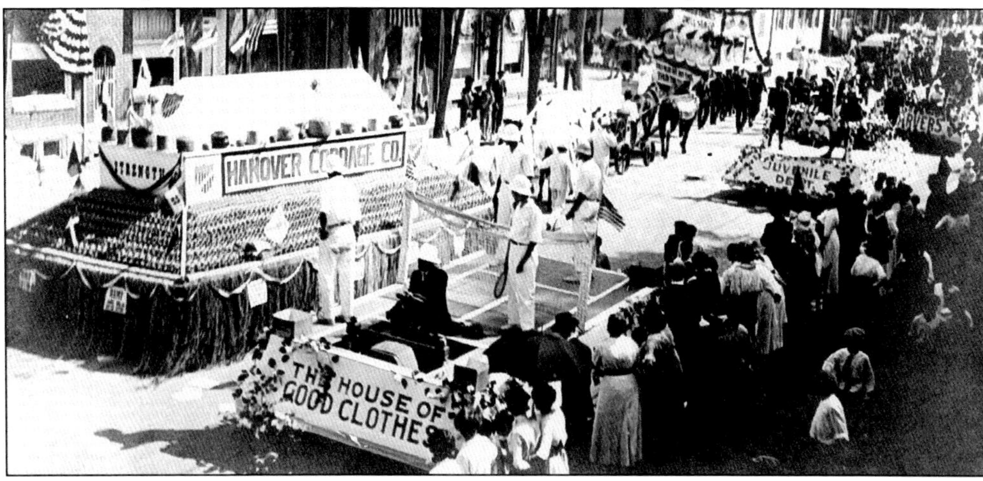

The morning of Saturday, September 18, began with a fantastic parade and masquerade carnival. As in all previous day's parades, prizes were awarded in a number of categories. Special prizes consisting of gold coins were given by several merchants to the best-costumed ladies. That evening at Wirt Park, a final concert was held, and a Jeffery six-cylinder automobile furnished by the Adams Sporting Goods House, 43 Baltimore Street, was given away to a winner, whose name was drawn from contributors that defrayed the costs of the Hanover centennial. The parade route came into town and departed downtown utilizing York Street, which is reflected here in a congested state. The float in the foreground approaching Broadway is one of several entered by N. B. Carver and Sons Department Store at 10–12 Baltimore Street. Two other Carver floats are in the right background. Hanover Cordage, with production located on East Chestnut Street, is heading out of town on the left (east) side of York Street, where the parade turned east on Middle Street.

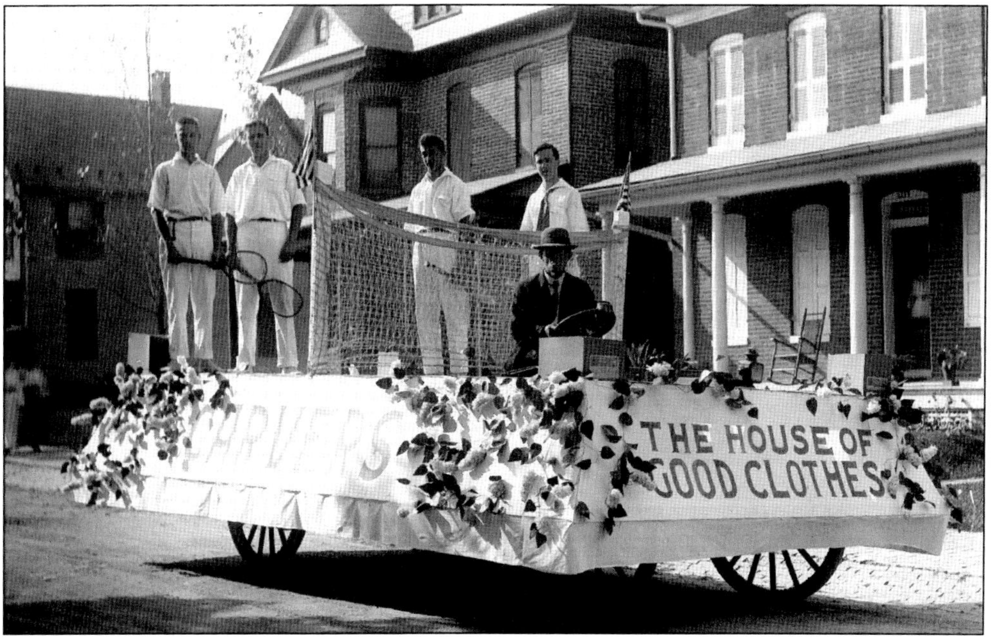

A close-up of the previous N. B. Carver's float reveals the sporting fashion statement of the day as well as the float's tennis racket design.

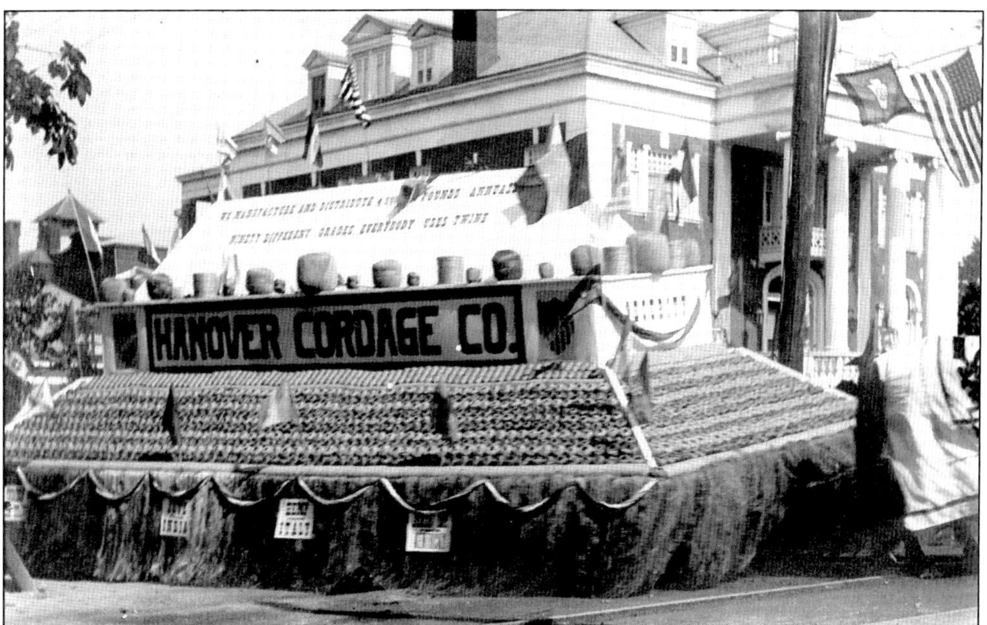

The Hanover Cordage Company float is seen here rounding the Frederick and High Street intersection with the Sheppard Mansion in the background. At the extreme left, the roofline of the Hanover Opera House at West Chestnut and Franklin Streets is visible. Hanover Cordage was incorporated in 1903.

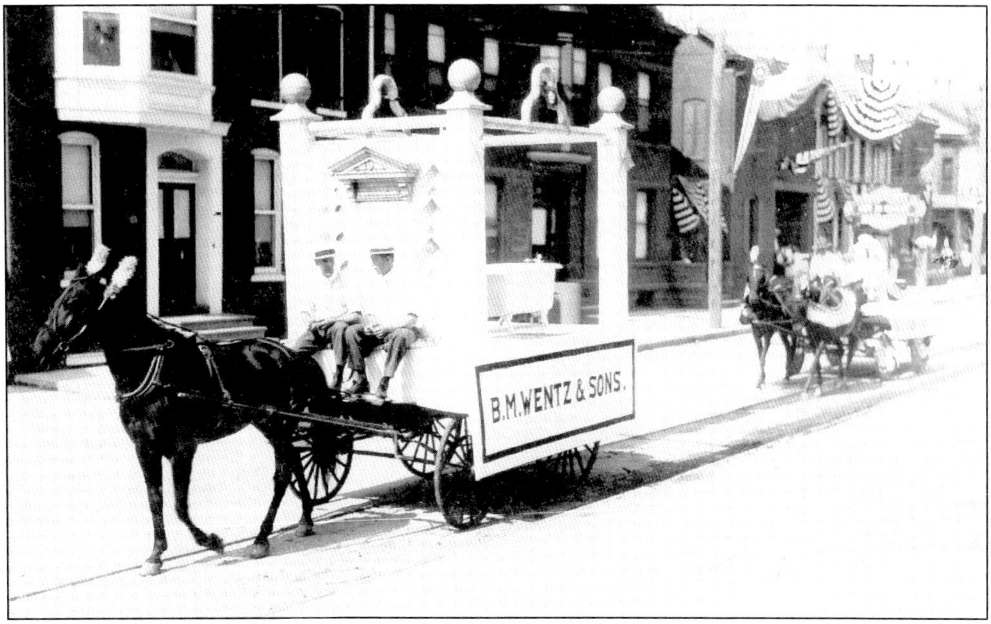

B. M. Wentz and Sons was a plumber and sheet metal fabricator located at 6 Baltimore Street. This Baltimore Street photograph depicts the rage of the day, an indoor plumbing bathtub, on the float. Due to the lack of spectators, the photograph was probably taken during the September 15 trade display parade.

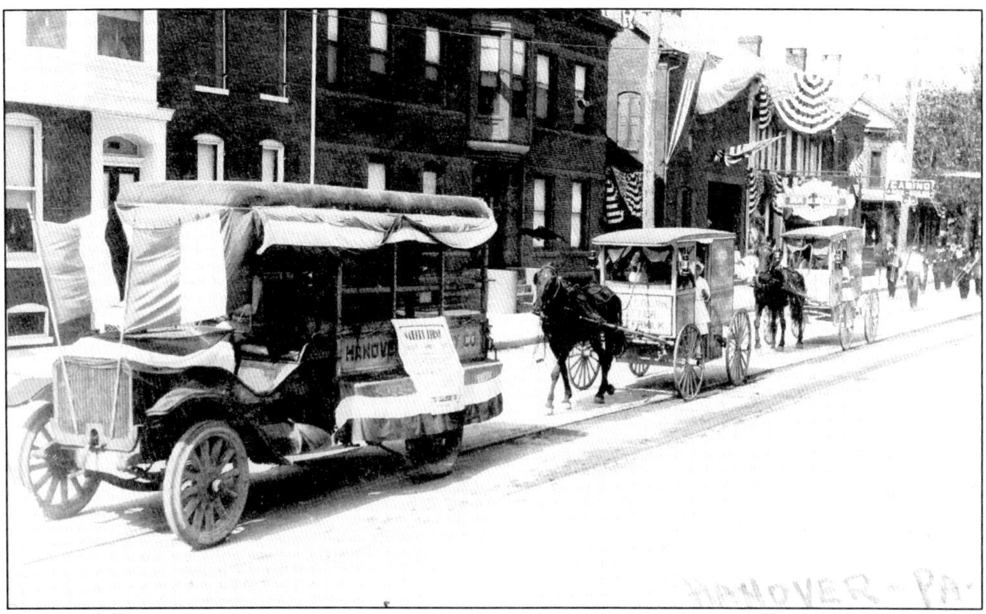

Another portion of the industrial and trade's parade on Wednesday, this is likely a display of the truck and delivery buggies of the Hanover Creamery Company, which was located on the north side of Poplar Street near High Street. The first buggy has ice cream, butter, and butter milk products listed on the carriage front. Henry M. Stokes was the company's treasurer, and this card was mailed, without any indication of the sender, to E. E. Stokes of Brooklyn, New York, announcing that the entrant had won third prize in the parade.

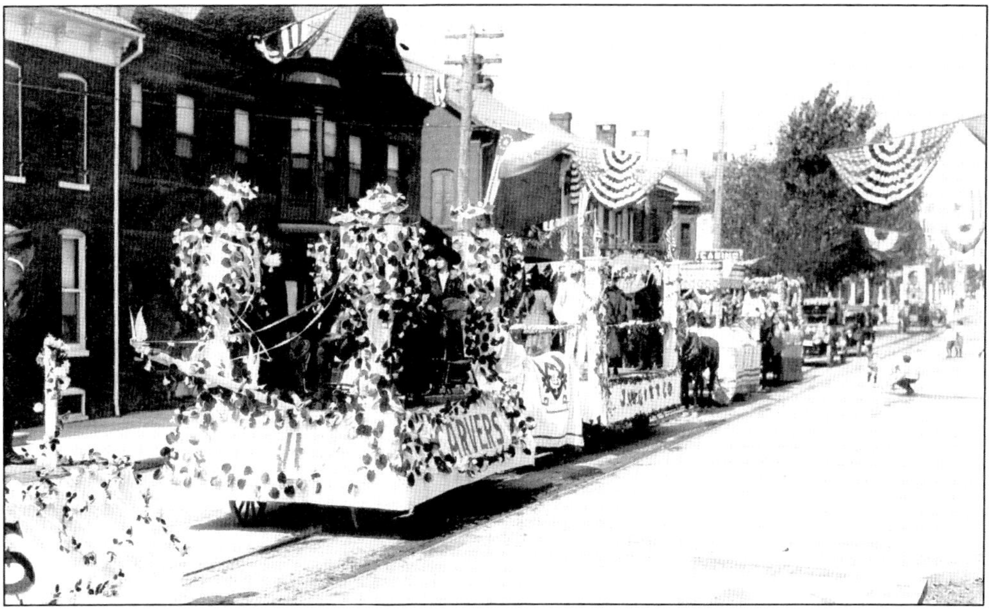

Once again taken on the west side of the 100 block of Baltimore Street during the trade parade of September 15, two Carver's Department Store floats are in the foreground followed by their competition across the entrance to Baltimore Street of J. W. Gitt and Company. Notice the Gitt float horses draped in medieval-era-looking white dressings from head to hoof.

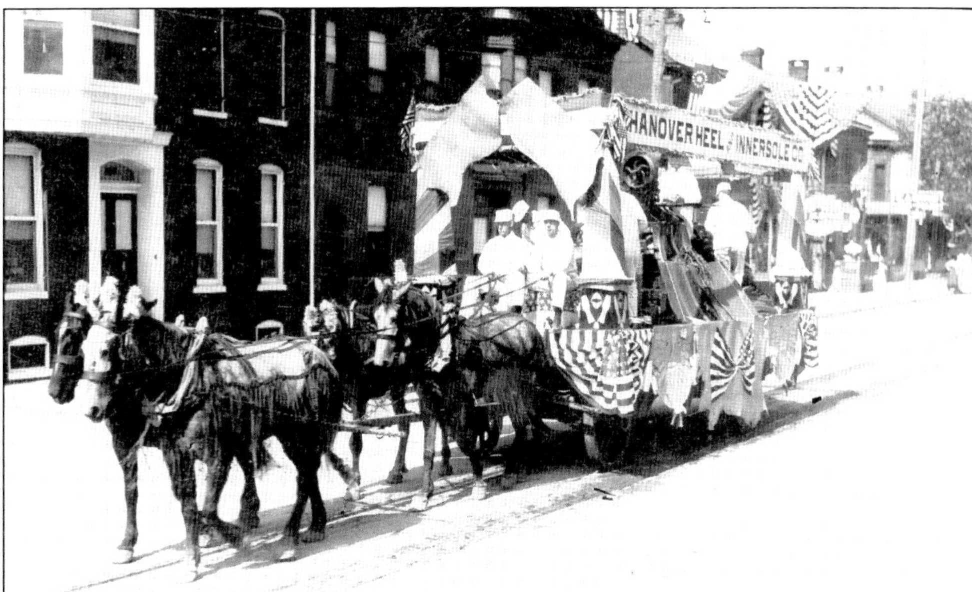

The Hanover Heel and Innersole Company float is carrying what might be industrial equipment to press out product for the local shoe industry. Incorporated in 1909, the plant was located on High Street with William E. Pitts, president and manager. Once again, taken on Baltimore Street, this is thought to be from the September 15 industrial parade.

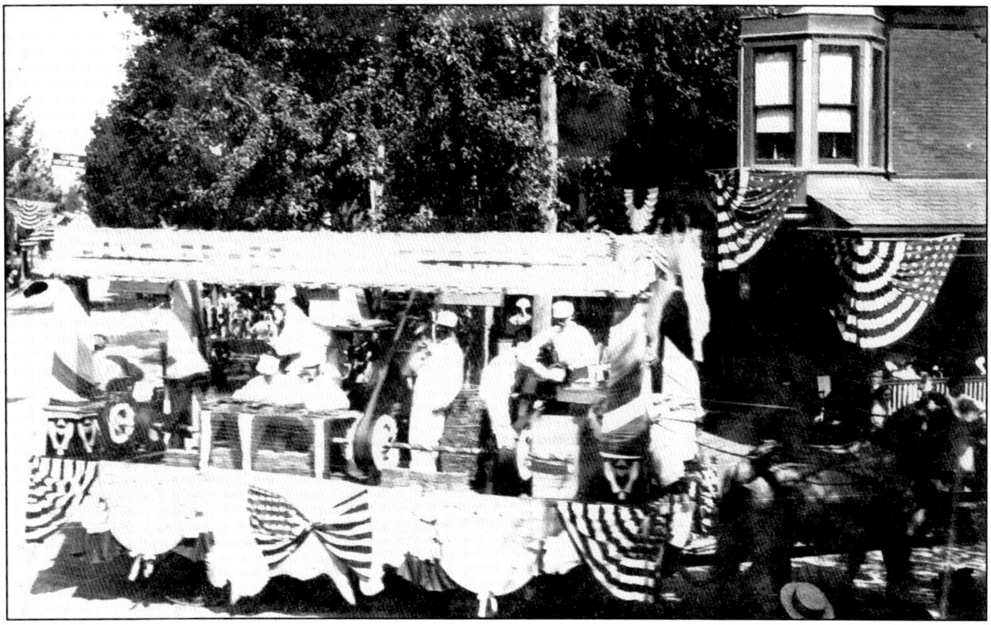

A side view of the previous Hanover Heel and Innersole Company float shows the simulated factory production theme of its float.

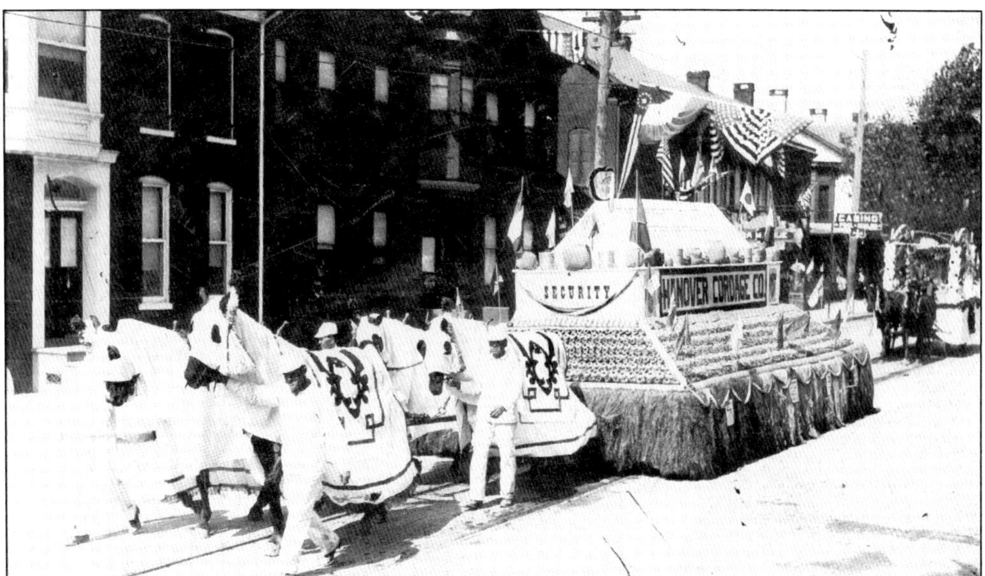

In the 100 block of Baltimore Street, this is the Hanover Cordage Company float with the handsomely decorated horses.

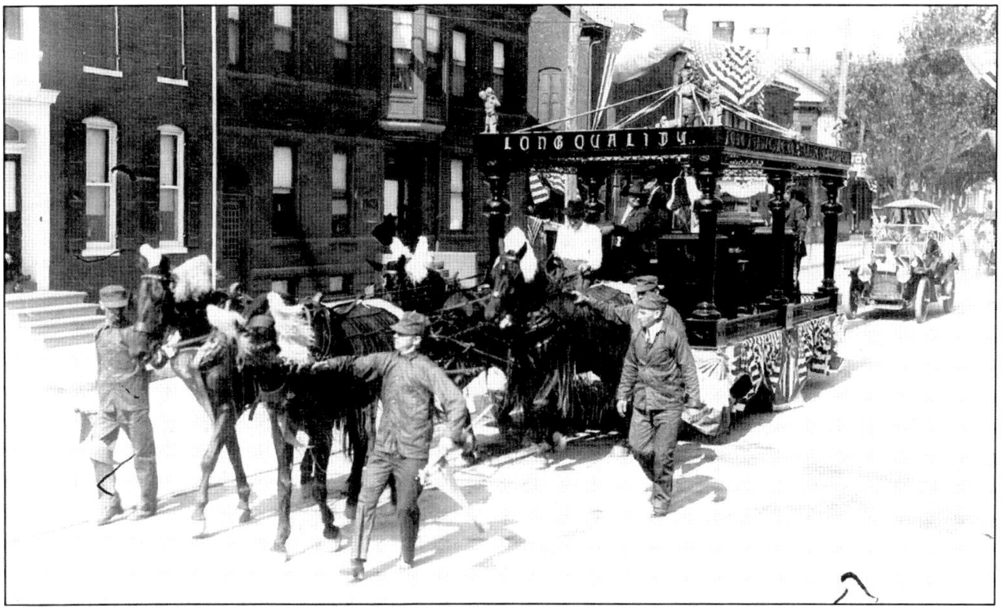

"Long Quality" on the front of the float on Baltimore Street refers to the Long Furniture Company, which manufactured dining room furniture such as tables and china cabinets, and the George A. Long Cabinet Company, which produced "talking machine cabinets" from a plant at Maple Avenue and High Street.

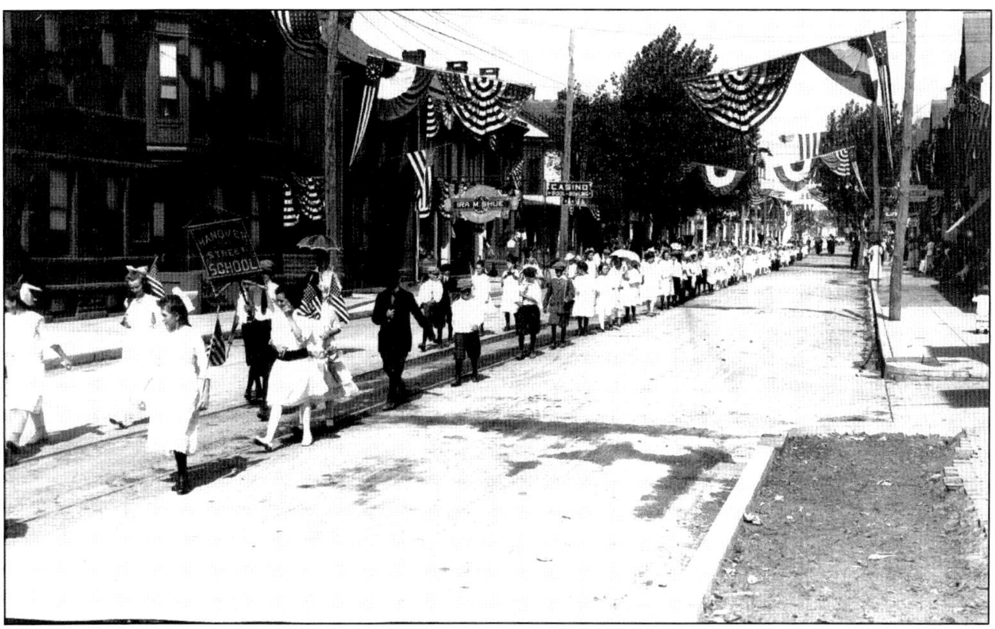

Part of the Tuesday, September 14 parade included these students from the Hanover Street School marching south on Baltimore Street.

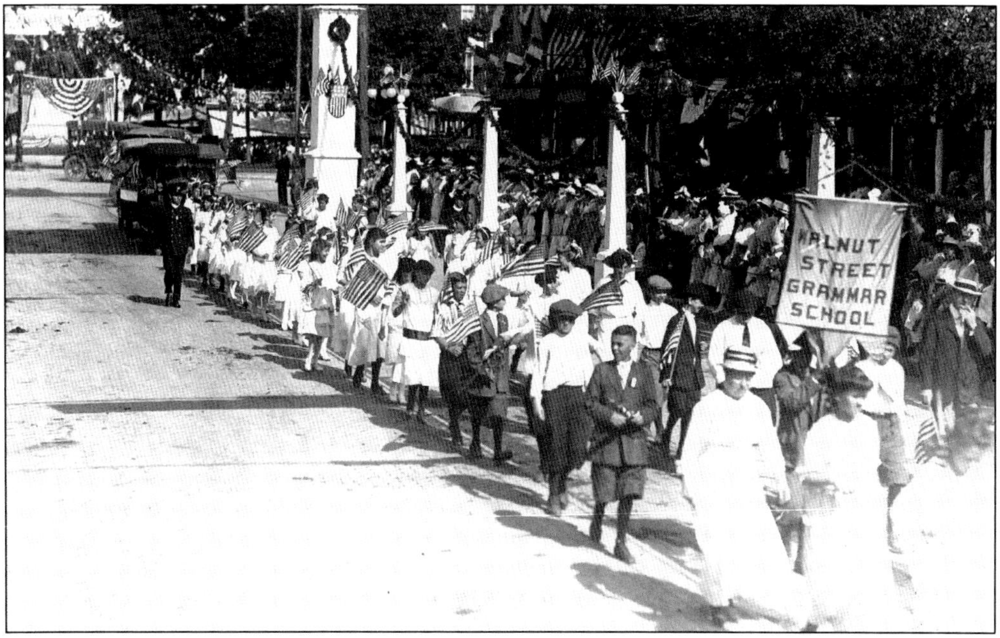

The Walnut Street Grammar School is starting its march down Baltimore Street from Center Square. For their efforts, each student got a free ticket to the fairgrounds and a soda from a downtown drugstore.

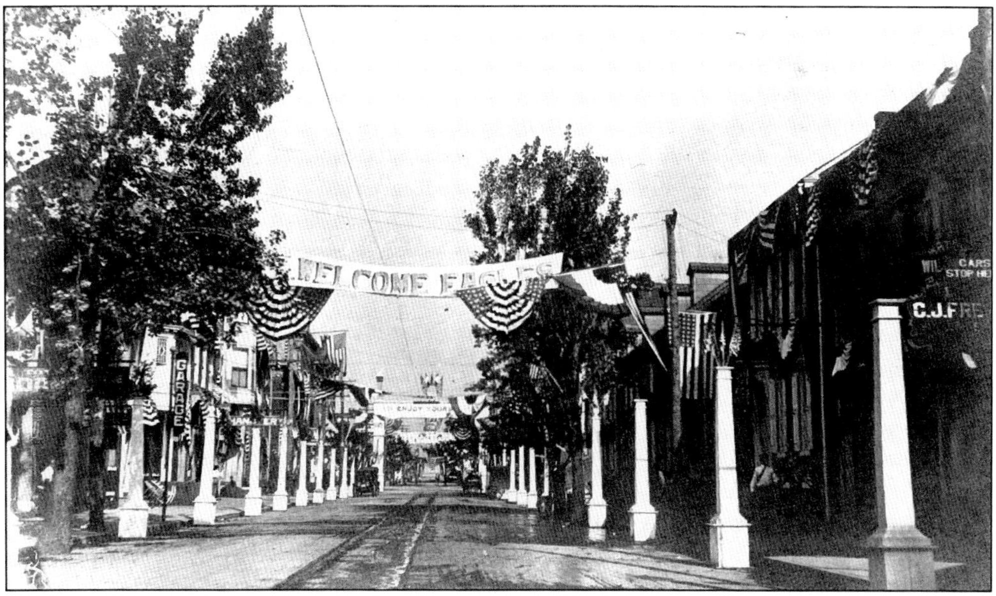

Baltimore Street, with the arched entrance to Center Square in the background, reveals the street lined with columns. The "Welcome Eagles" sign is strung across the street at the Eagles Home on the right at 38 Baltimore Street. C. J. Frey and Company, a ladies' furnishings store at 44 Baltimore Street, is apparent in the right forefront. Behind that is the John H. Wildasin watch repairing sign at 42½ Baltimore Street. Ten columns on each side of the four arteries leading onto the square are evident on Baltimore Street.

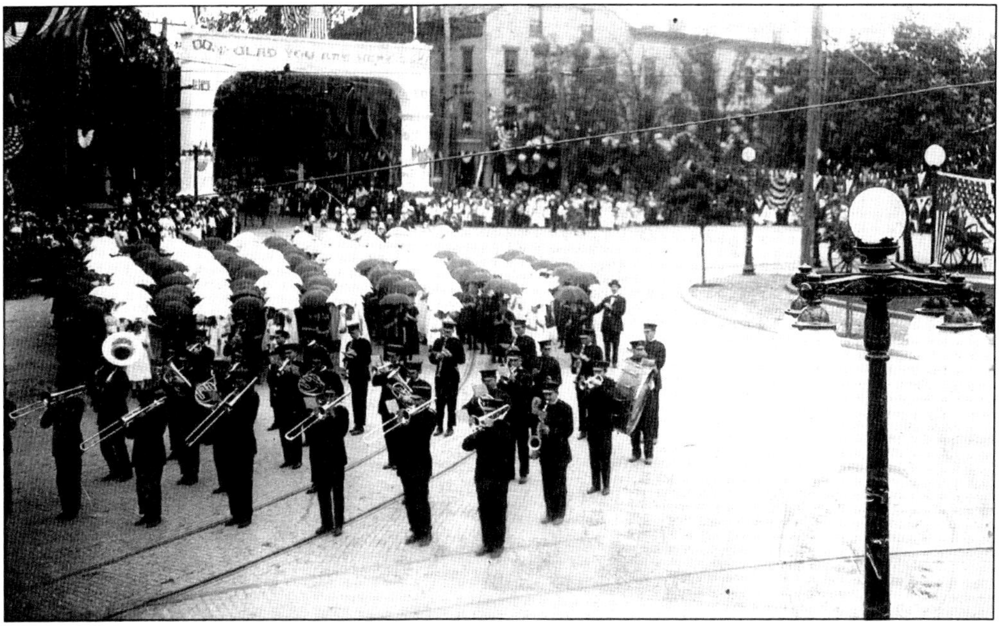

A parade scene on Center Square on Saturday, September 18 was taken looking toward Frederick Street, with the Central Hotel as a backdrop.

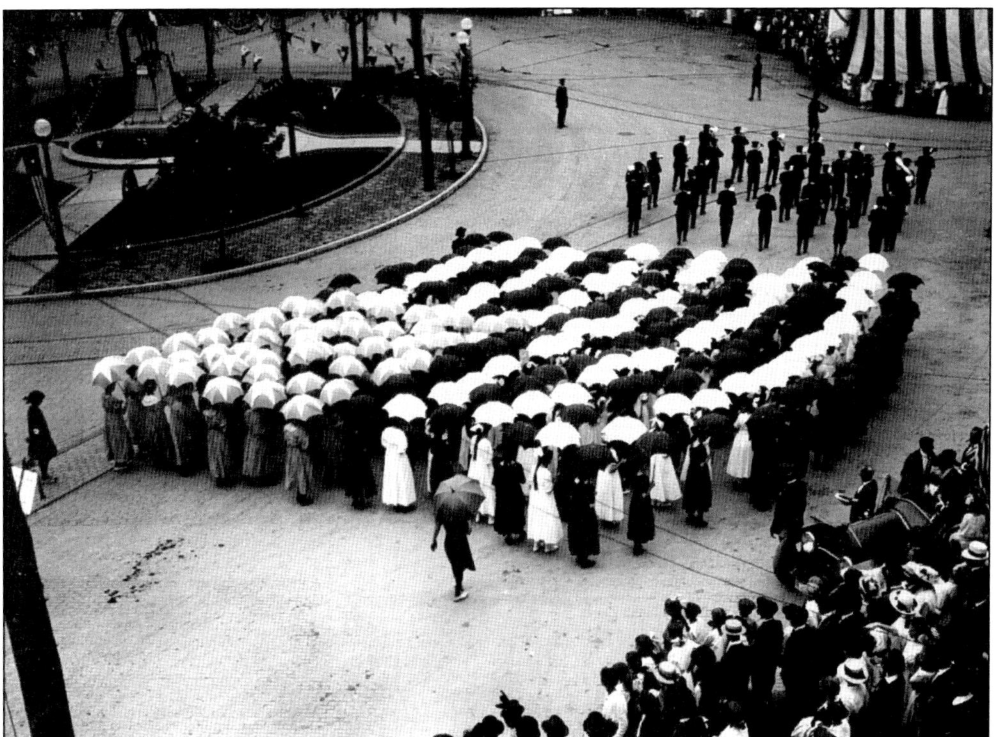

Another view from the rear of the previous group shows the display of the American flag created by varying colored umbrellas.

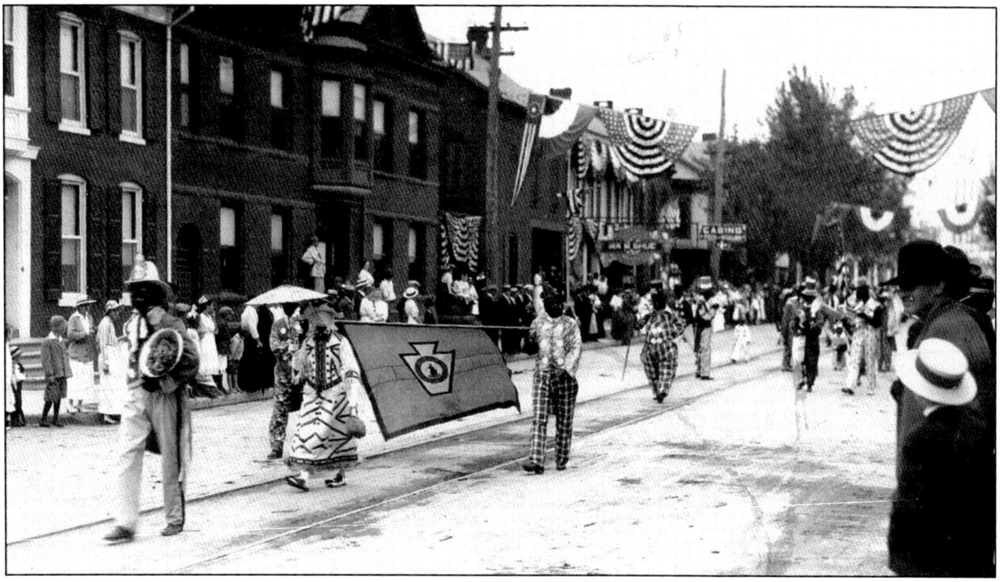

The Lime Kiln Club marches on Baltimore Street. The group was affiliated with Hanover Fire Company No. 1. The lead marcher is wearing a fireman's hat and carrying an early fireman's horn filled with a floral bouquet. See page 28 for another photograph of the group.

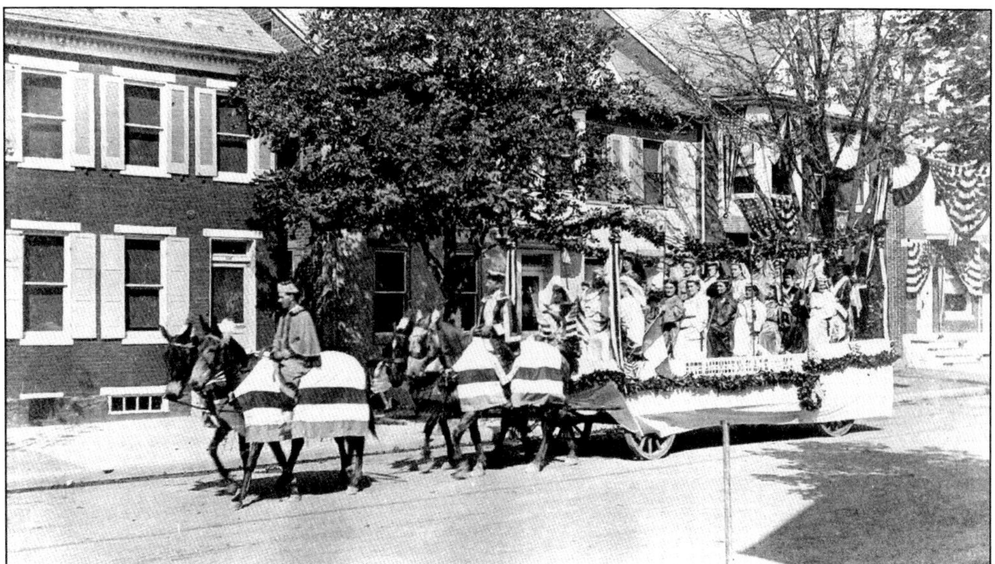

The float on York Street is identified as the Ruth Assembly Council No. 50, of the Ancient Order of Knights of the Mystic Chain. The group met every Tuesday evening in the Melhorn Building at 18–20 Carlisle Street.

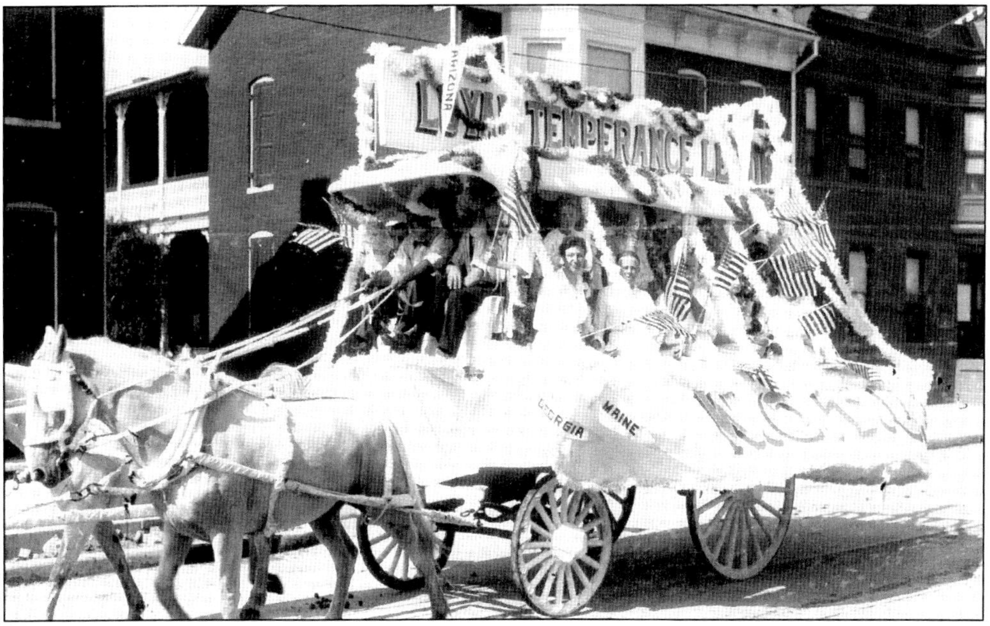

The Loyal Temperance Legion float displays banners along its side that indicate the states in which it conducts its activity.

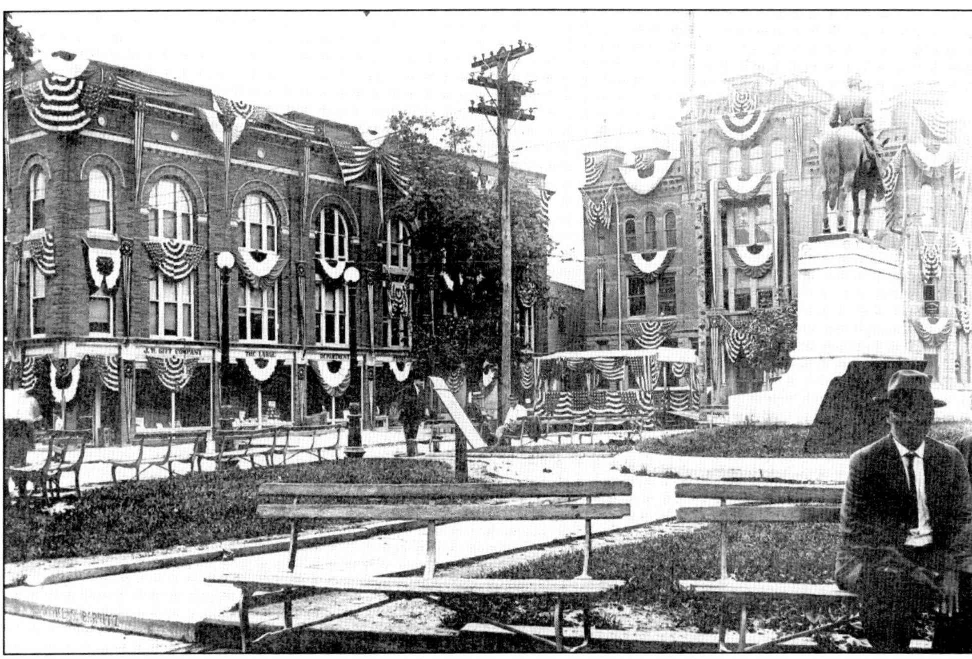

Decorations in the southwest quadrant of Center Square reveal a judge's platform in the center.

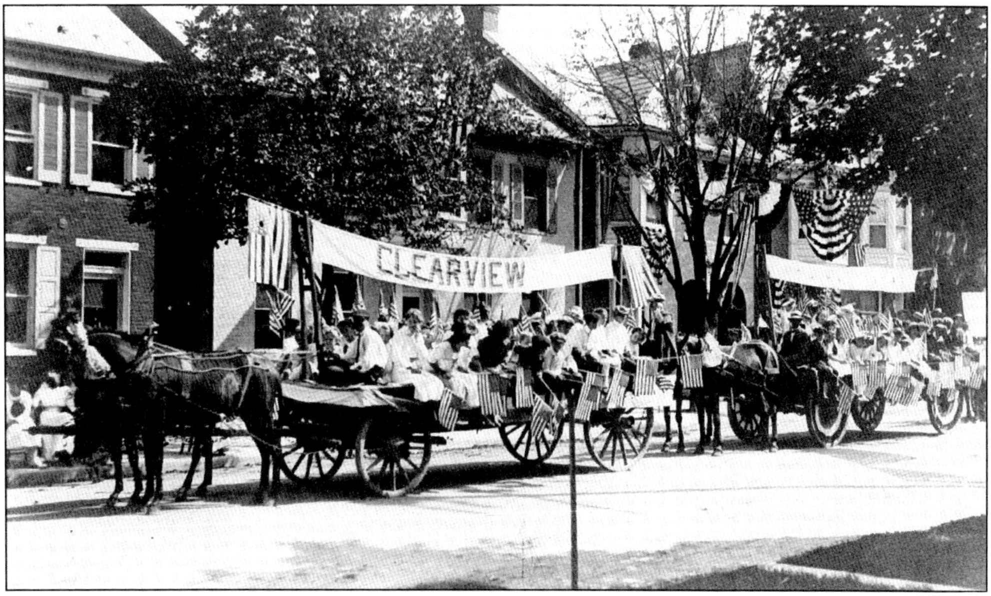

The Clearview School students enjoy a wagon ride for their participation in the celebration.

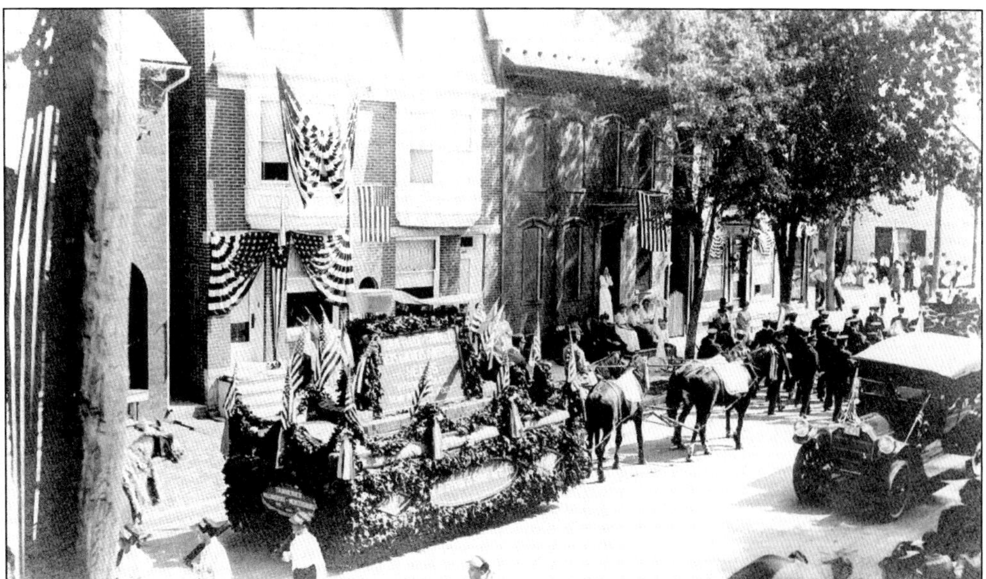

W. O. Byron and Sons Manufacturing Company was located on the corner of High Street and Linden Avenue. They produced shoe bottom stock. The top of their float states "oak bark tanned mens and womens innersoles and heels." This is York Street approaching Middle Street with the parade going in both directions.

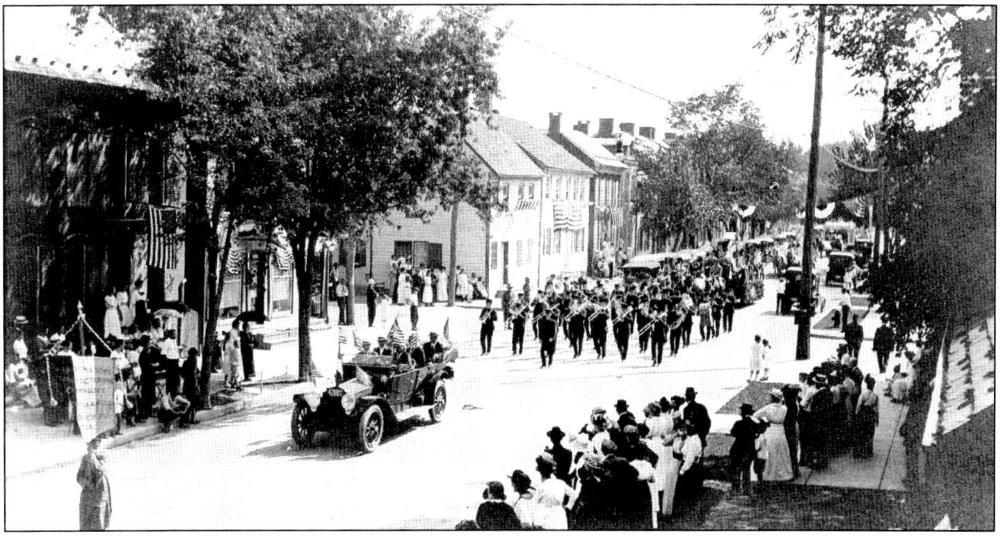

Marching groups and automobiles probably represent the beginning of the Saturday parade as it proceeds on York Street at the Middle Street intersection heading toward Broadway.

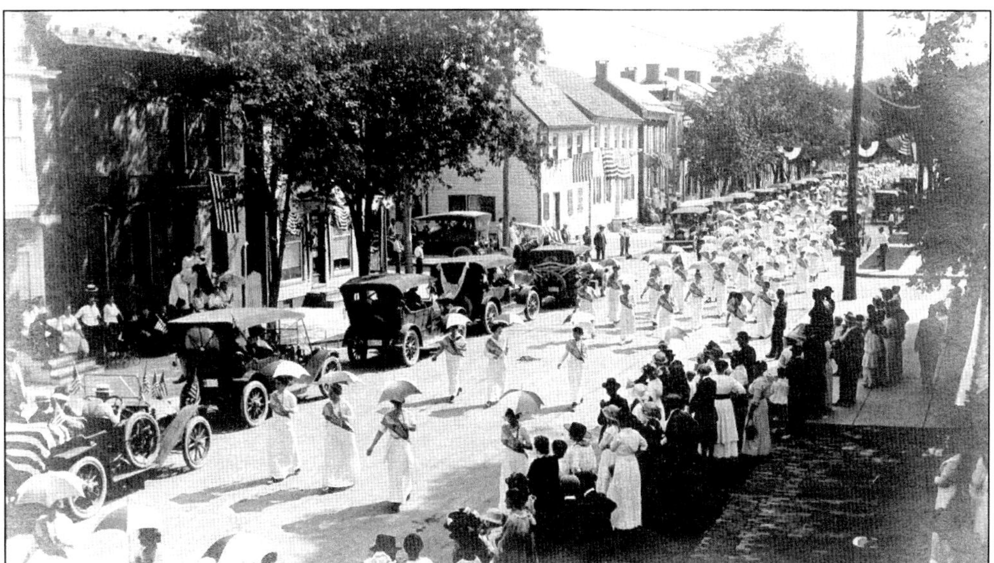

The automobile portion of the parade leads out of town on York Street, turning left (east) on Middle Street as additional groups progress into downtown on the right side of the street.

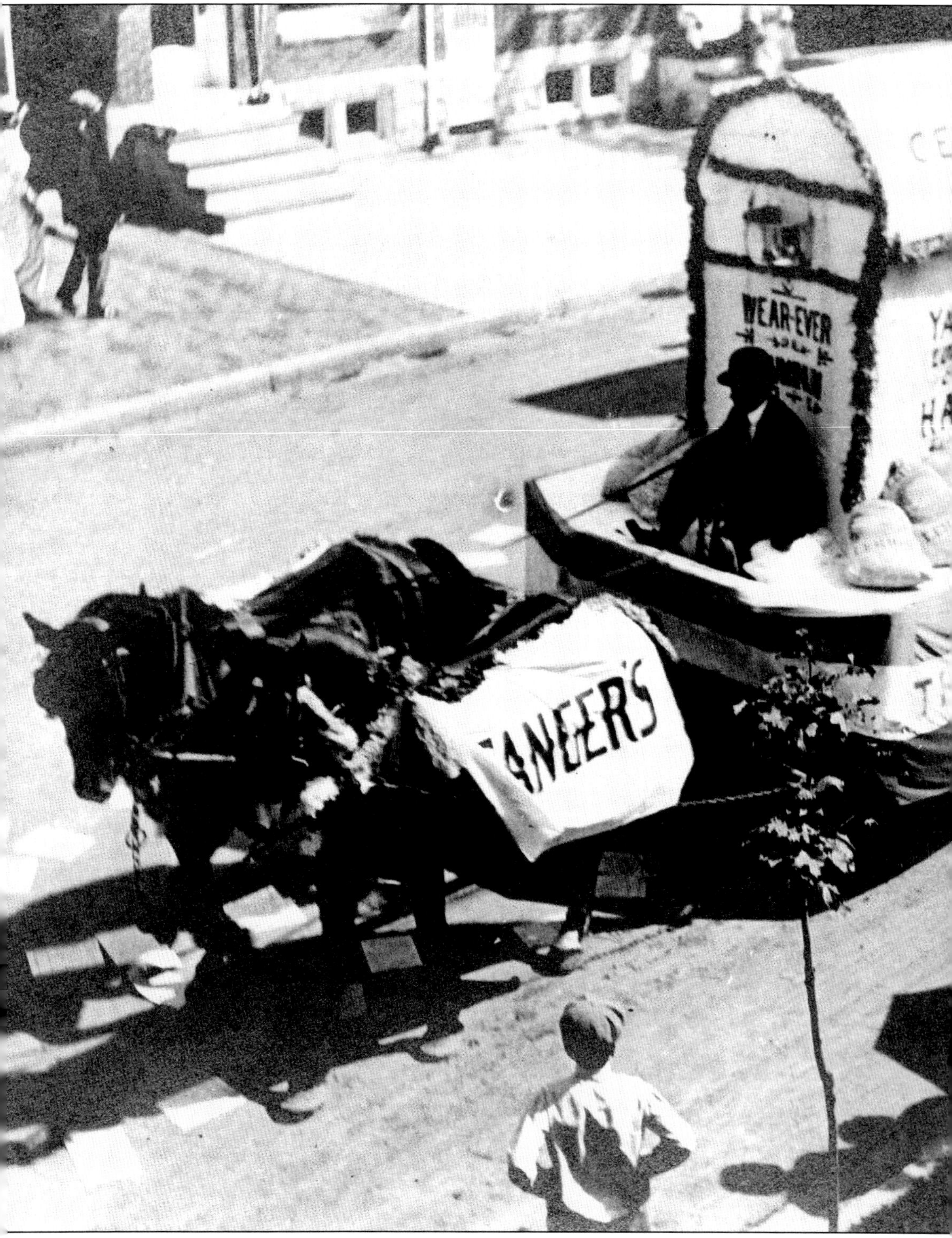

Seen on York Street heading toward Broadway from near Middle Street, the J. C. Tanger Company float with its business located at 37 Broadway, already in business for 77 years,

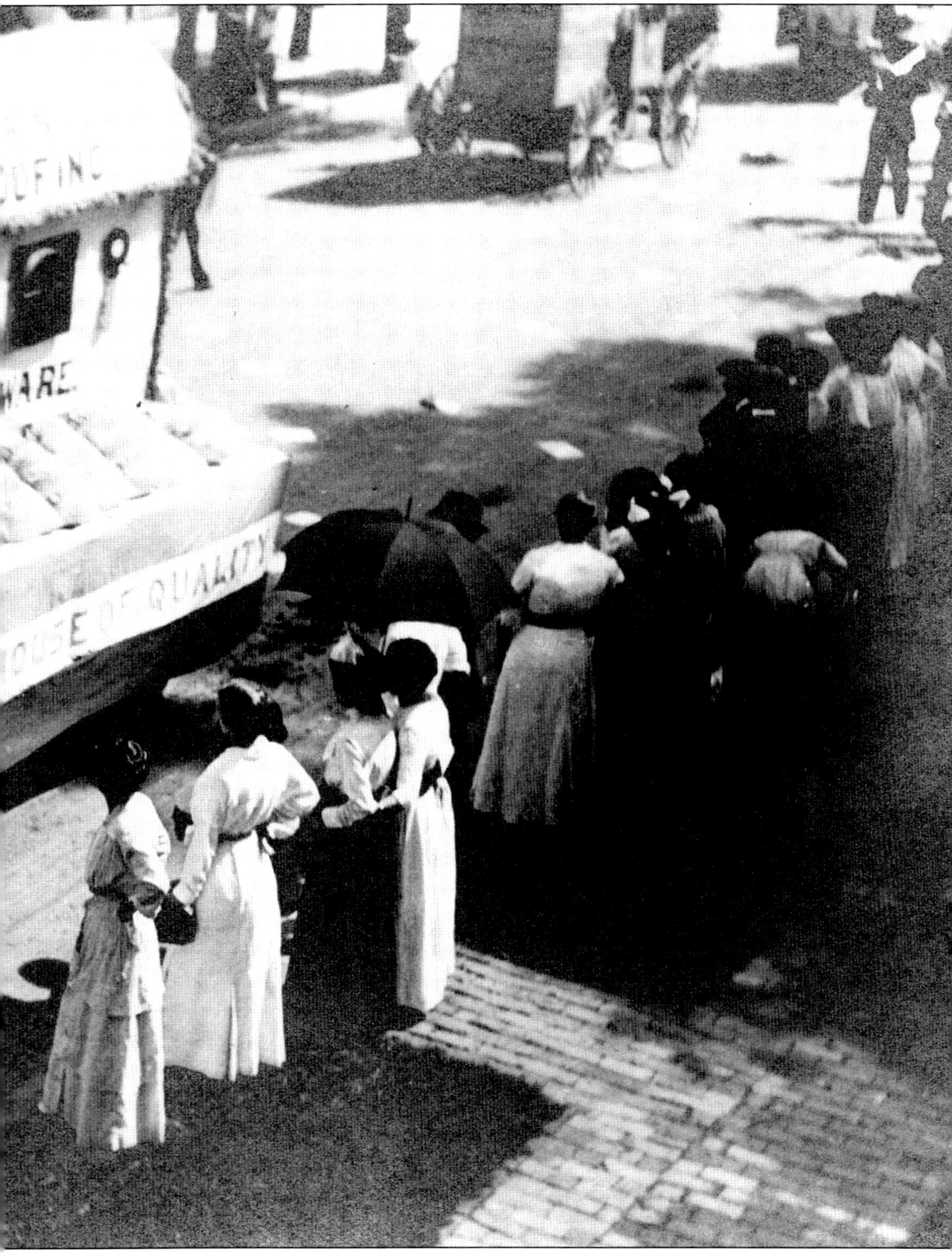

promotes brand-name products of the day such as Certainteed Roofing, Yale Hardware, and Wear Ever.

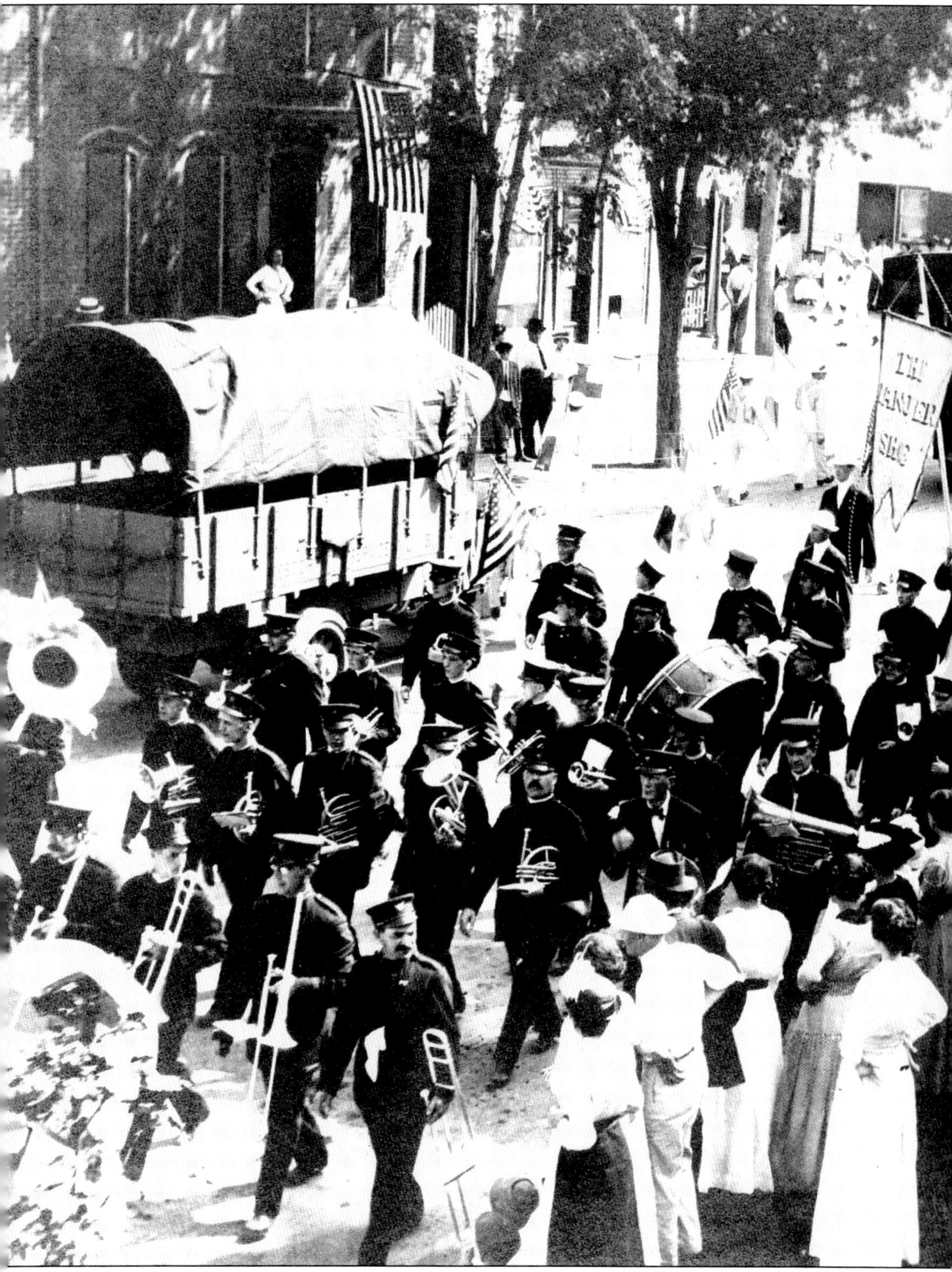

A crowded street reveals parade traffic in both directions on York Street. The Hanover Shoe

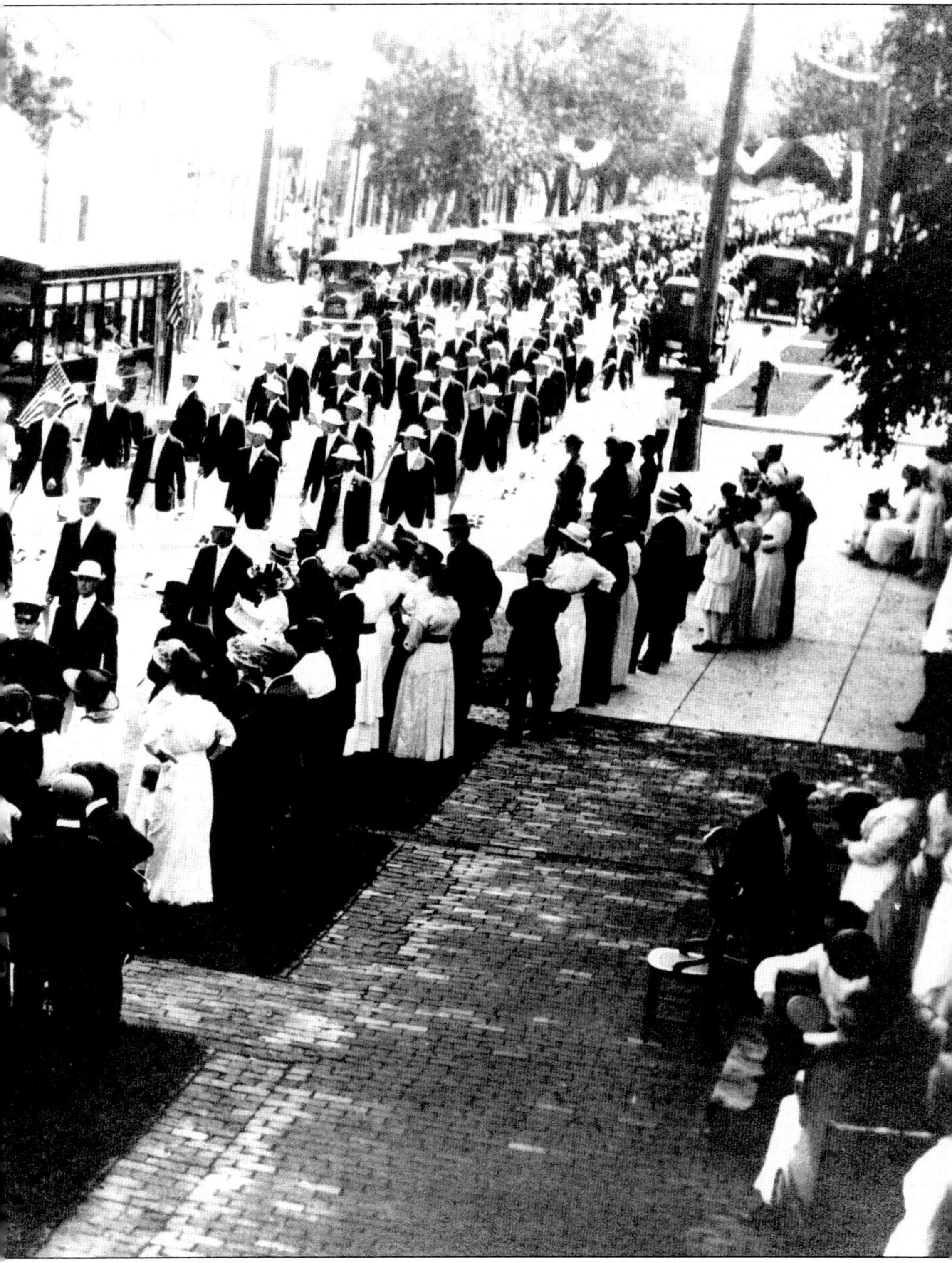

Factory marchers are heading into town and are evident as far as the eye can see.

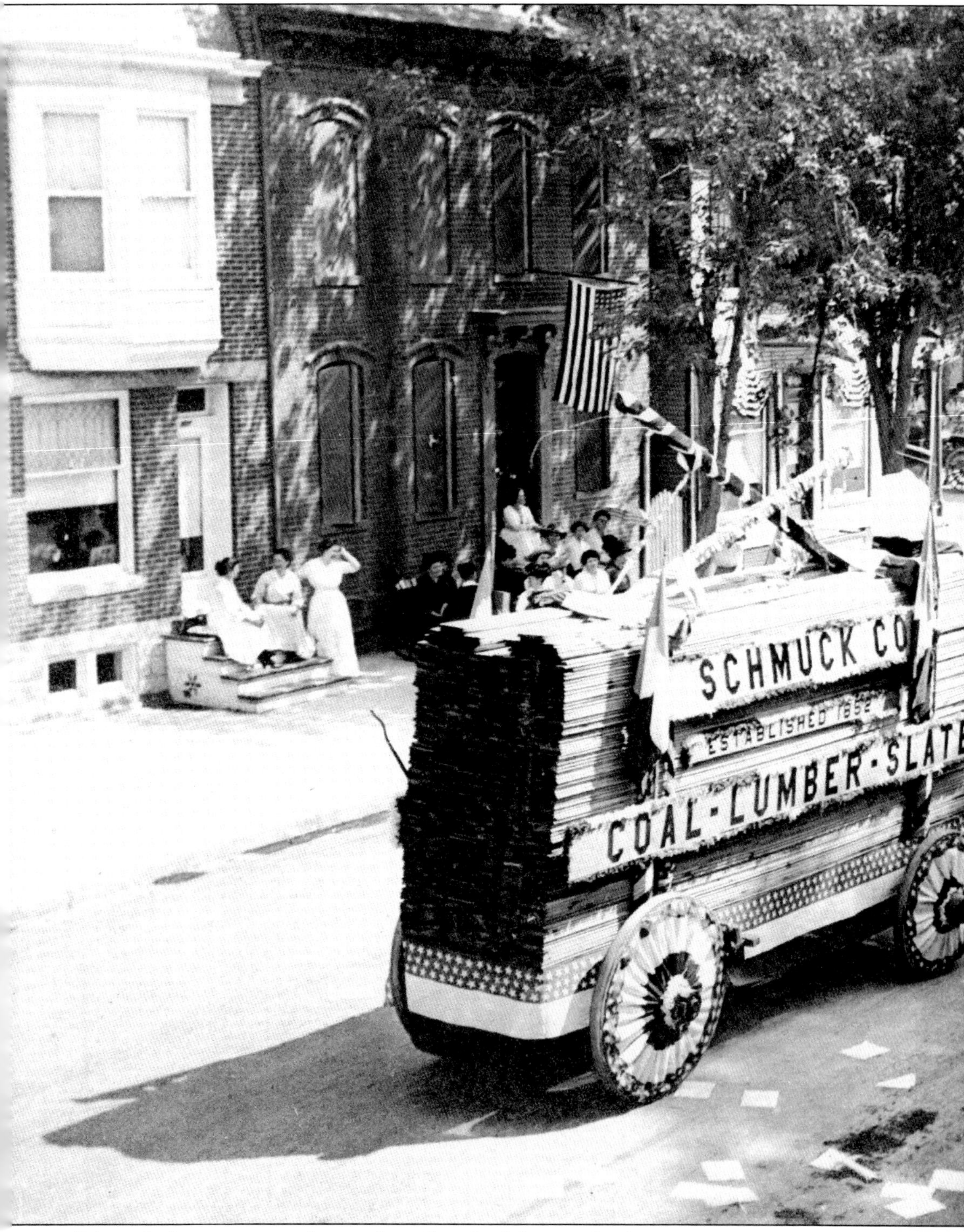

Schmuck Company must be on the tail end of the parade since no groups are continuing into town on York Street and crowds are beginning to dissipate from earlier photographs. Schmuck Company, operated by Joseph H. Schmuck and Charles Y. Brough, was established

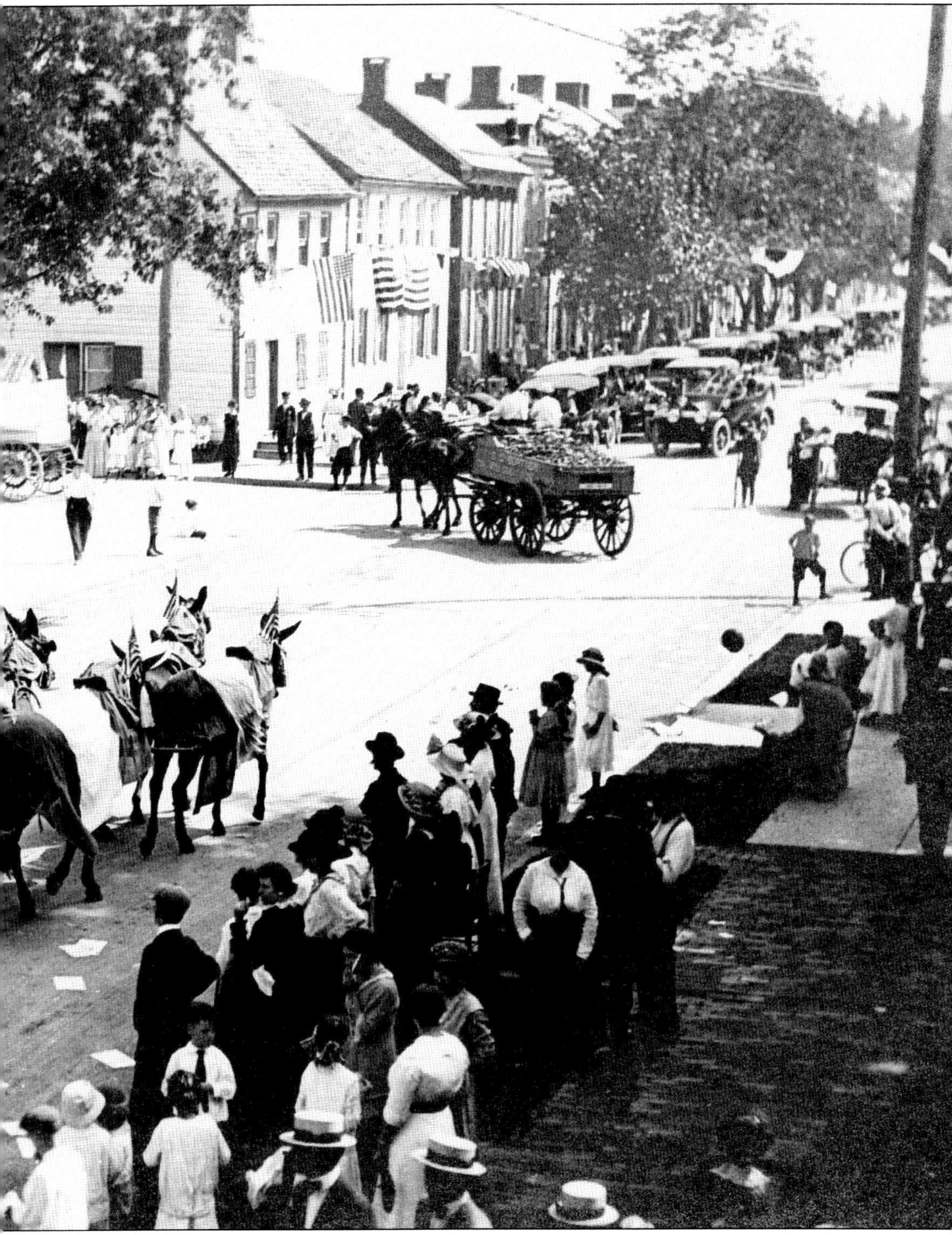

in 1852, offering coal, lumber, and slate. The company continues to prosper to this day as a building supply company, successfully competing with mass merchants such as Lowe's and Home Depot.

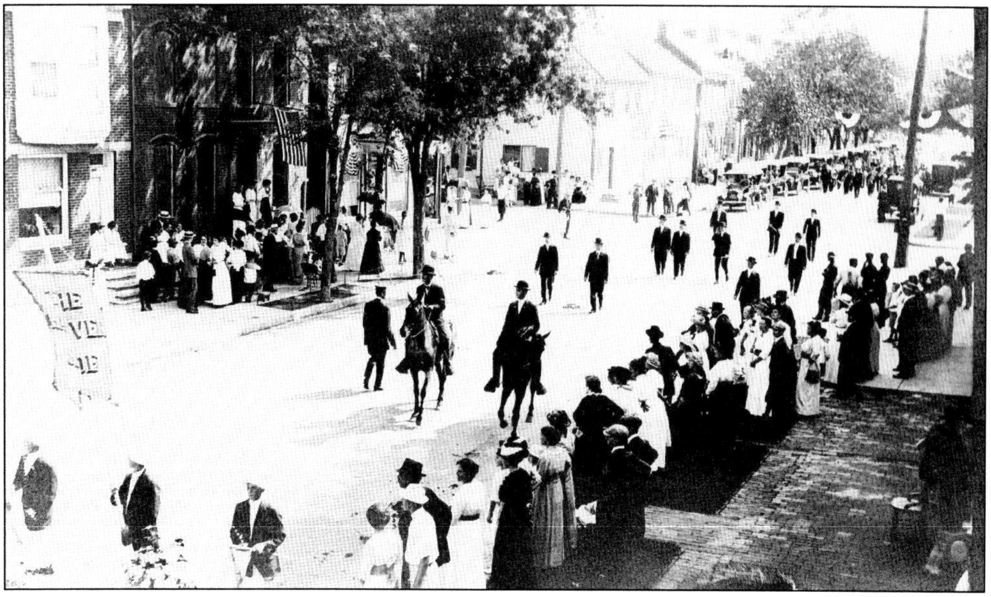

The Hanover Shoe Company is led on horseback by owners Harper O. Sheppard, president, and Clinton N. Myers, secretary and treasurer.

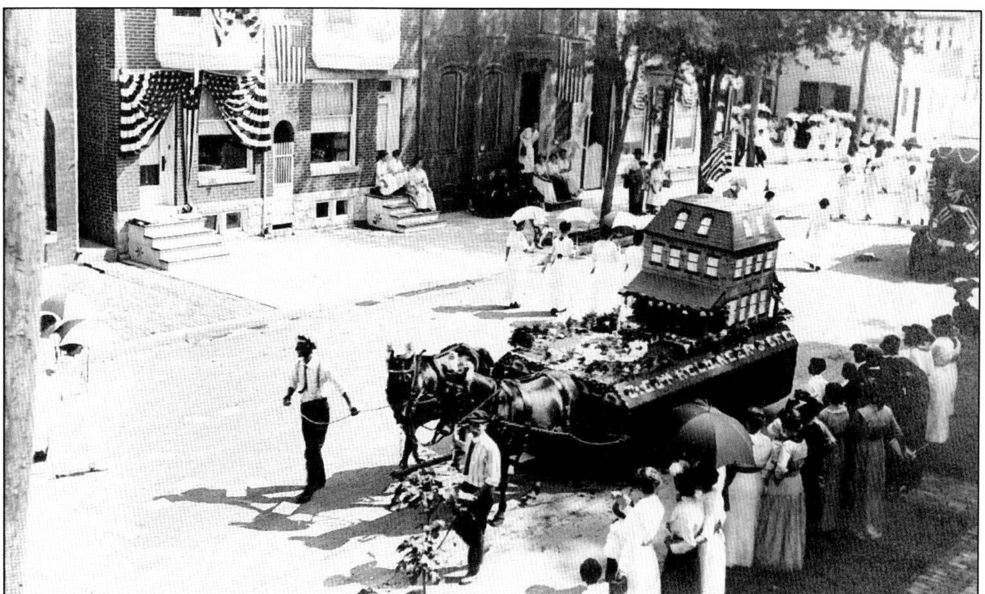

The D. Guy Hollinger and Brothers float has moved in front of the photographer on York Street. The business offered real estate, investments, and insurance to the public from its office on the second floor of the Sheppard and Myers Building at 17 Carlisle Street.

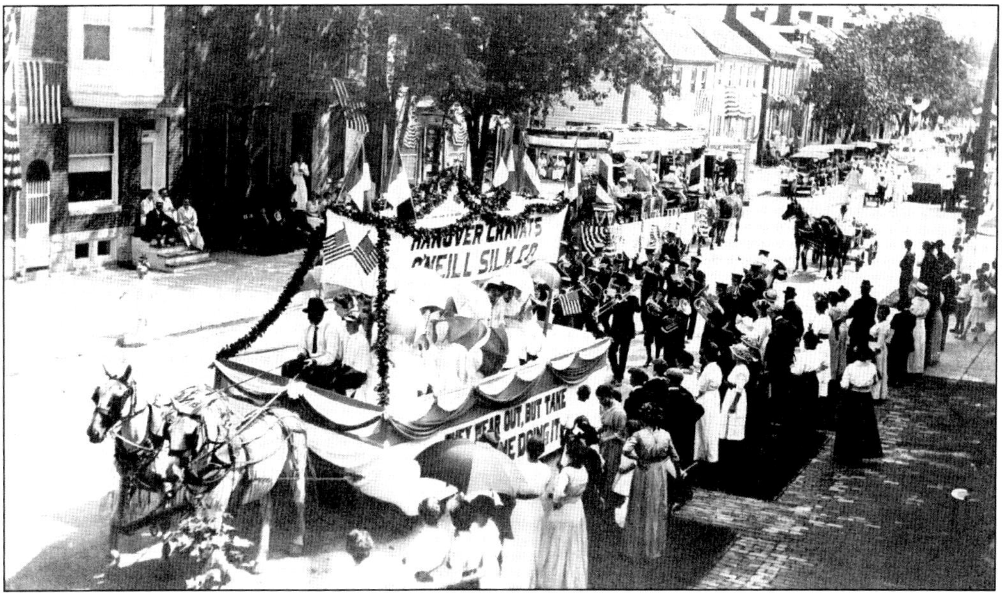

The Hanover Heel and Innersole Company float heads east on York Street, beginning its left turn onto Middle Street while, in the foreground, the O'Neill Silk Company float proceeds up York Street to the center of town. Maker of Hanover Cravats neckwear, the factory was located near Ridge Avenue and East Walnut Street along Silk Mill Alley. Today it has been converted into apartments.

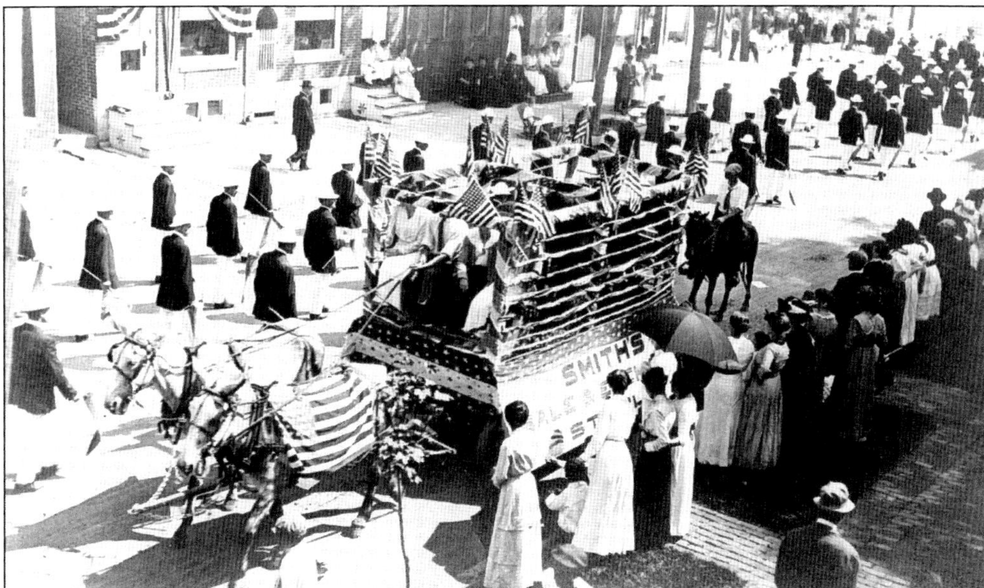

The Hanover Shoe workers march in the background. Smith's (Harry A.) Sale and Exchange Stables, a livery stable located at East Chestnut and Railroad Street, promotes its stock in the foreground float.

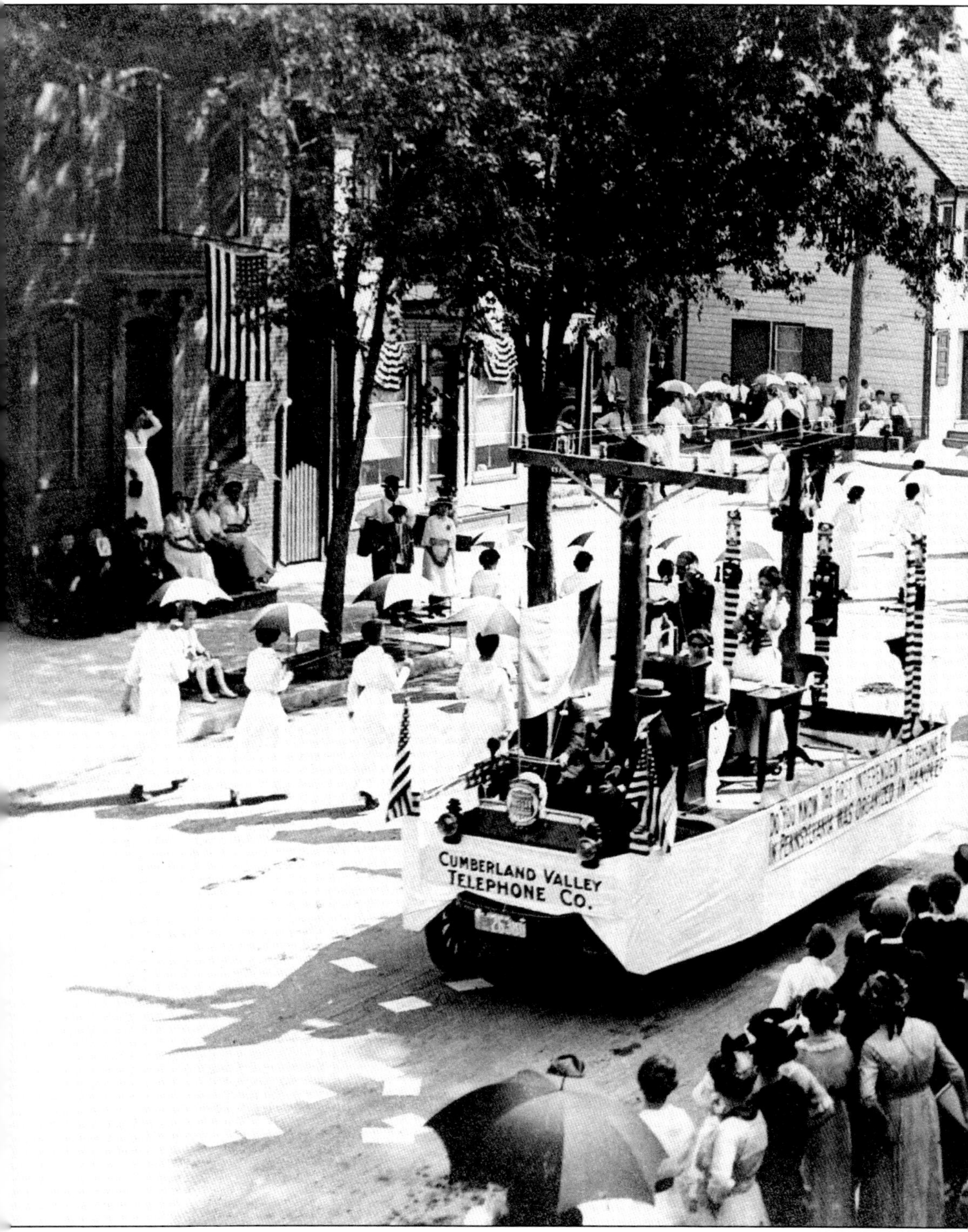

The Cumberland Valley Telephone Company of Pennsylvania, in the foreground, includes several female telephone operators in action with two utility poles standing on the float. The phone company, which was previously the American Union Telephone Company, was located on the

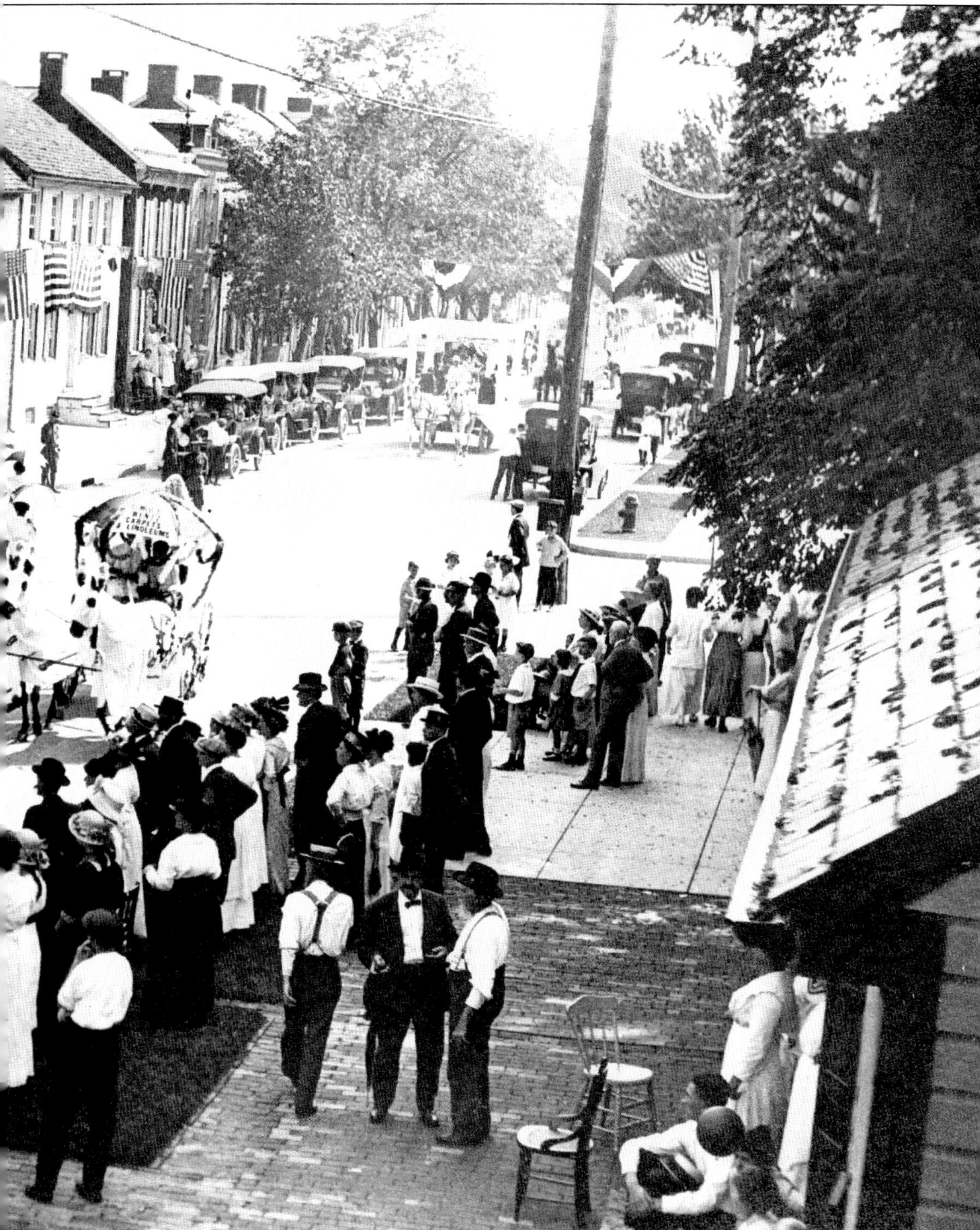

third floor of the Gitt building on Center Square. By the 1920s, Hanover had three telephone companies, including Bell Telephone and the Penn Rural Telephone Company. The following float represents the Elmer E. Wentz dry goods store advertising carpets and linoleum.

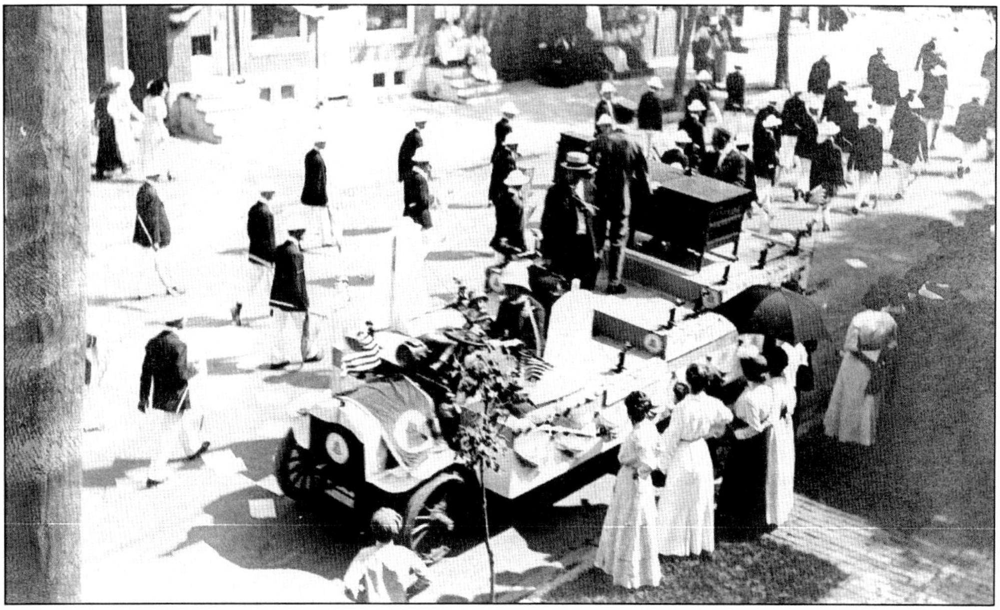

More Hanover Shoe workers continue down the left side of the street, with the float in the foreground possibly the Bell Telephone Company float. The bell trademark emblem appears in several places, and the rear of the float may be depicting an office desk with a standing phone in front of the seated individual behind the desk.

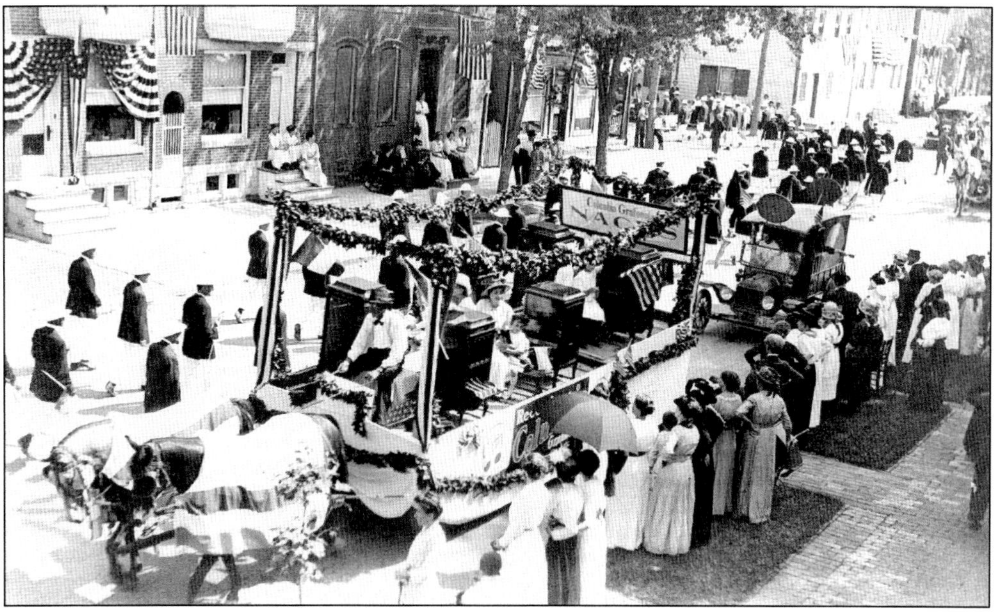

When will the Hanover Shoe employees all get through town? The float in the forefront represents G. B. Nace Sons and Company department store located at 11–13 Carlisle Street. The float displays a number of Columbia grafonolas with record players on top and record storage in the cabinet beneath. Their centennial program advertised grafonolas, the rage of the time, from $17.50 to $500 and an inventory of 2,000 records for 65¢ each. At a price of $500, it must have represented cutting-edge technology of the time, and with no remote control.

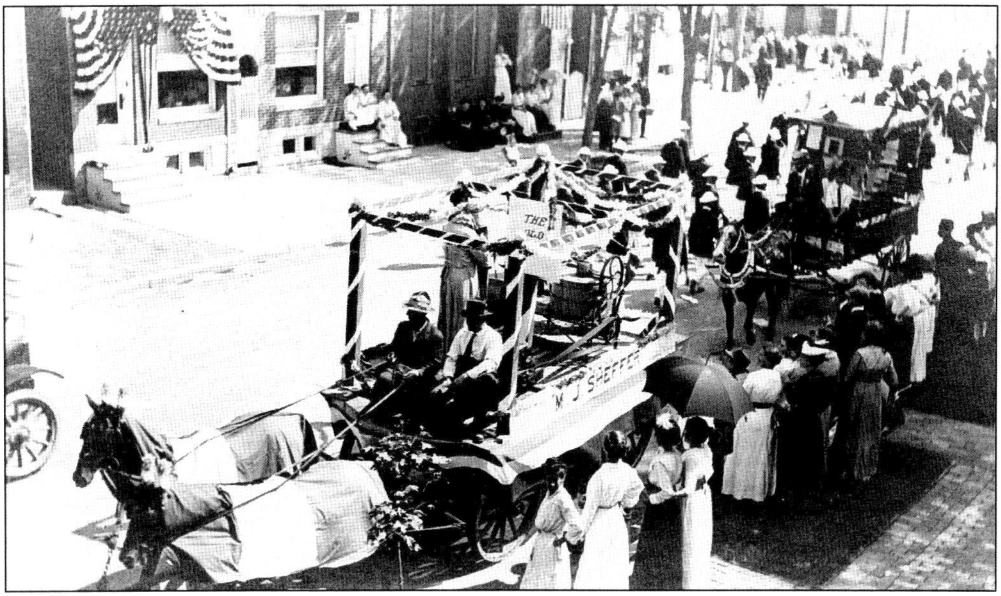

The last Hanover Shoe employees depart in the rear as the M. (Melvin) J. Shaffer float passes in the foreground. Melvin Shaffer was a fertilizer, farm equipment, and machine dealer located in the northeast corner of Railroad and Chestnut Streets. It appears that the float is promoting a belt-driven, wooden barrel–type washing machine (on the right) over hand washing (the woman on the left).

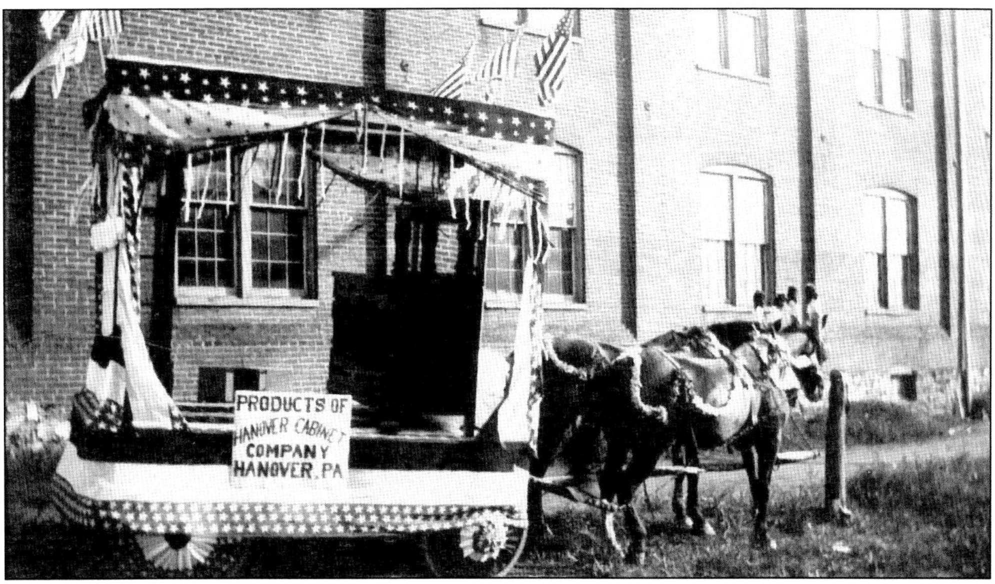

With its factory at Elm Avenue and the Western Maryland Railroad as a backdrop, the Hanover Cabinet Company float was photographed. A sideboard or buffet is evident on the wagon, reflecting the type of products made.

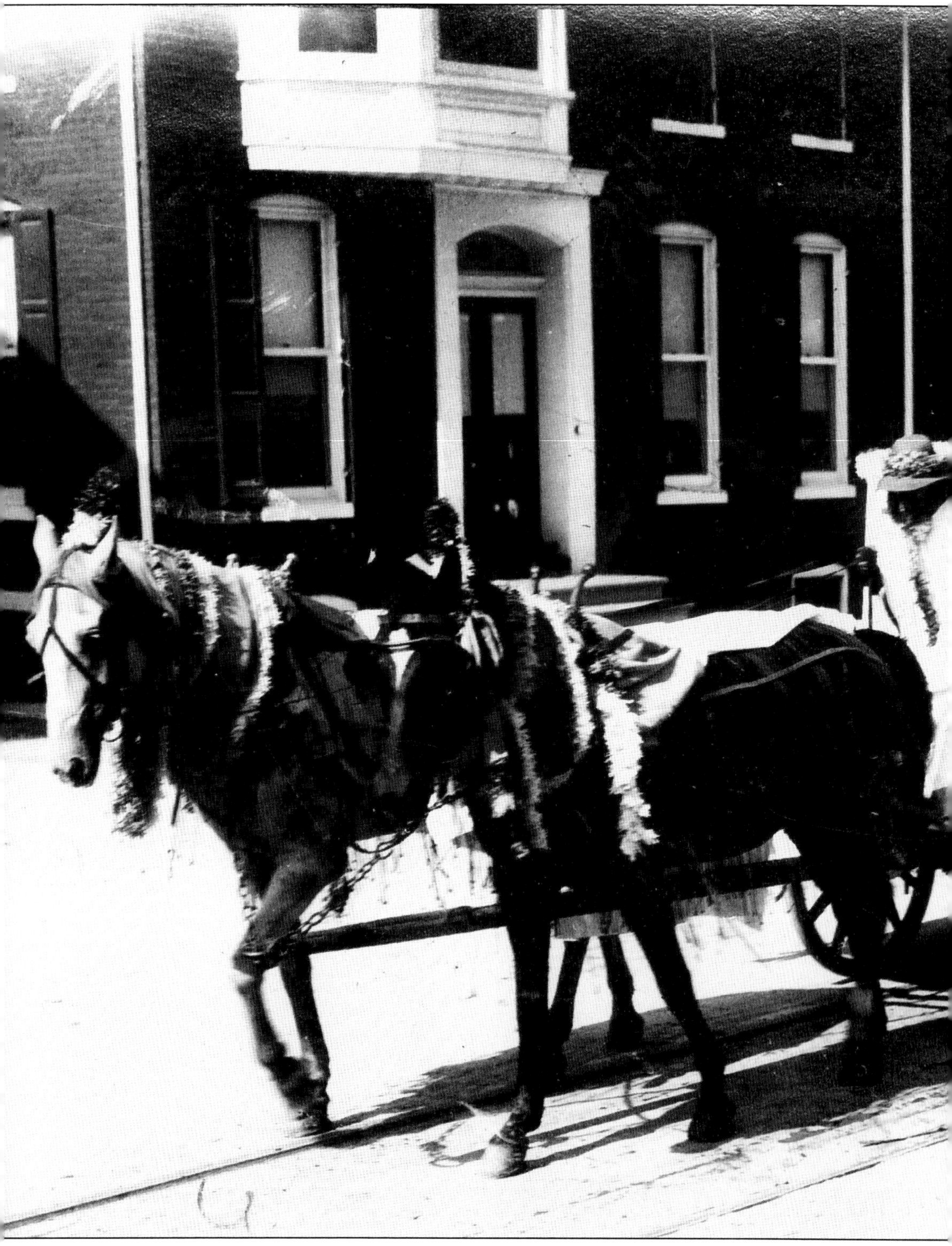

One of the few businesses to survive the last 90 years is Hanover Ice Company. At the time owned by Cornelius R. McCosh, it was located on Poplar Street near Spruce Street. Its product was

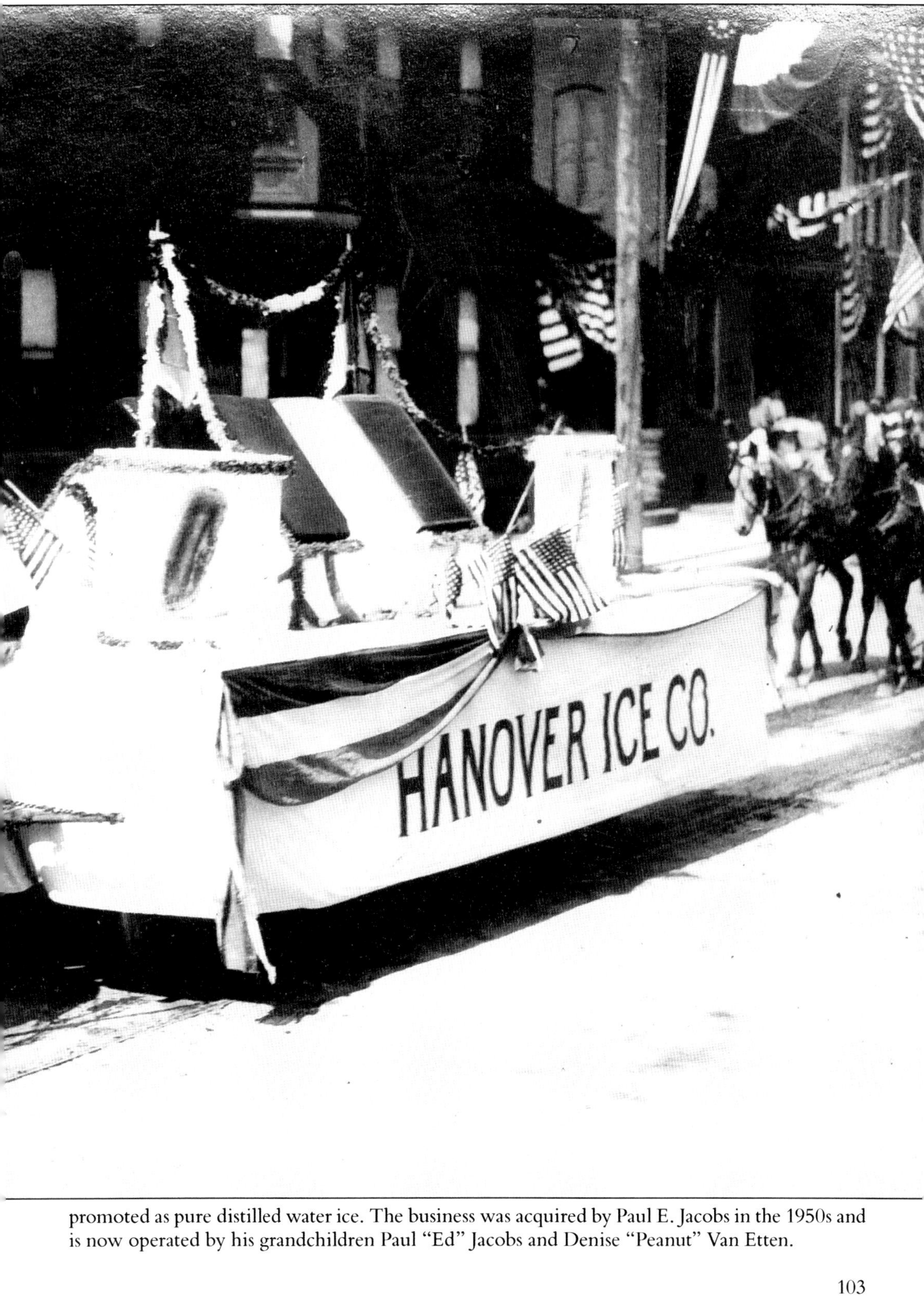

promoted as pure distilled water ice. The business was acquired by Paul E. Jacobs in the 1950s and is now operated by his grandchildren Paul "Ed" Jacobs and Denise "Peanut" Van Etten.

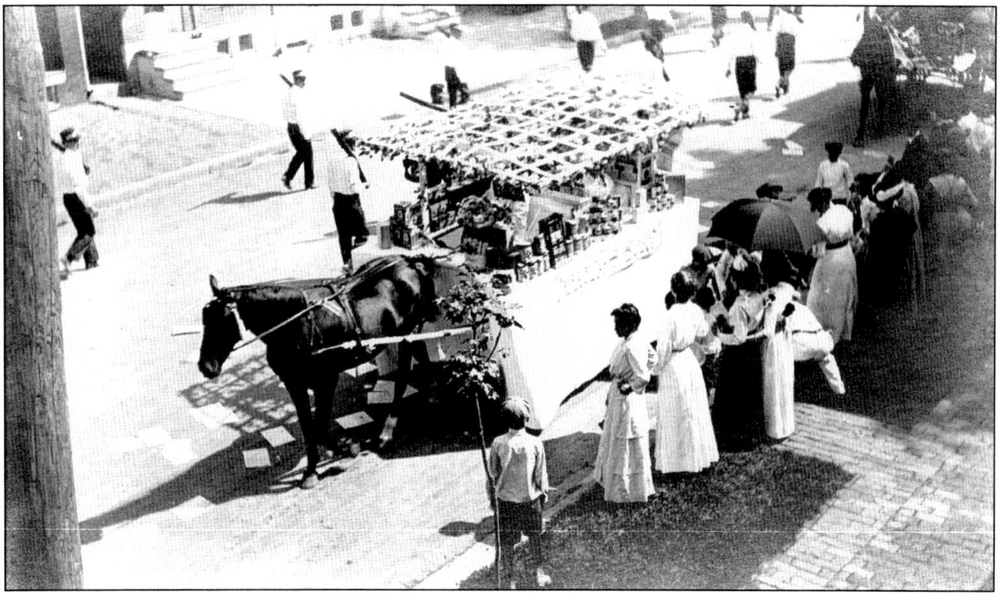

Trone and Sons grocery store at the northeast corner of York and Middle Streets entered this float.

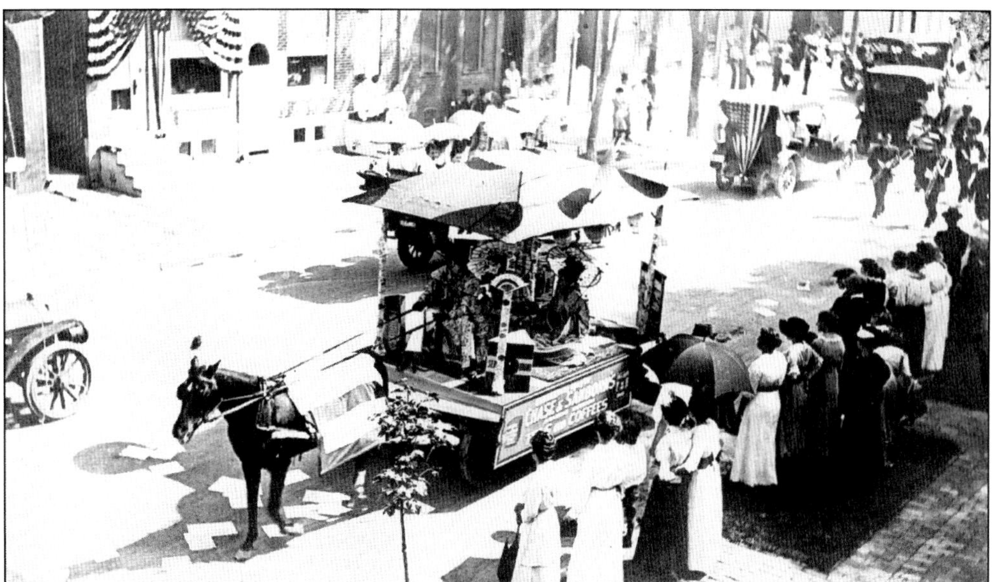

The float representing an unknown business is promoting Chase and Sanborn's Teas and Coffees.

Five

OTHER EARLY-20TH-CENTURY CELEBRATIONS

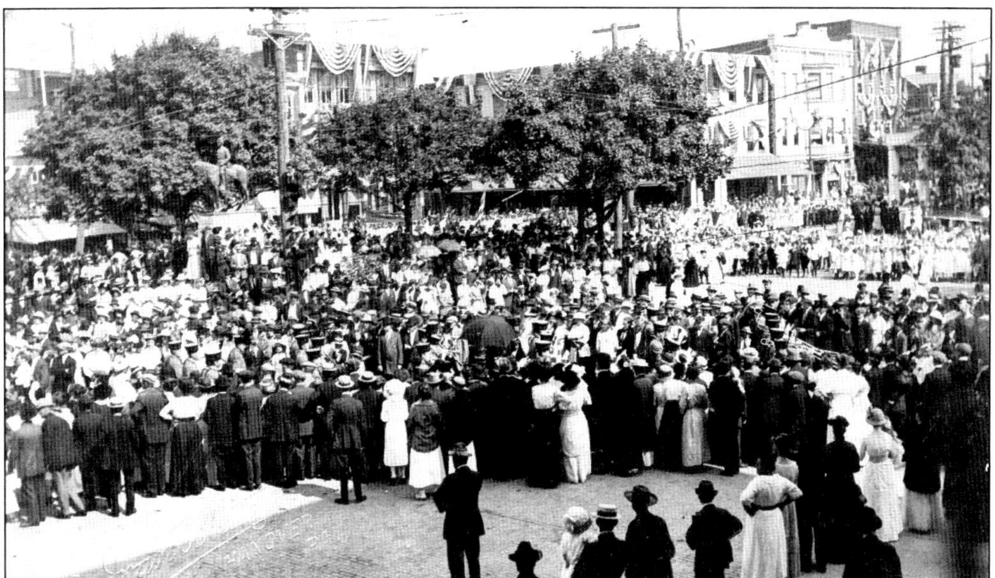

Before the 1915 centennial celebration, there was a practice or confidence-builder for the later. The community had for decades focused its festivities around the annual September Hanover Fair, which began in 1884. Therefore, the 1914 fair would be the 30th and an excuse to party. On September 19, 1914, the Hanover community witnessed a parade of massive proportions. This postcard demonstrates the popularity of the event from the crowds gathered at Center Square for ceremonies, with the northeast quadrant of Center Square as the backdrop and Broadway to the right.

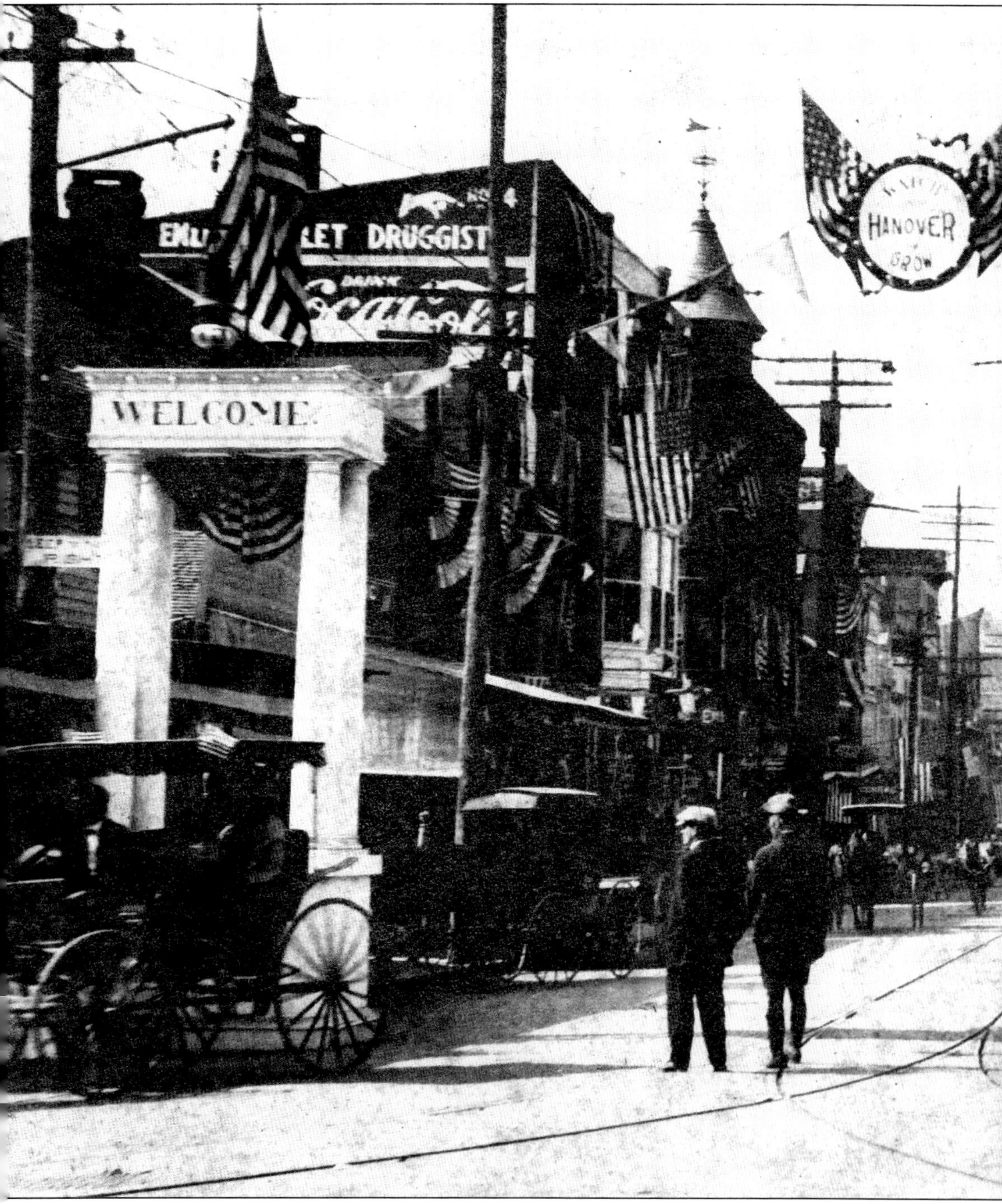

The September 1914 event was known as Civic Celebration Day. The parade committee consisted of T. S. O'Neill, Paul Winebrenner, Harry S. Ehrhart, C. N. Myers, C. F. Moul, and F. W. Delancey. The parade route was over three miles long, snaking around town, going out Carlisle Street to Park Avenue to High Street then to Frederick Street and Center Square. Then the parade proceeded out Baltimore Street, across Pleasant Street to York Street to Abbottstown Street (now known as Broadway) to Fulton Street turning down East Chestnut and up Carlisle Street to

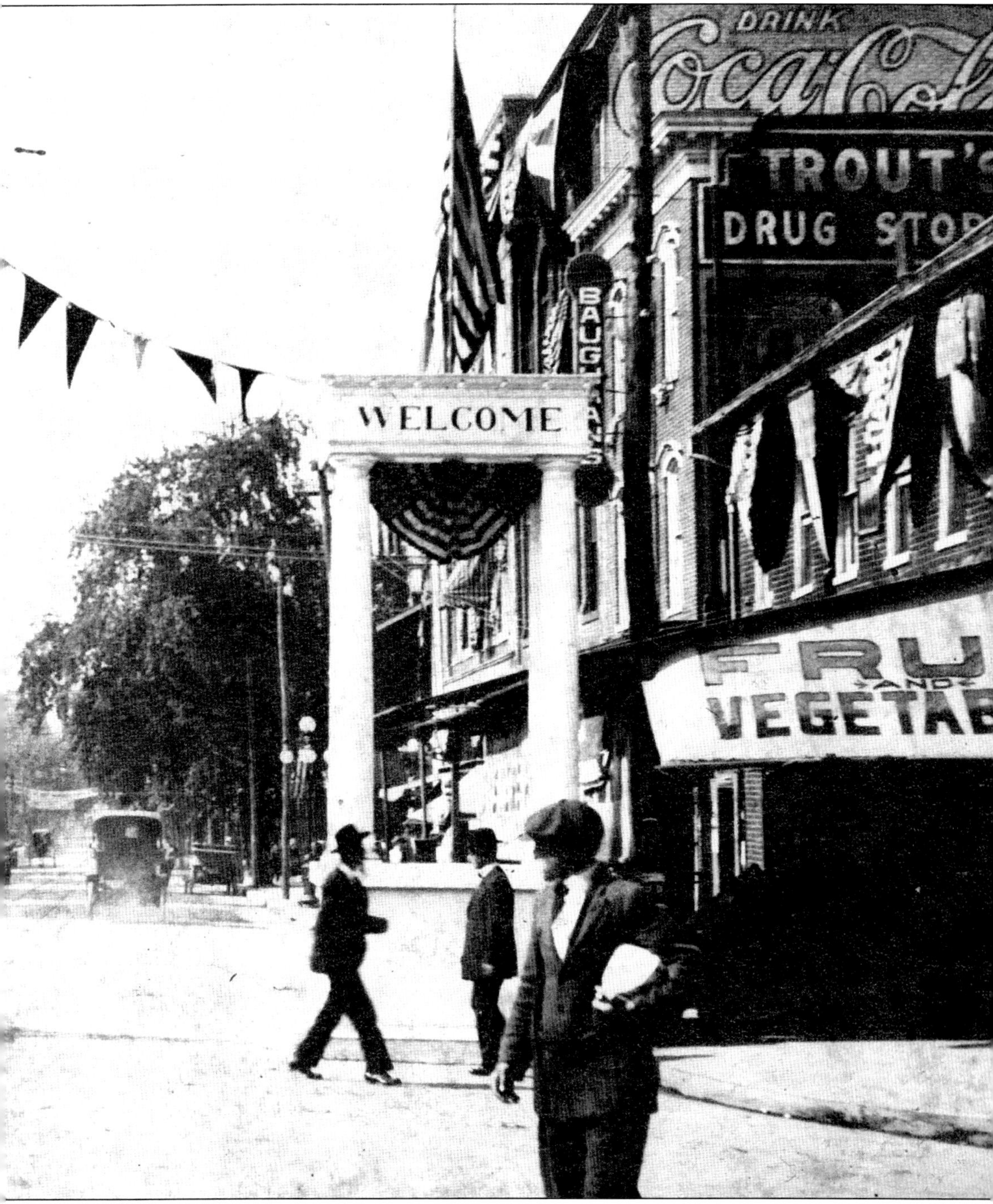

Center Square. The parade dismissed at Center Square, where the school children, of which 3,000 participated in the parade, sang National Airs accompanied by all the parade bands massed together for the presentation. This postcard reveals the 1914 decorations placed on Carlisle Street at Center Square in preparation for the festivities. These photographs are frequently misidentified as 1915 centennial celebrations. But compare the pillars in this scene with the 1915 parade arches on pages 75 and 76 to recognize the distinctive features to identify the respective celebrations.

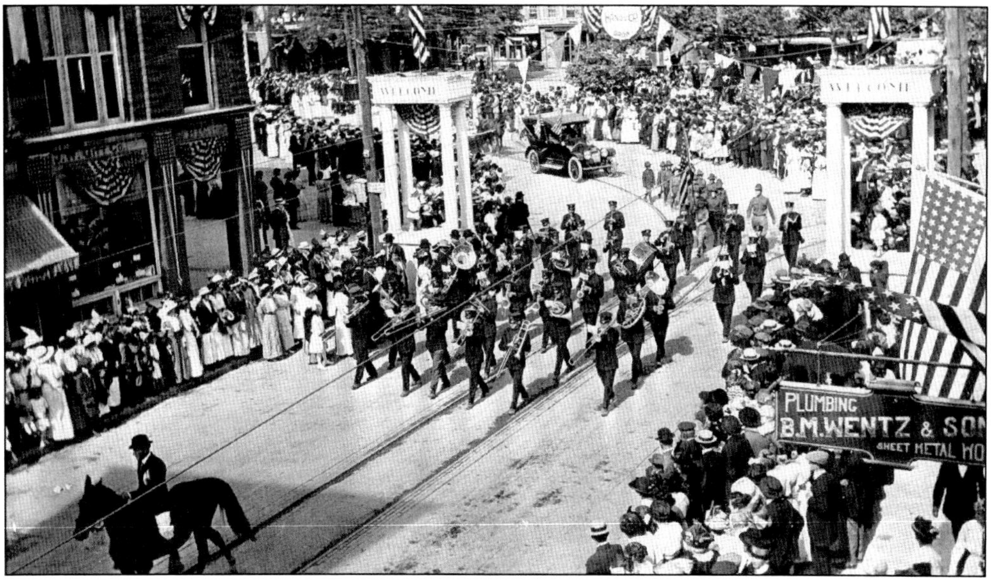

The parade organizers offered numerous prizes to the parade participants. Perhaps the most unusual was $10 to the farmer who hauled the largest number of people to Hanover for the event in a four-horse wagon. Newspaper articles boasted of over 40 floats sponsored by manufacturers and businesses. Here the Patriotic Order Sons of America Band in the second parade division leaves Center Square departing on Baltimore Street after passing through the arches. Forty-eight-star flags are proudly displayed to the right, two years after Arizona and New Mexico achieved statehood.

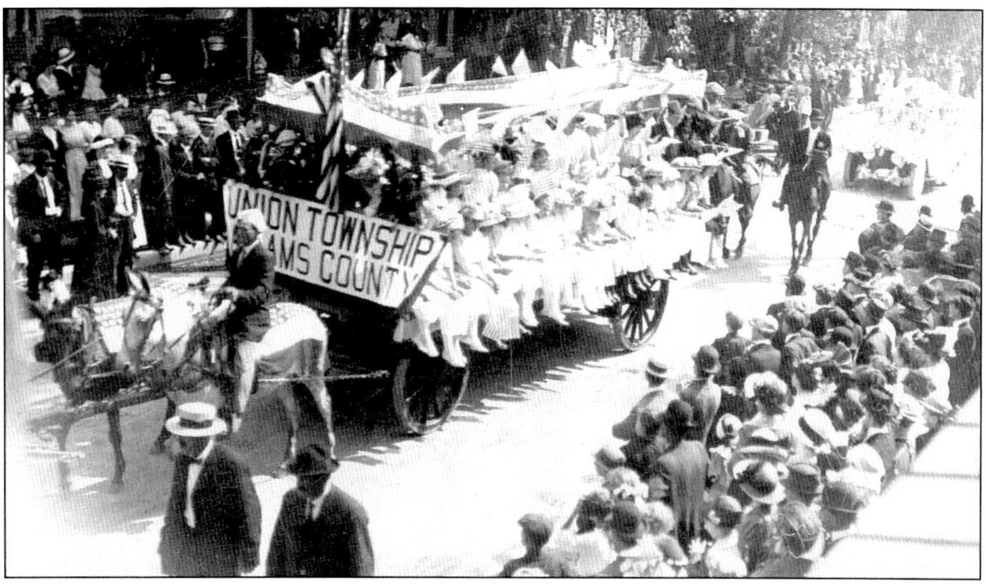

The schools of Union Township, Adams County, ride in the third division on a decorated hay wagon drawn by four mules. The card's writer, Dorothy, sent the card to E. J. J. Gobrecht and announced that she was the second student from the front of the wagon. The fifth division begins behind the wagon with marshal H. O. Baughman and aide Holi Smith riding horses. The decorated automobile of Stewart and Shaffer, men's clothiers at 22 Carlisle Street, driven by Louis B. Hafer of 54 Frederick Street, follows.

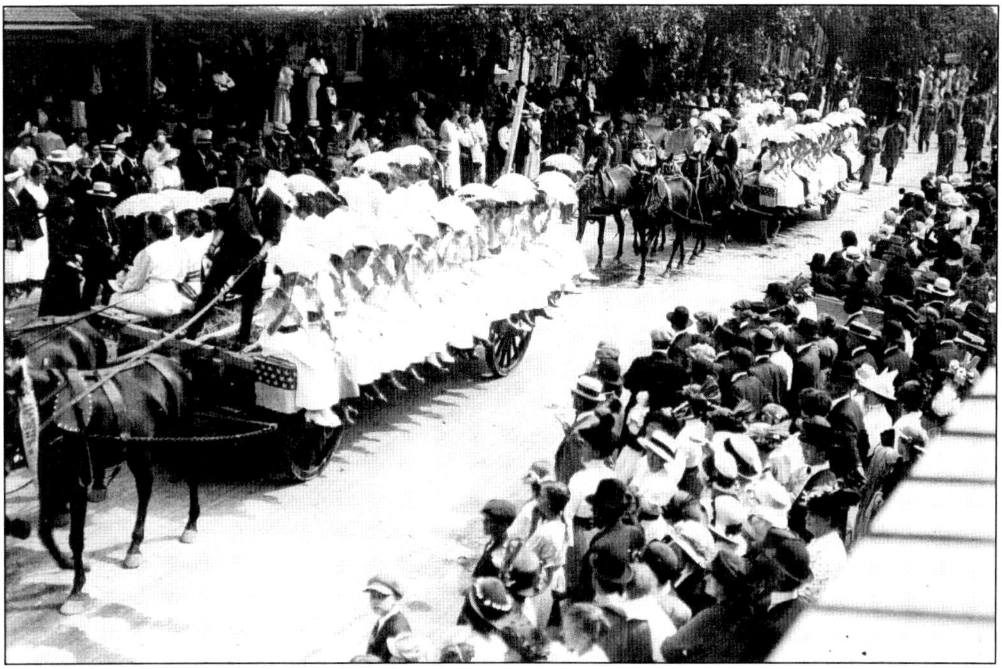

These two wagons of umbrella girls are believed to have represented the Civic League of Hanover, which met the first Monday of each month at 16 Center Square.

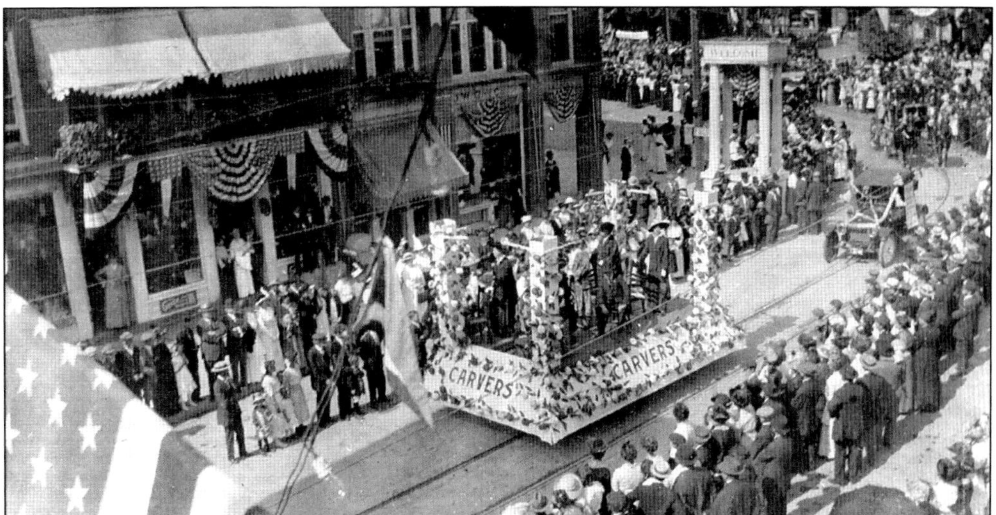

A series of postcards exist with photographs of various floats taken at this precise location, looking over the parade from a high vantage point. This one was entered by N. B. Carver and Sons, a department store just to the opposite side of the street at 10–12 Baltimore Street. The J. W. Gitt Company department store is behind the float. A *Record-Herald* newspaper article on September 21, 1914, provides an excellent report of the parade for anyone desiring more information about the event.

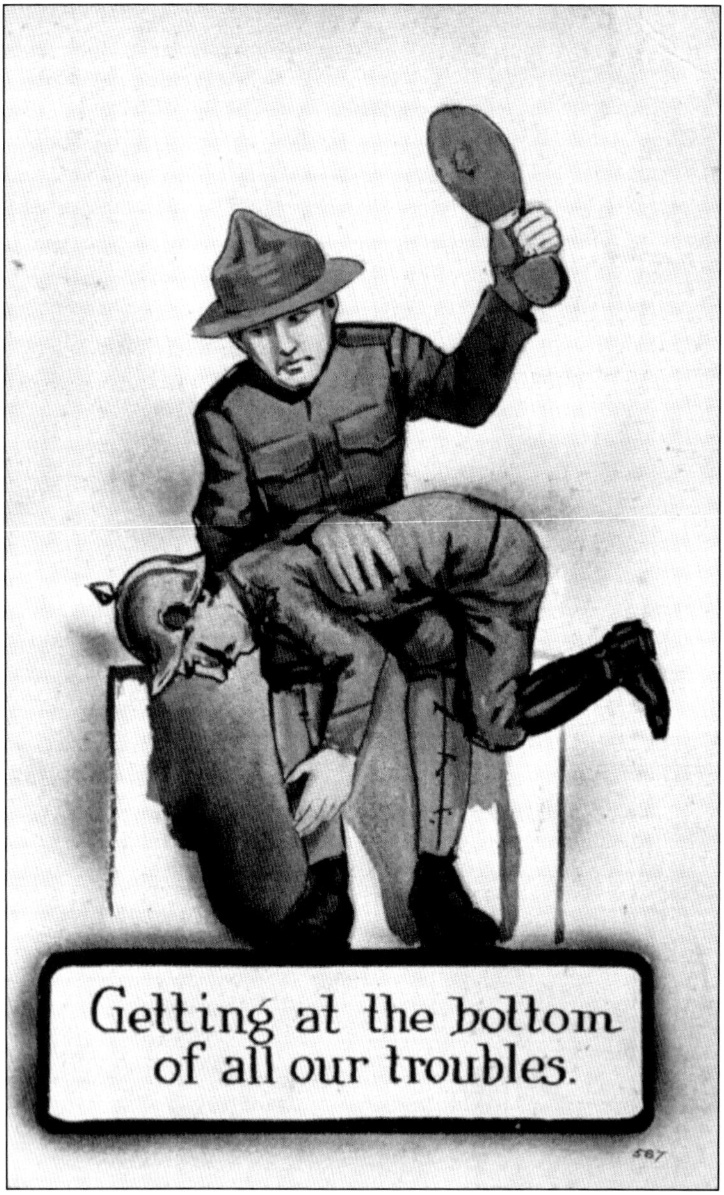

On June 28, 1914, in the little town of Sarajevo, Bosnia, Archduke Francis Ferdinand, heir to the crown of Austro-Hungarian Empire, was shot dead. This became the catalyst for the beginning of the World War, as it was then simply known. On April 2, 1917, Pres. Woodrow Wilson addressed Congress in what became the basis for the eventual declaration of war with Germany and the sailing of the U.S. fleet for Europe on April 6. York County would eventually send over 6,000 individuals to serve its country in the battle. The United States mobilized nearly 4.3 million men, and almost 68,000 of them were killed. Germany surrendered November 11, 1918, ending the war. One year later on November 11, 1919, York County held a Welcome Home celebration for its service men. The local sentiment regarding the Germans was depicted in this postcard. It was sent from Camp Meade, Maryland, on February 12, 1918, from recently enlisted soldier and Hanover native Charles Diller to his father. He reported "we have our uniforms now and like camp life. Some great things happen here. 2,200 came in when we did."

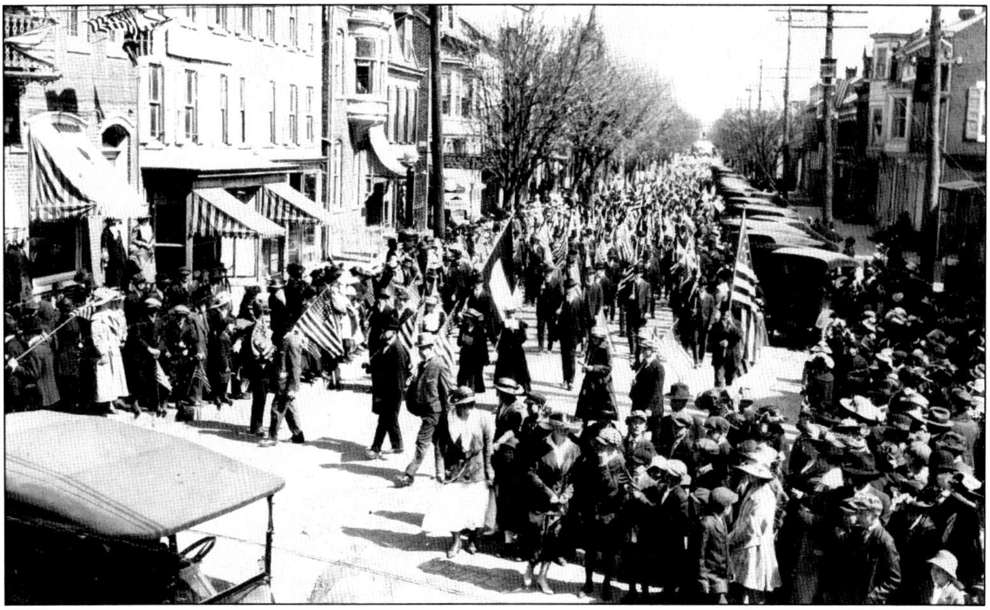

This postcard of a photograph taken of York Street looking southeast from Broadway is reported to be a parade celebrating one year in the war, thus suggesting it was taken in April 1918. It clearly demonstrates the patriotism and support for the war effort overseas.

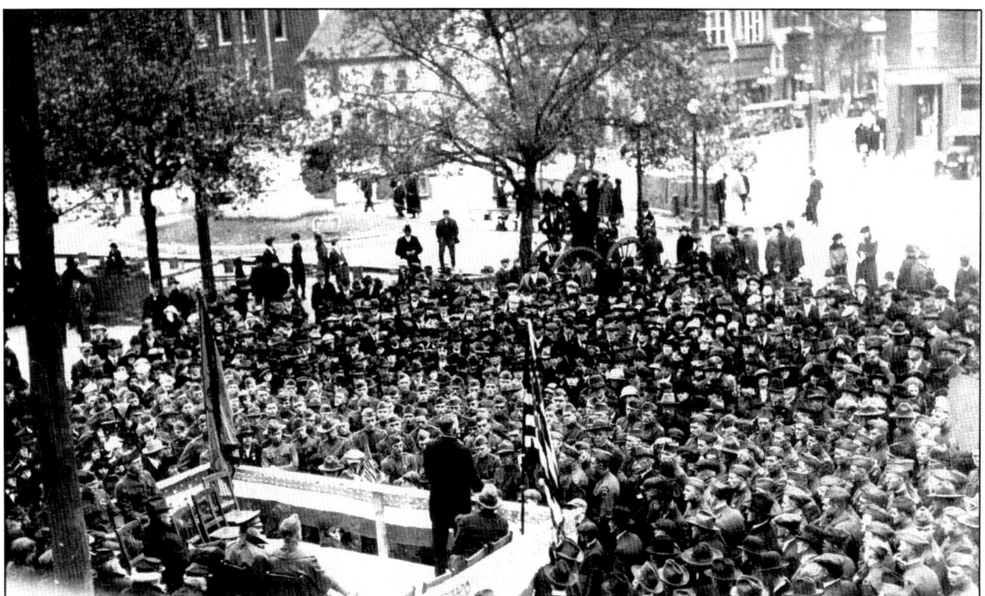

The Hanover November 11, 1919, Welcome Home celebration program is conducted in the northwest quadrant of Center Square and is well attended.

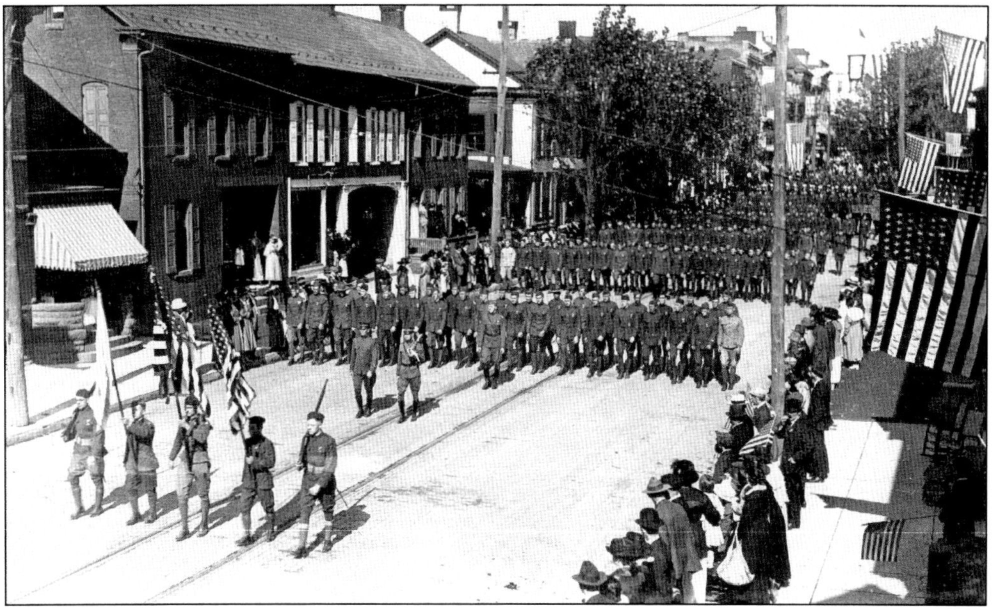

Soldiers paraded down Baltimore Street decorated with numerous flags, reflecting the pride in the U.S. military's achievement.

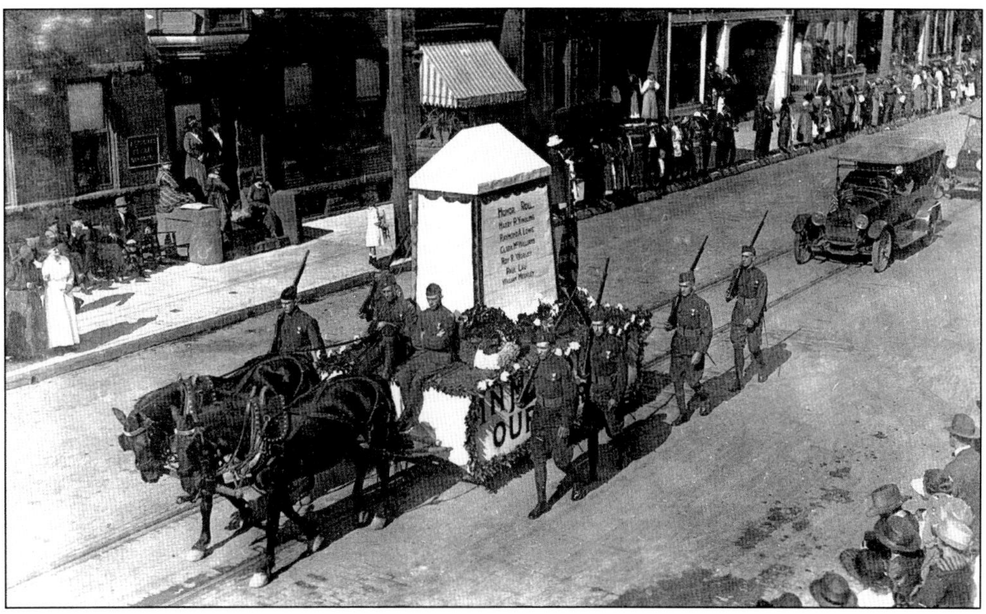

This float lists names on the so-called honor roll, those Hanover-area natives who lost their lives in the war. Those listed are Harry R. Yingling, Raymond A. Lowe, Clark McWilliam, Roy R. Worley, Paul E. Lars, and William H. Meckley. It is possible that additional names were posted on the other side of the float since it is known that other Hanover servicemen also perished during the war.

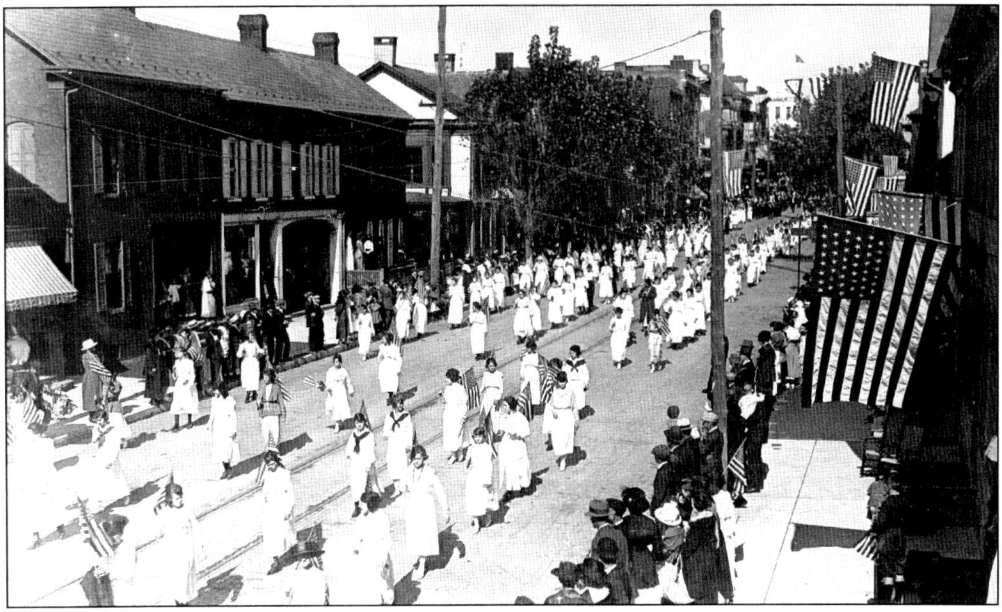

Numerous other groups marched in the soldiers' Welcome Home parade to reflect the appreciation and pride for the U.S. military might.

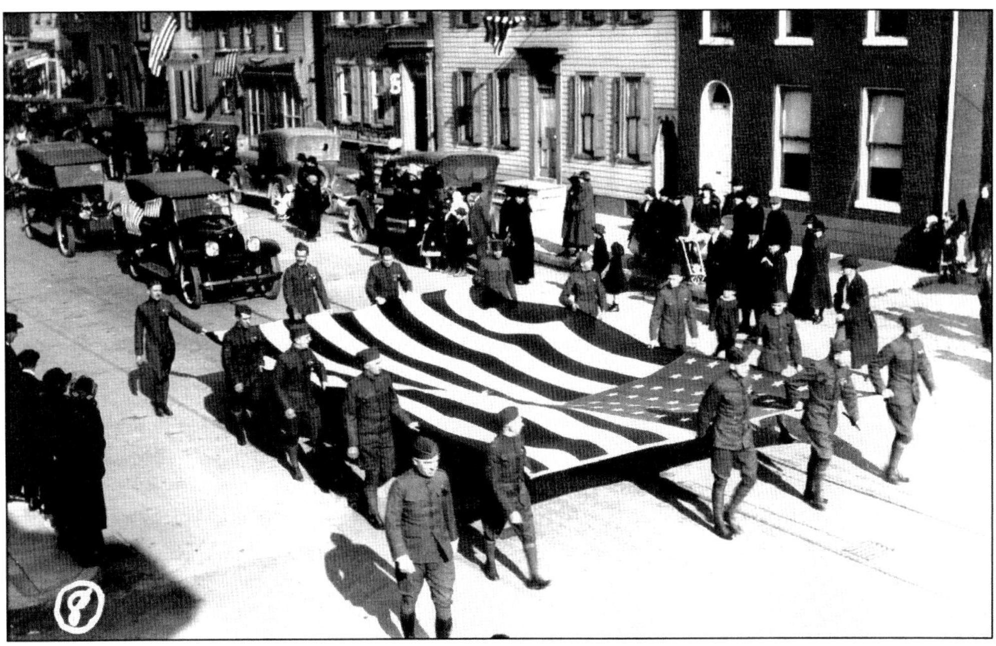

Annual recognition of Armistice Day followed, such as this 1920 observation.

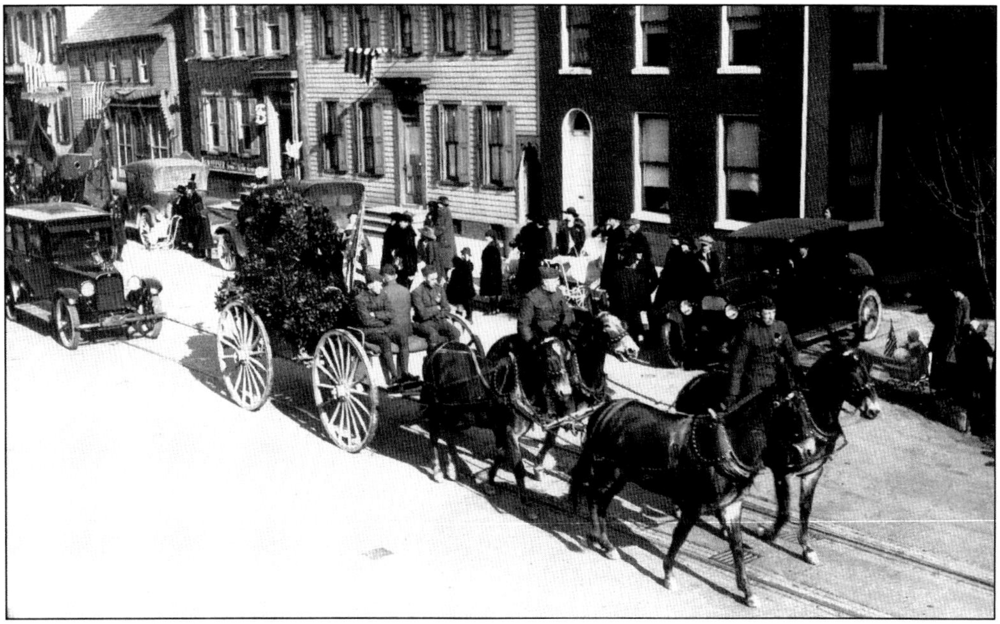

This 1920 Armistice Day parade caisson includes lead mule rider Paul Luckenbaugh, saddle mule rider John Teel, and George Miller and Milt Anthony siding on the caisson.

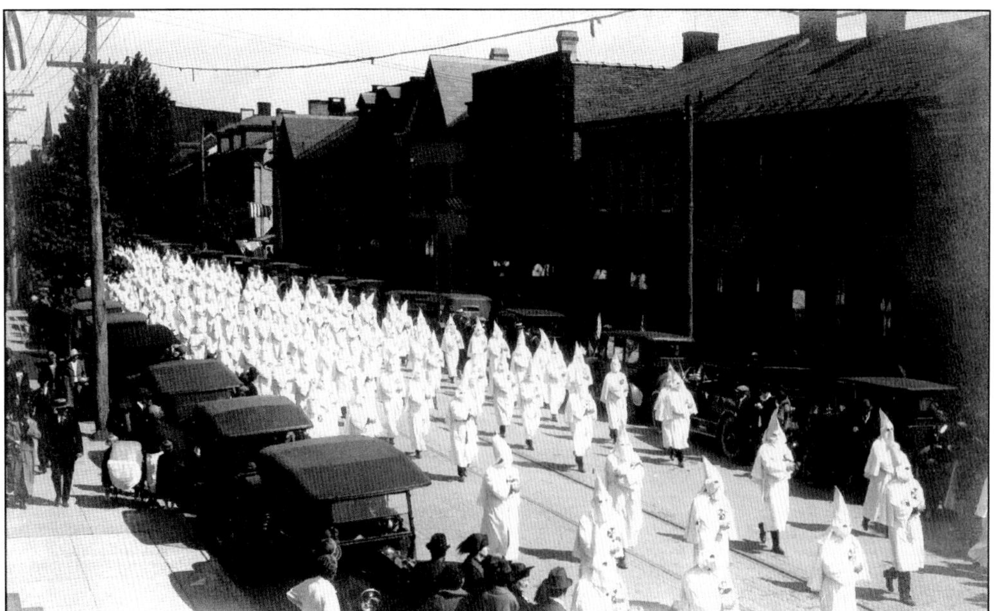

Hanover had moments of shame to balance the euphoria of its proud achievements. This Ku Klux Klan group marched south on Baltimore Street in the May 30, 1925, Memorial Day parade.

Six

The 1932 Washington Bicentennial

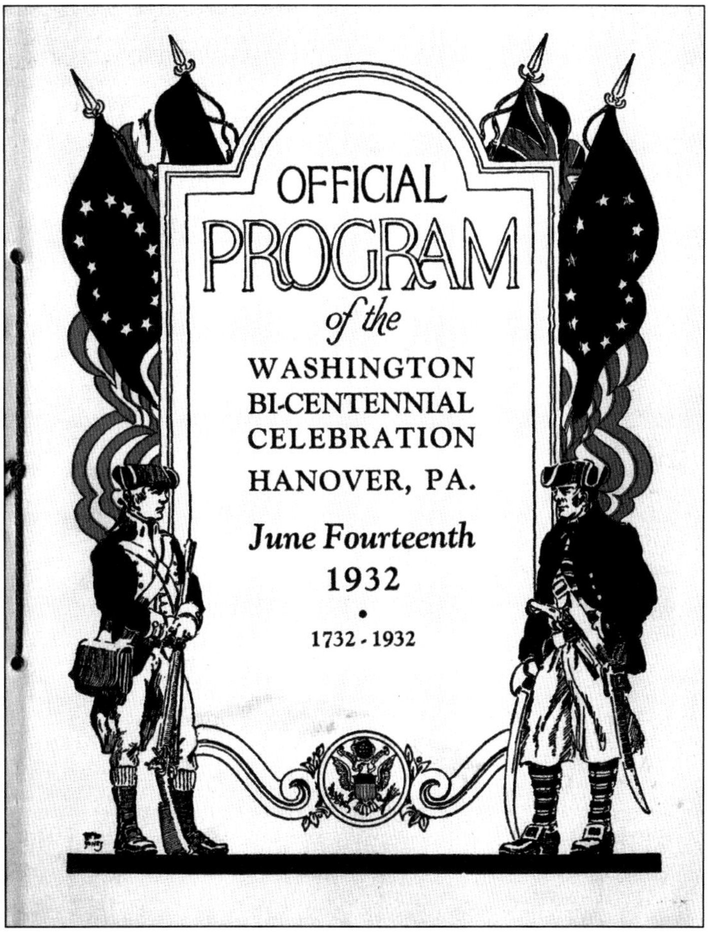

Hanover celebrated with the rest of the nation on June 14, 1932, when the bicentennial of George Washington's birthday was recognized. A pageant and a memorable parade centered around Washington's life were held. Evidence of the festivities is shown here in the program cover and the following series of postcards, which is perhaps one of a mere two sets in existence to record the event.

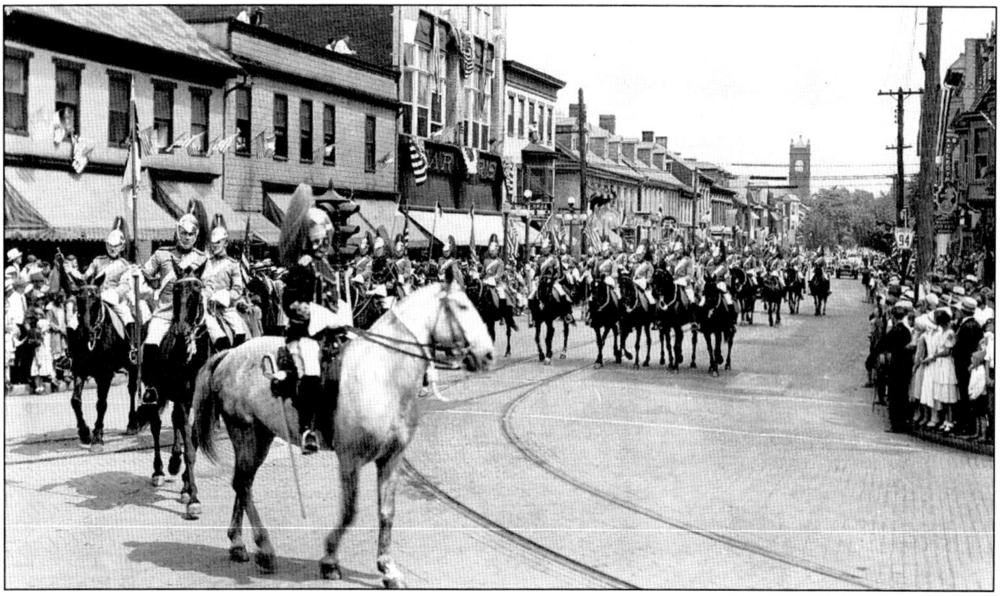

The parade chief marshal L. B. Sheppard leads the parade, followed by the Patriotic Order Sons of America Band and then the Governor's Troop, pictured here entering Center Square from Baltimore Street.

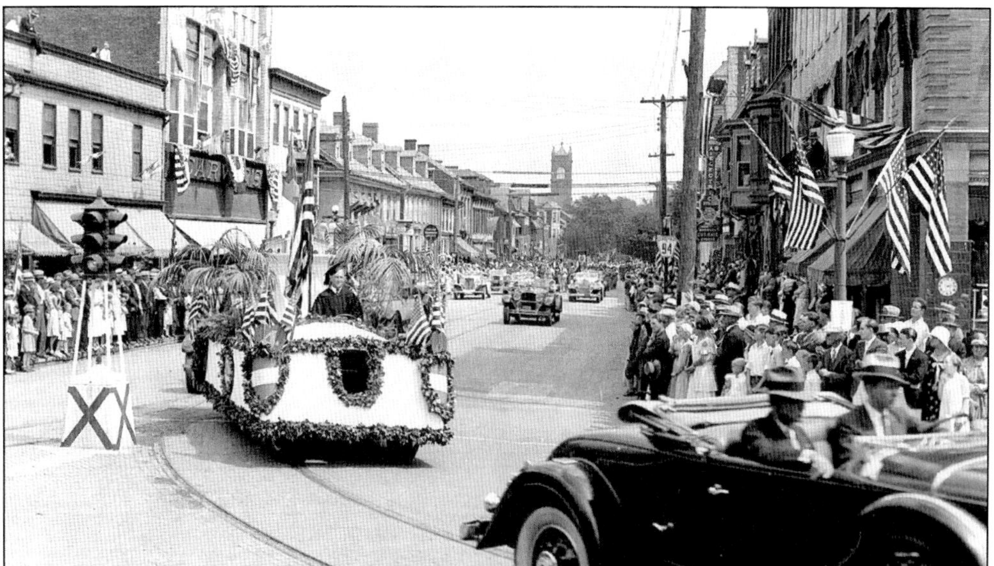

The founder of Hanover, Col. Richard McAllister, was a soldier in Washington's army and George Washington himself visited Hanover on July 2, 1791. The committee dedicated a bronze tablet to memorialize Washington's stop at an inn, which was then located on the 1932 site of the Hanover Trust Company buildings on the northwest corner of Center Square. This, the first float in the parade, was sponsored by the churches of Hanover and is followed by cars carrying the ministers. The passenger in the car preceding the float is Marine Maj. Gen. Smedley D. Butler, the honorary marshal and main speaker.

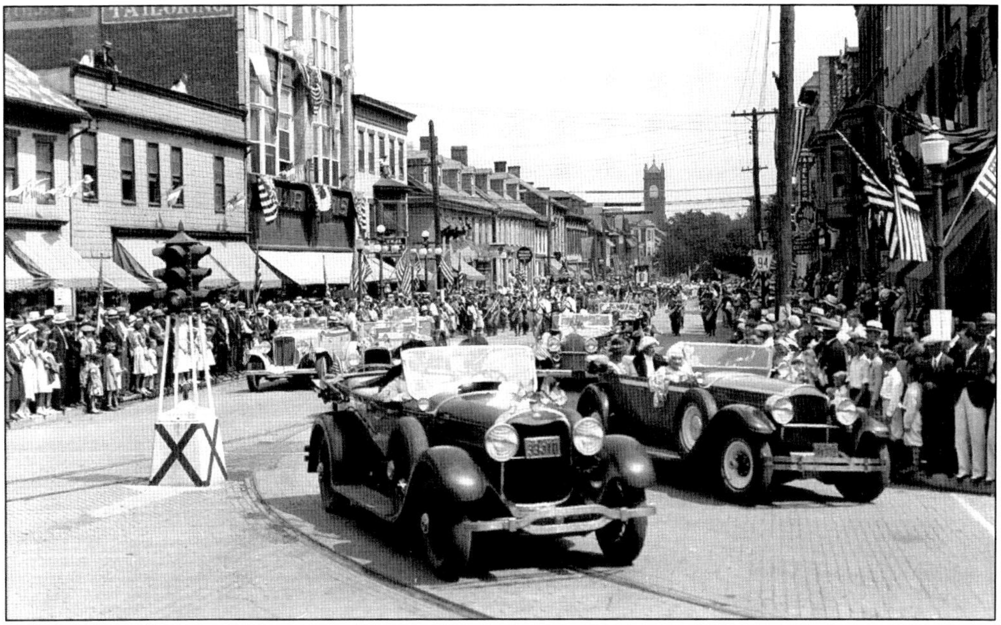

A number of cars follow, carrying dignitaries and parade committee personnel.

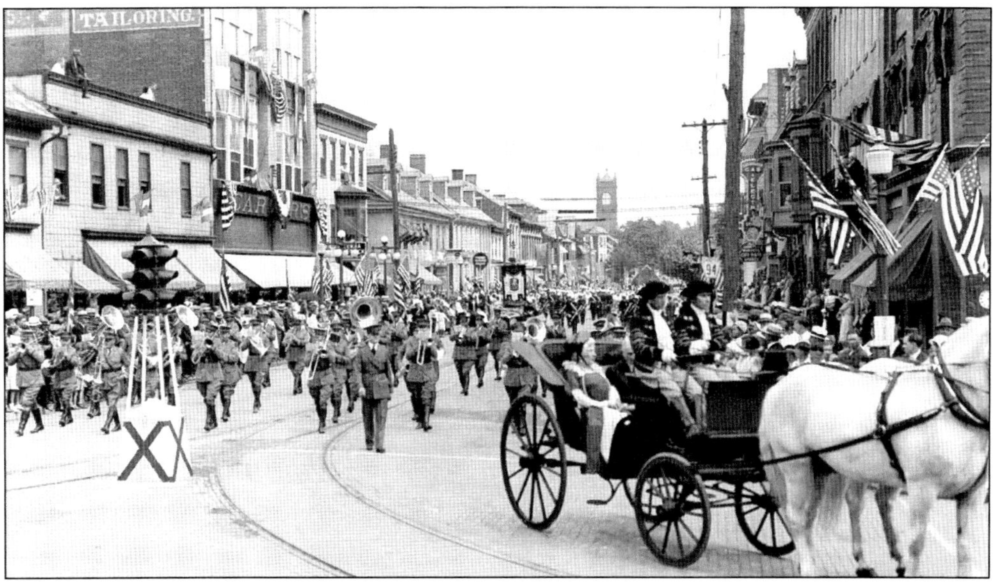

Judge Henry C. Niles, chairman of York County's bicentennial observation, appointed H. (Henrietta) D. Sheppard as Hanover's chairman. This carriage carries county committee chairman Judge Henry C. Niles and Hanover chairman H. D. Sheppard. They are followed by the Westminster Band under the direction of John L. Schweigert.

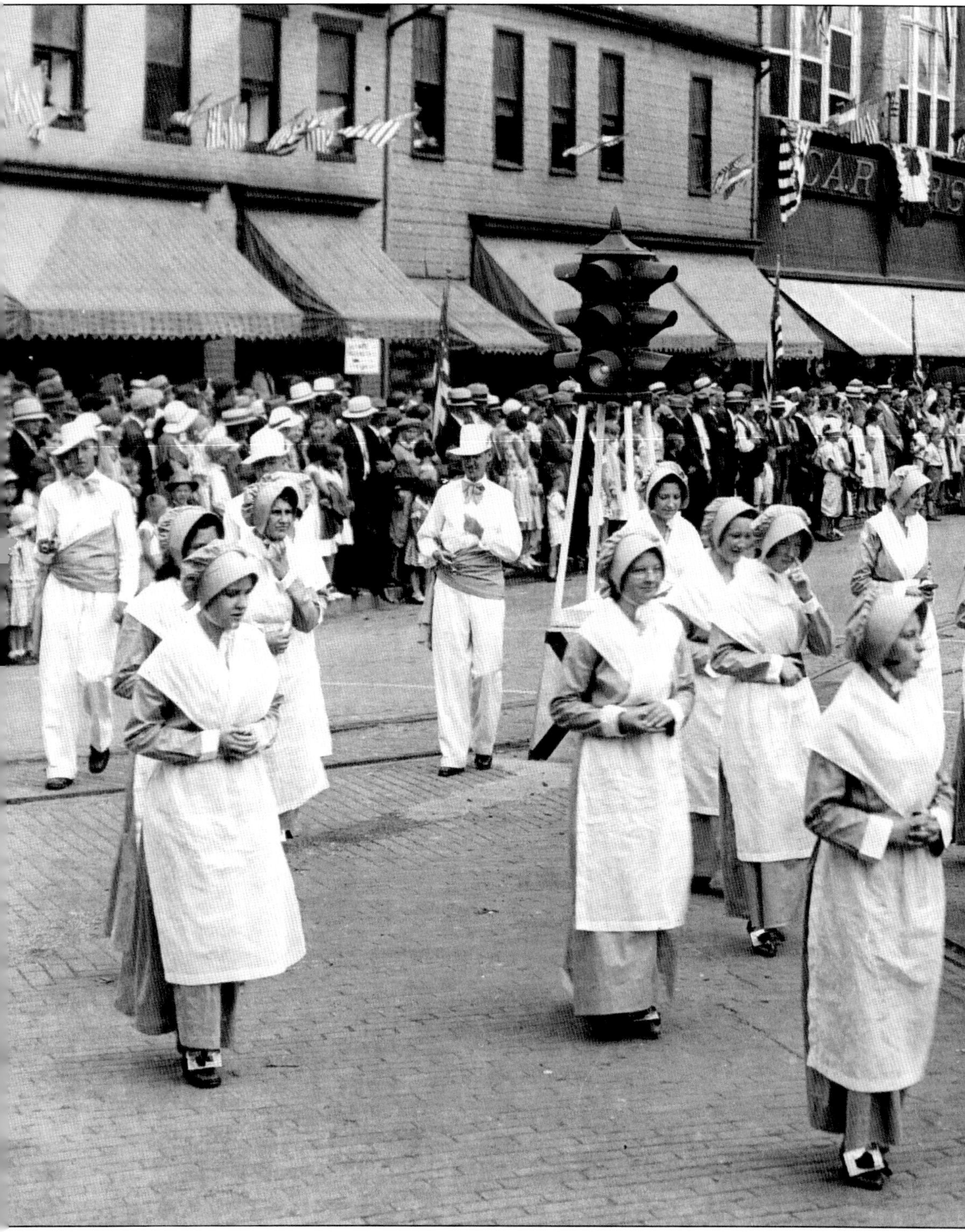

The parade formed at the Hanover Fairgrounds and proceeded down Baltimore Street to Center Square, then out Frederick Street to High Street. From High Street, the parade crossed Park Avenue to Carlisle Street, again crossing through the square and down York Street to return to

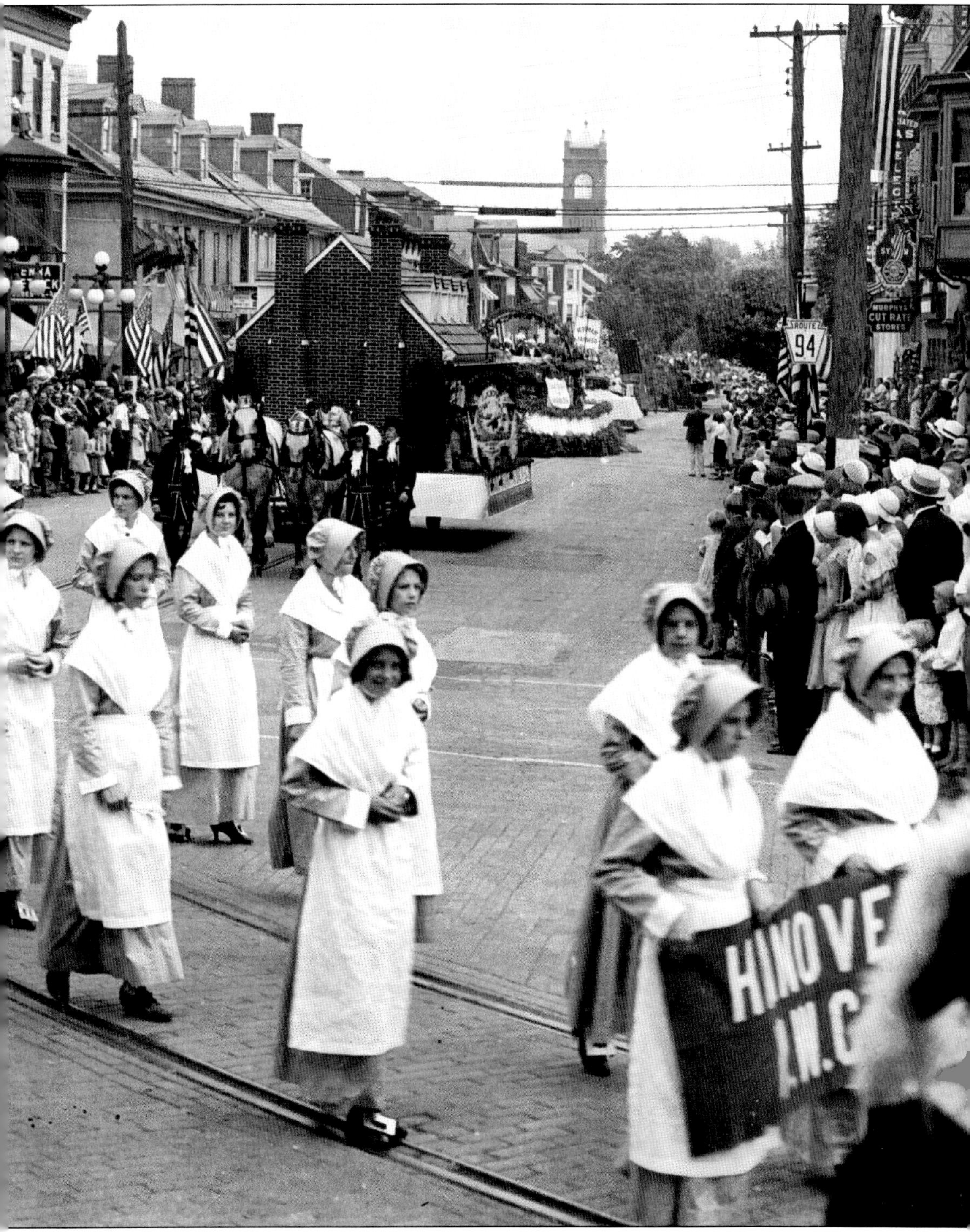

the east fairgrounds entrance. A grand colonial ball was held that evening at Forest Park. The YWCA members, seen here, enter the parade depicting the Mayflower Pilgrims of 1620.

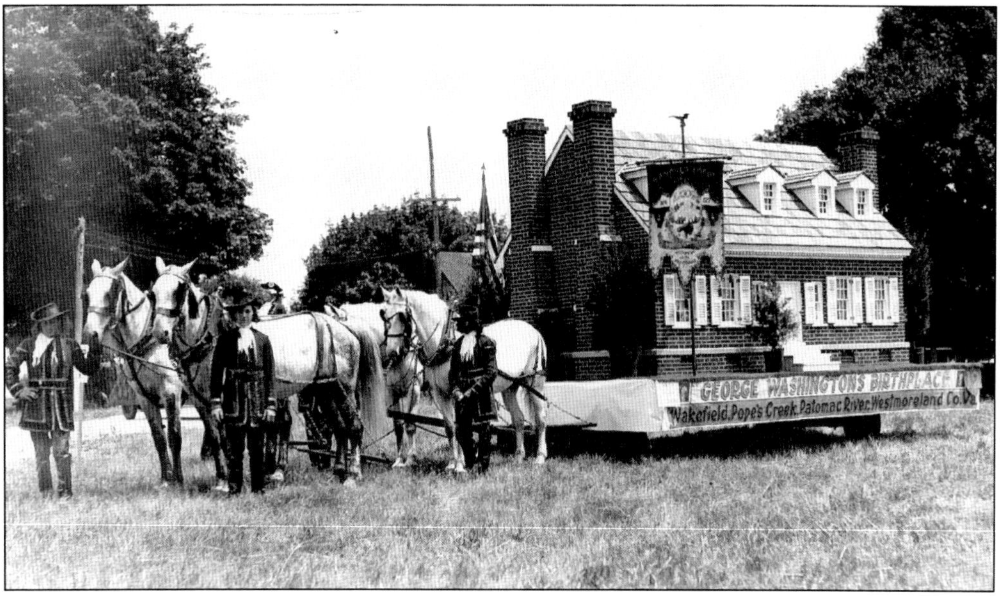

The parade concluded at the fairgrounds where the pageant and other exercises were held. George Washington's birthplace home at Wakefield, Virginia, is represented by this float, which was entered by the Loyal Order of Moose with Walter Kale as the dictator. The coachman was George Shultz Jr. The photograph is believed to have been taken in the fairgrounds.

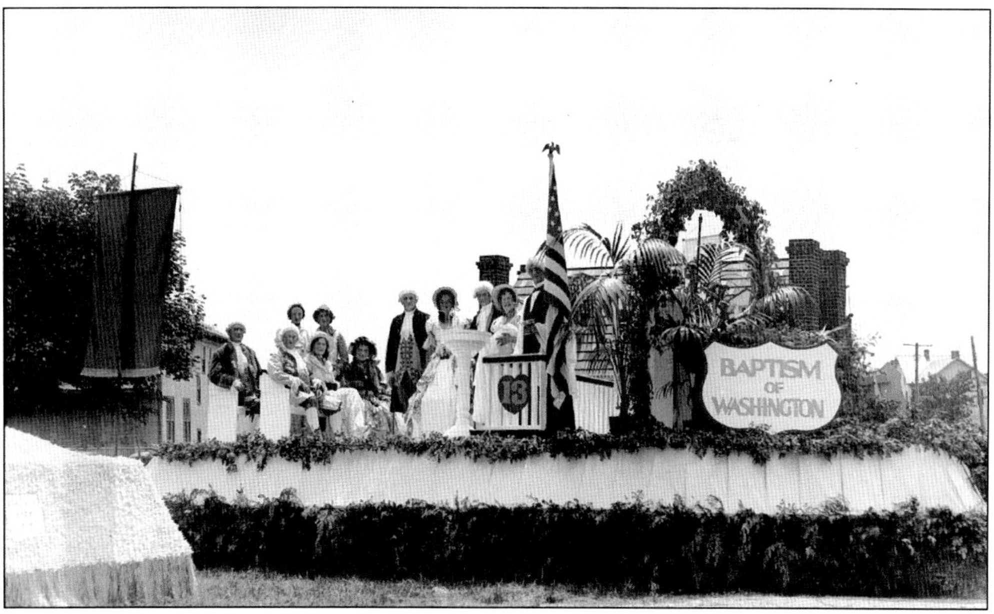

The order of these cards is the same as the parade order, as determined by the official program, and put the events of Washington's life in sequential order. This photograph is of a float depicting the baptism of Washington at White Chapel, Virginia. The Hanover General Hospital Auxiliary, Mrs. Malcolm W. Myers, president, sponsored the float. Charles Y. Brough was president of the hospital board and is on the float.

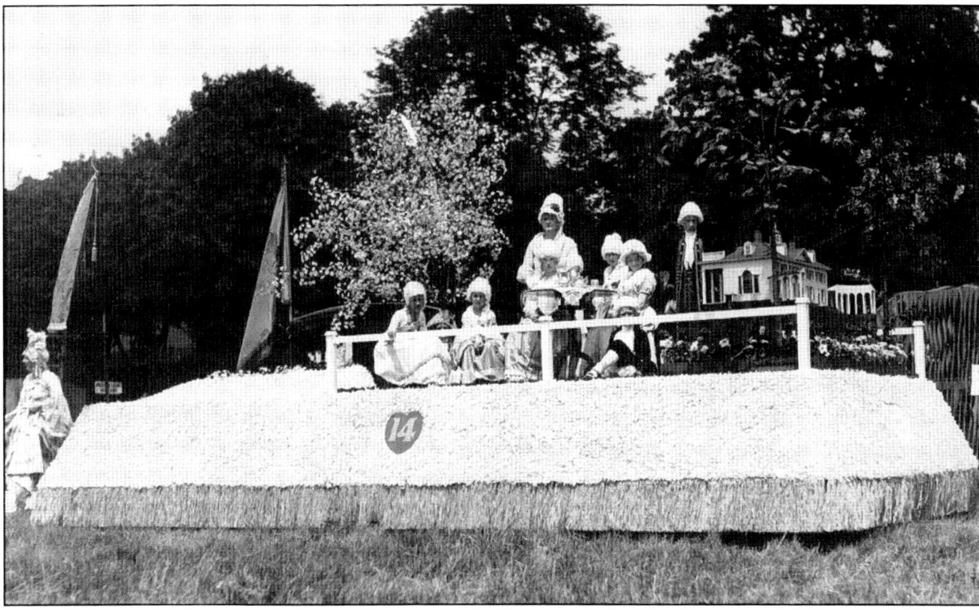

This miniature of Mount Vernon was created by the National Society United States Daughters of 1812, of which H. D. Sheppard was the state president. The heart-shaped 14 on the float indicates its position in the parade. The prior card also shows its entrance number of 13.

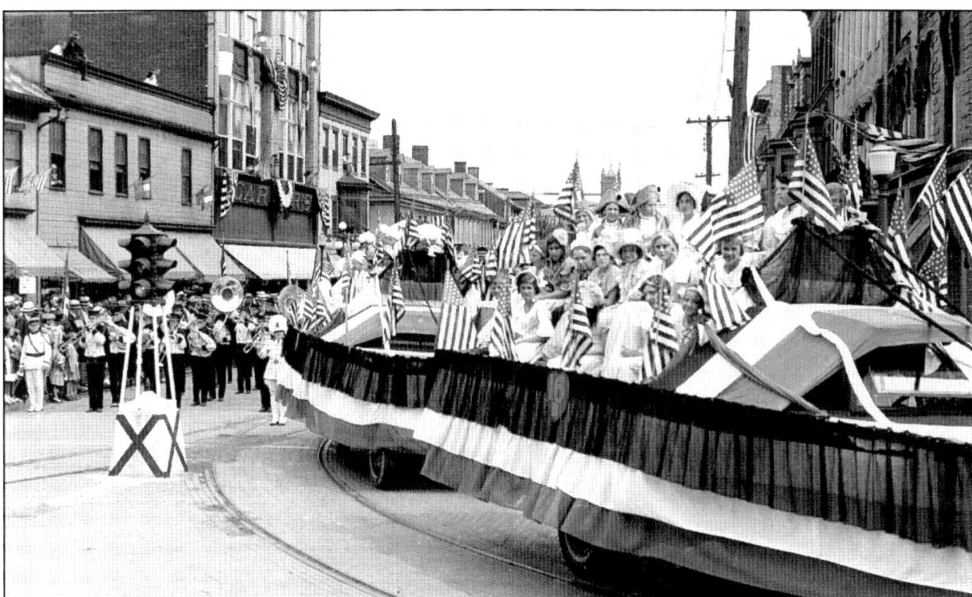

Subsequent floats No. 14B, Washington cutting down the cherry tree, and No. 15, Washington's boyhood, entered by the Boy Scouts are not available in postcards. Float number 16, pictured, shows the Hanover Grade School students.

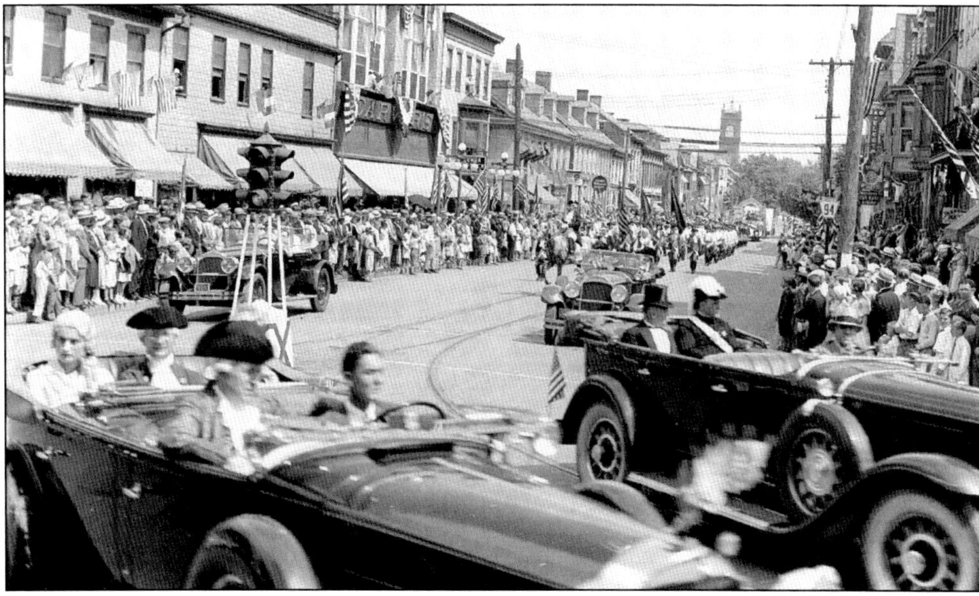

Parade group No. 3, per the program, was led by Congressman Harry L. Haines, John W. Young, former Congressman Andrew Brodbeck, and their driver in the right car. It appears one of them is absent. The left car is driven by Robert C. Myers, with general committee member passengers Hazel H. Henry (recording secretary), E. Fred Carver (treasurer) in the rear seat center, and Emma P. Little (corresponding secretary) and Hugh B. Hostetter (marshal) in the front seat.

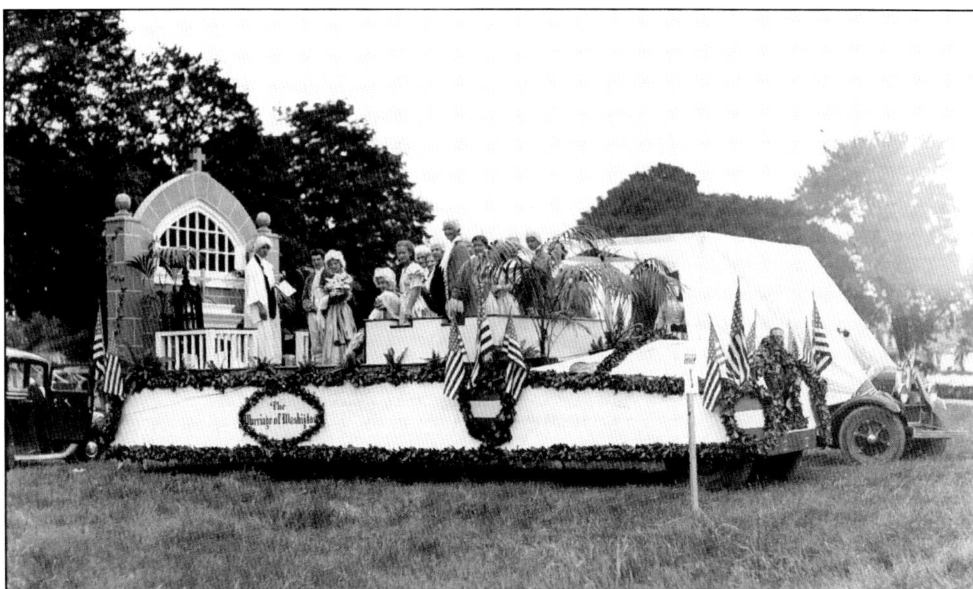

Float No. 23 depicts the marriage of Washington and was sponsored by the Manufacturers of Hanover, A. Ross Hostetter, chairman.

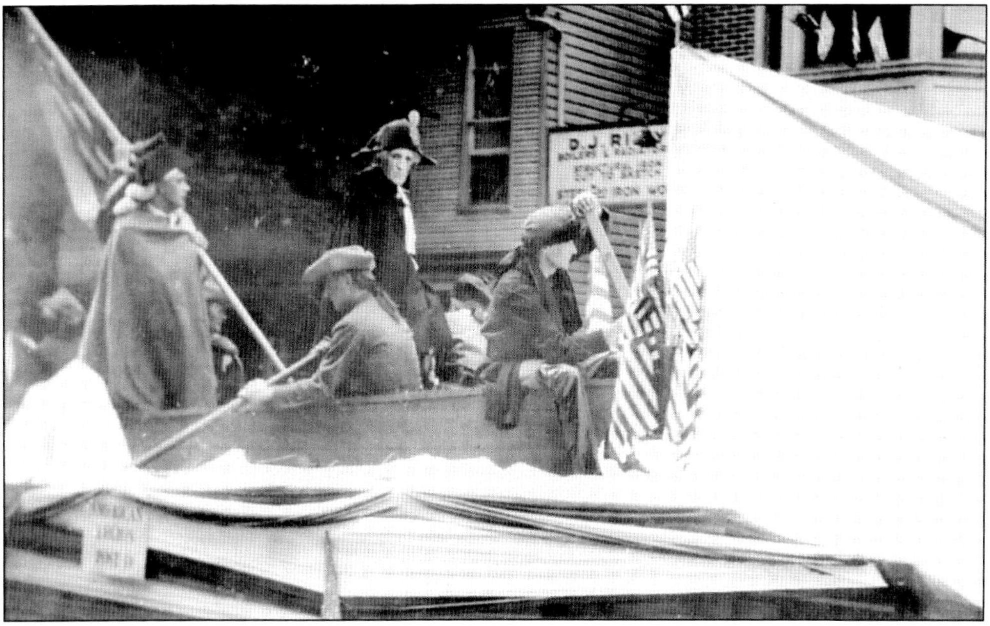

Washington crossing the Delaware River on the morning of December 25, 1776, is depicted by this float, which was entered by the American Legion Post No. 14, James H. Dillon, commander. George Washington is portrayed by George Wildasin. The building sign is for a machinist David J. Riley, who operated his business from 18 York Street.

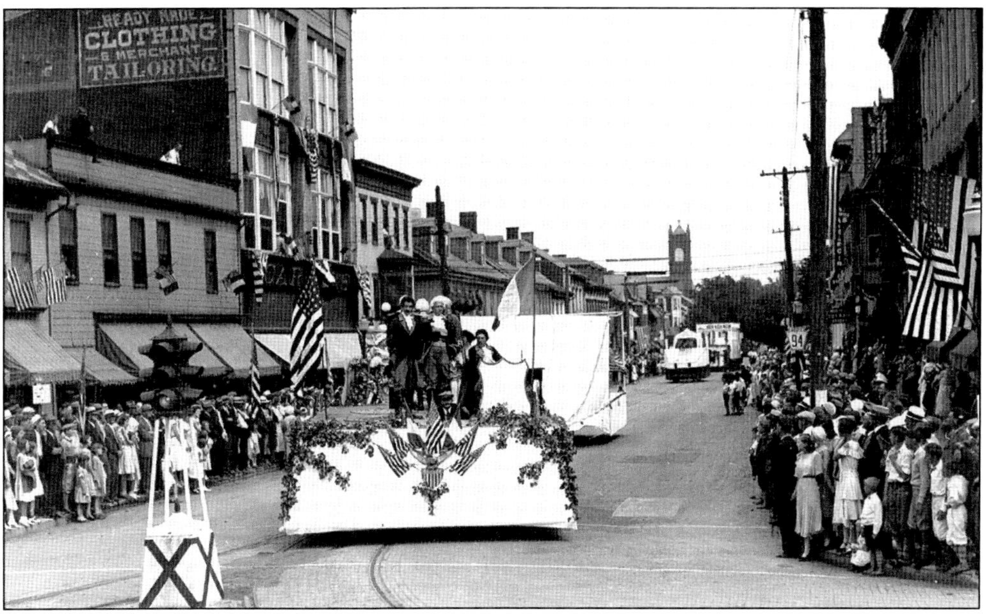

Entrant No. 29 was a float representing the Oath of Allegiance of the Continental Officers, constructed by the Merchants Club, E. Fred Carver, chairman. Coincidently the photograph, taken at Center Square looking south on Baltimore Street, shows the N. B. Carver and Sons building on the left with the clothing advertisement. The Carver sons referred to are E. Fred Carver and Daniel S. Carver. General Washington is played by C. L. Swope and Mrs. Washington is played by Viola L. Carver.

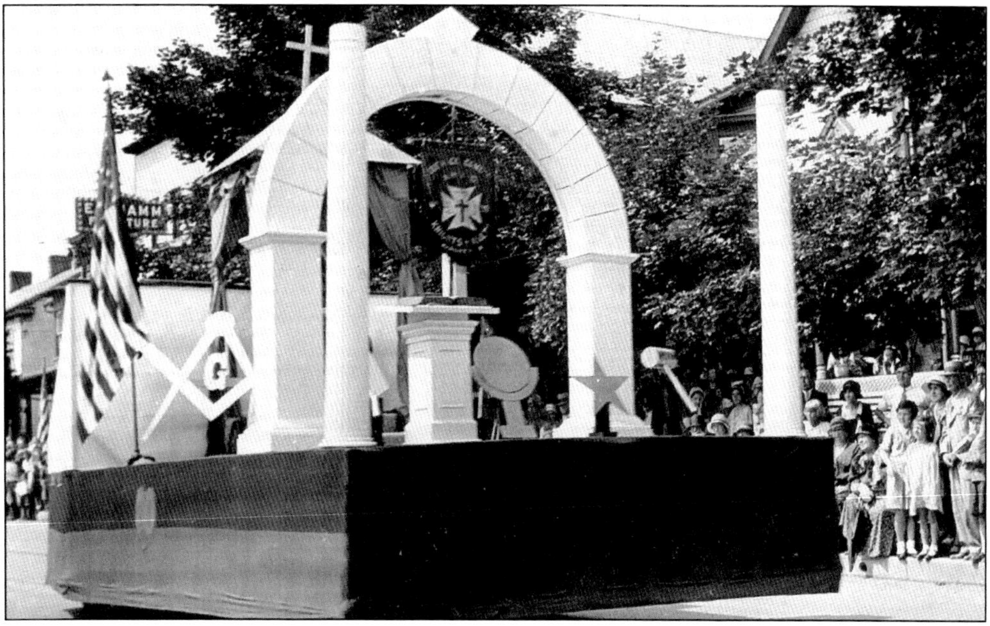

Float 30 was titled "Washington as a Fraternity Man." It was prepared by Defiance Commandery No. 380, Knights of Malta, F. W. Gebensleben, recorder. George Washington is impersonated by Luther A. Harner. The E. E. Hamm Furniture sign in the background suggests the photograph was taken near the store at 408 Baltimore Street heading toward Center Square.

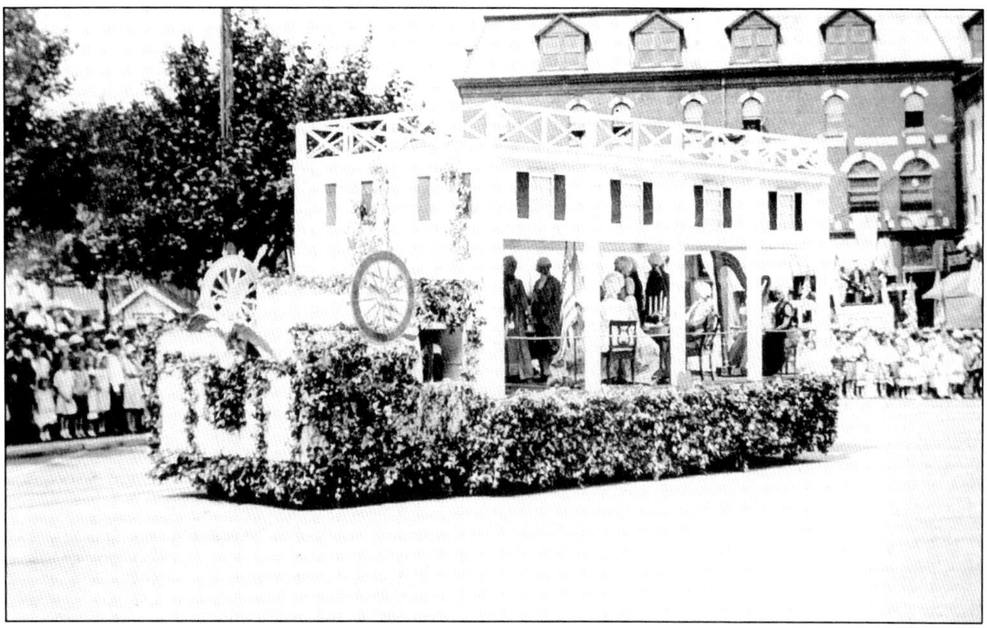

The 31st entrant was this float depicting a "Parlor Scene at Mount Vernon." The Col. Richard McAllister Chapter of the Daughters of the American Revolution, Mrs. George P. Ard, regent, was responsible for its erection. It was taken on Center Square with the Hanover Hotel in the background in the southeast corner of Broadway and Center Square. George Forney was George Washington, and Estelle Fitz was cast as Martha Washington.

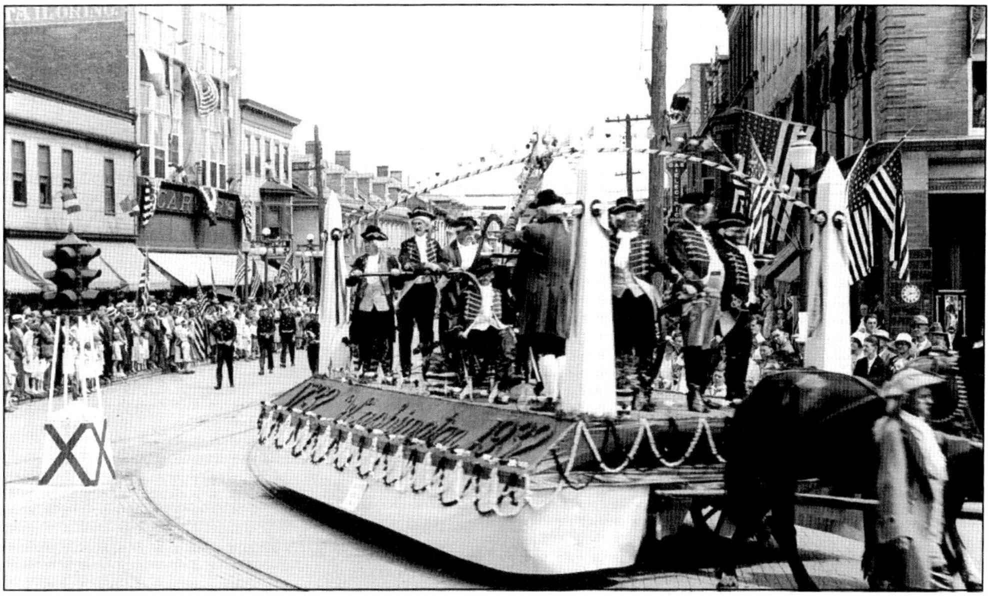

Entry 38 was made possible by the Hanover Fire Company No. 1, Samuel C. Garber, president, and Rev. John S. Tome, chaplain. The float is entering Center Square from Baltimore Street in front of the J. W. Gitt Department Store on its way to Frederick Street.

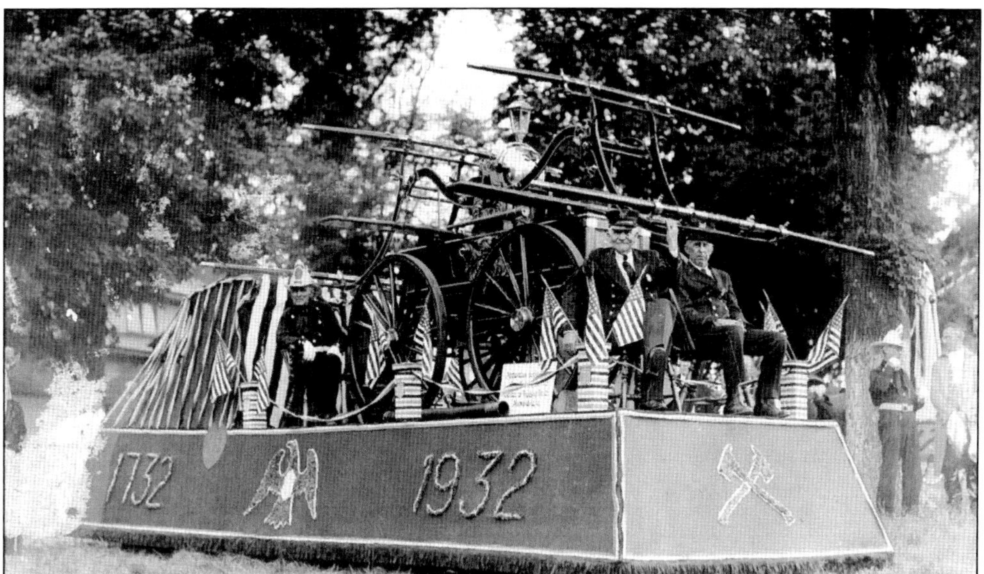

The Hanover Eagle Fire Company followed next with their float titled, "Friendship Fire Company of which Washington was a Member." David Musselman was the Eagle Fire Company president.

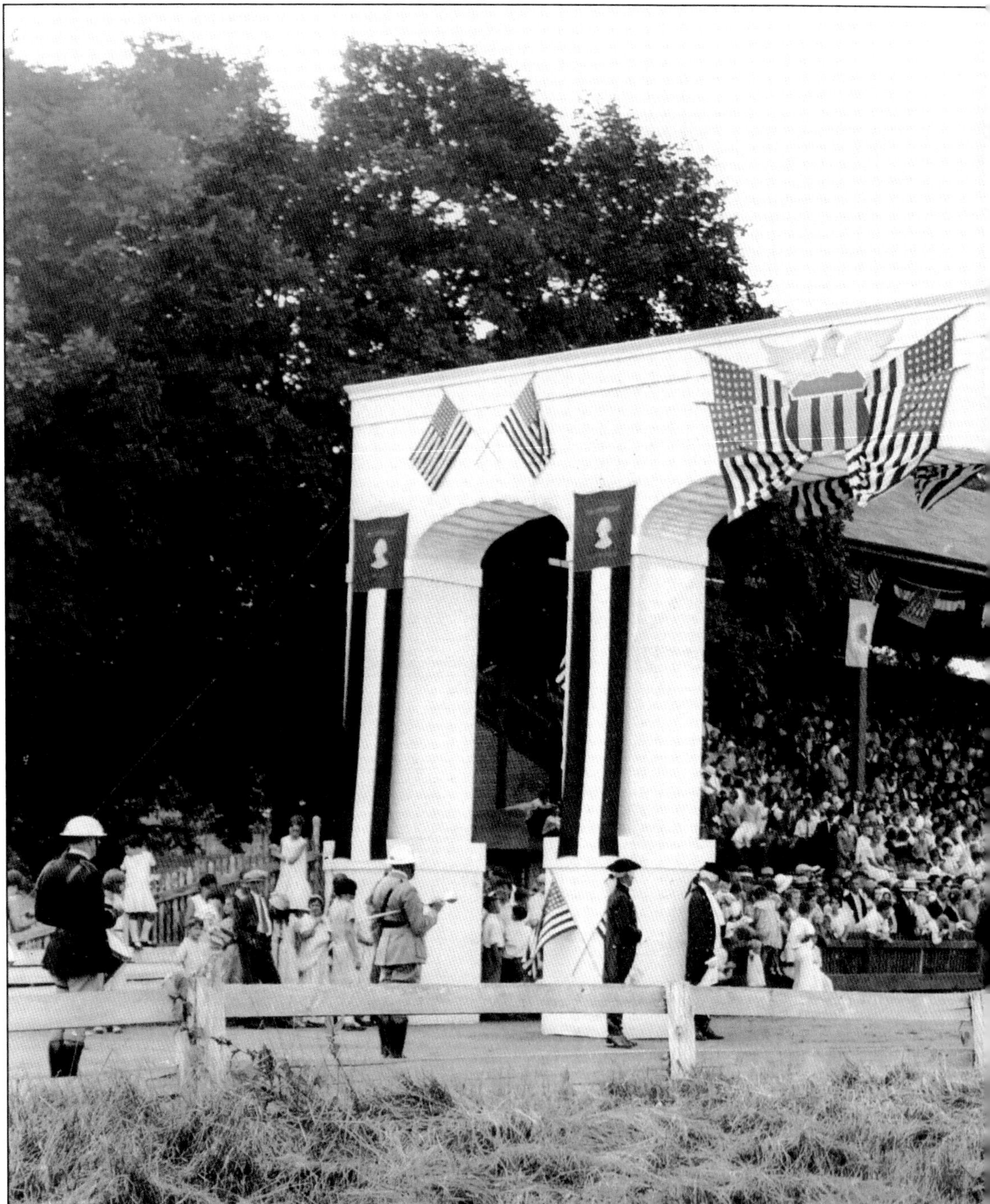

The parade ended at the Hanover Fairgrounds where this elaborate arch was constructed.

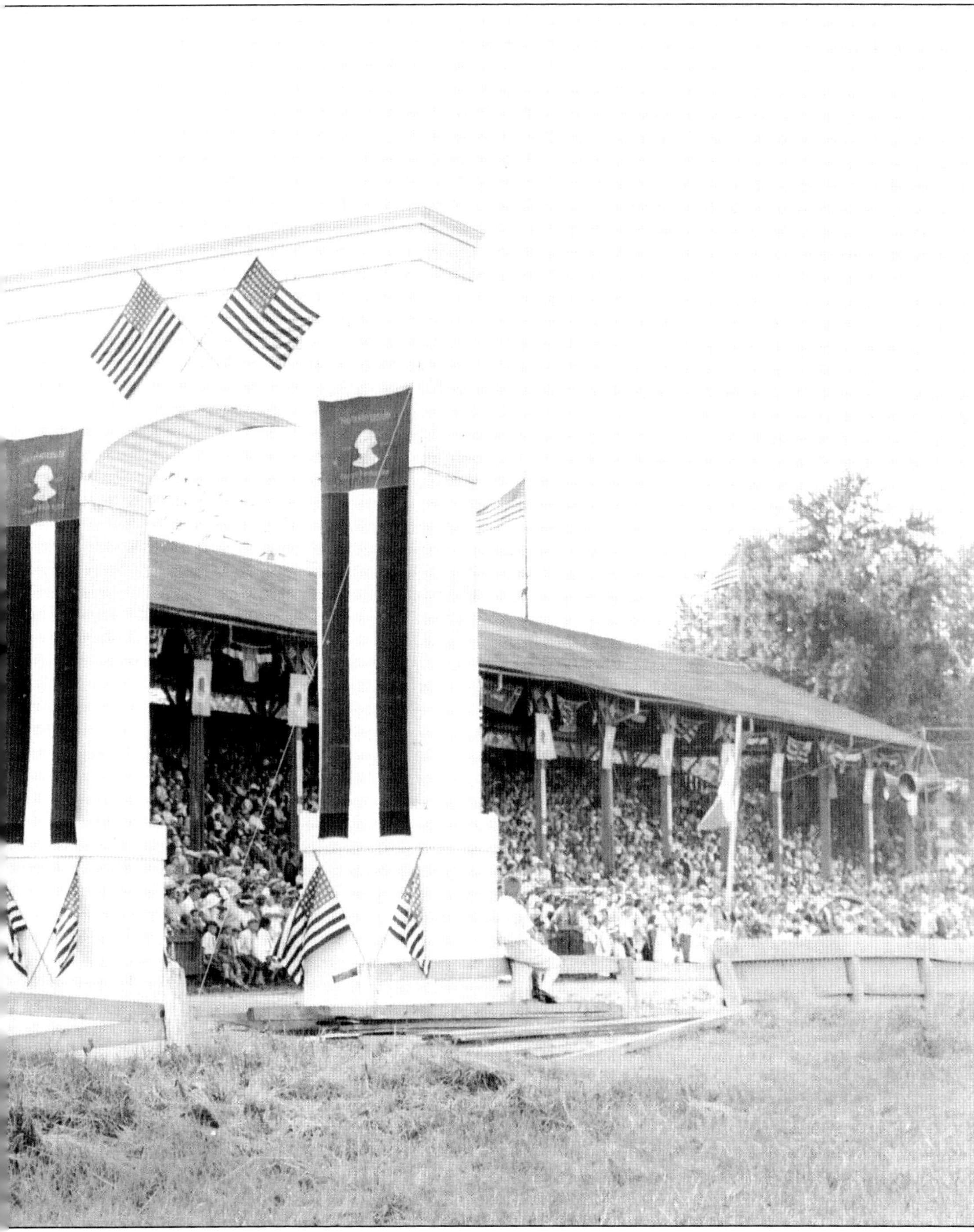

Pageant festivities held at the fairgrounds followed the parade.

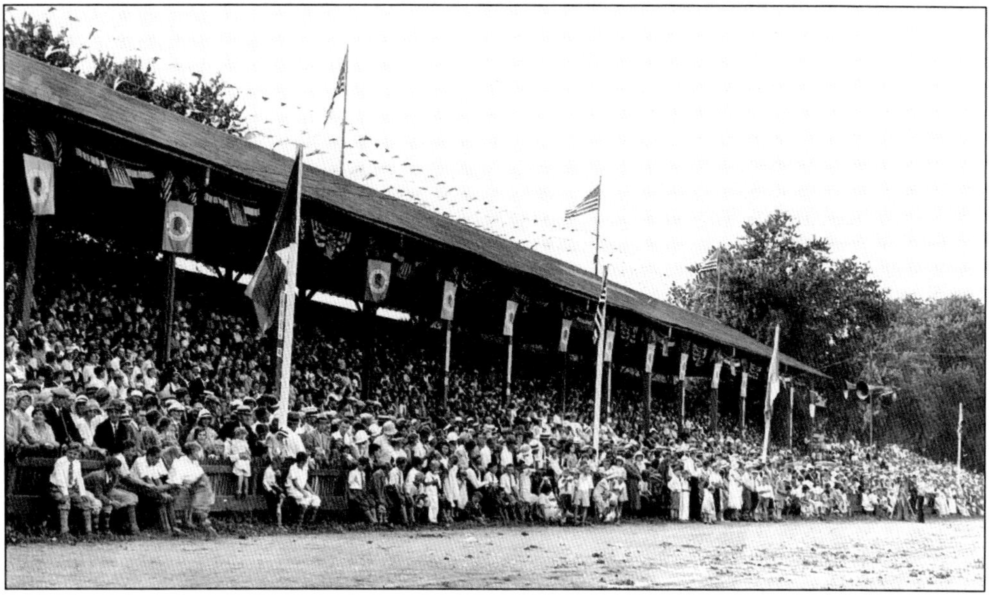

Based upon this scene of the crowds awaiting the finale of the parade and the ensuing pageant, the day's celebration was a very popular event for the community.

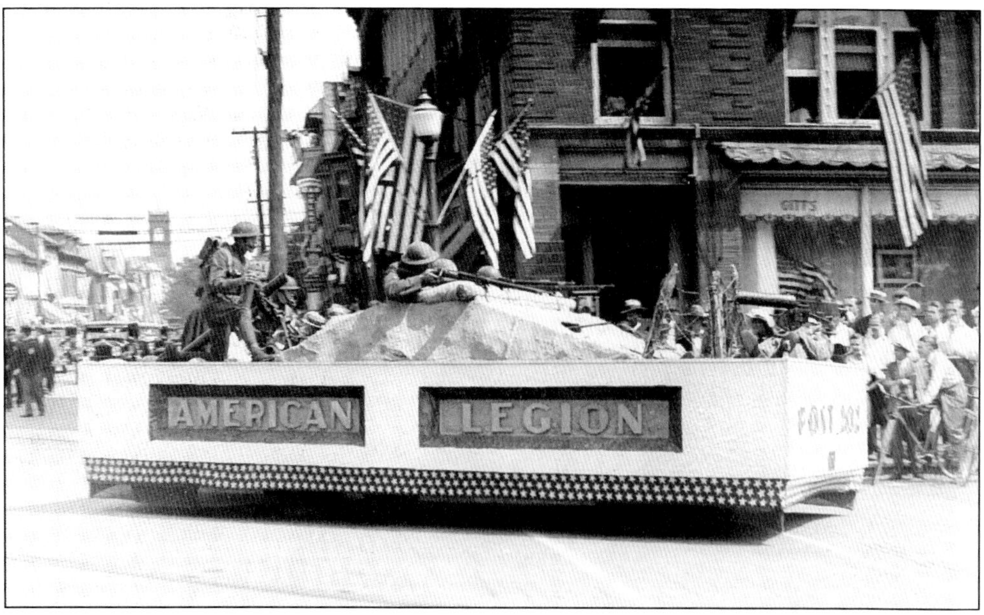

Judging from their uniforms, a visiting American Legion post float perhaps depicts a World War I scene. This float followed three groups of marchers, the Degree of Pocahontas Council No. 37, the Minnewaukaree Tribe No. 250, Improved Order of Red Men, and the Woodmen of the World, social clubs of the era.